EVIL DEEDS IN HIGH PLACES

Evil Deeds in High Places

Christian America's Moral Struggle with Watergate

David E. Settje

NEW YORK UNIVERSITY PRESS

New York

NEW YORK UNIVERSITY PRESS
New York
www.nyupress.org

References to Internet websites (URLs) were accurate at the time of writing. Neither the author nor New York University Press is responsible for URLs that may have expired or changed since the manuscript was prepared.

Library of Congress Cataloging-in-Publication Data
Names: Settje, David E., 1970–   author.
Title: Evil deeds in high places : Christian America's moral struggle with Watergate / David E. Settje.
Other titles: Christian America's moral struggle with Watergate
Description: New York : New York University Press, [2020] |
Includes bibliographical references and index.
Identifiers: LCCN 2020015041 (print) | LCCN 2020015042 (ebook) |
ISBN 9781479803149 (cloth) | ISBN 9781479803170 (ebook) |
ISBN 9781479803156 (ebook)
Subjects: LCSH: Watergate Affair, 1972–1974. | Christianity and politics—United States—History—20th century. | Nixon, Richard M. (Richard Milhous), 1913–1994. | United States—Politics and government—1969–1974.
Classification: LCC E860 .S47 2020 (print) | LCC E860 (ebook) | DDC 973.924—dc23
LC record available at https://lccn.loc.gov/2020015041
LC ebook record available at https://lccn.loc.gov/2020015042

New York University Press books are printed on acid-free paper, and their binding materials are chosen for strength and durability. We strive to use environmentally responsible suppliers and materials to the greatest extent possible in publishing our books.

Manufactured in the United States of America

10 9 8 7 6 5 4 3 2 1

Also available as an ebook

In loving memory of Allen D. Settje

CONTENTS

Introduction

Watergate and American Religion

Americans fretted about the state of their country. It seemed as if every-one read the newspaper and sat riveted to the television as a tale of government misdeeds unfolded before their eyes. Some wondered if the nation could survive the constitutional crisis, while at a minimum many believed the president would be removed from office. By the end, even stalwart defenders of the chief executive found his behavior wanting. The US government, many feared, had fallen into an abyss of unethical and immoral activity.

For just over two years, Watergate gripped the United States in a dev-astating chasm of executive branch misdeeds. It ended only after the first resignation of a president in American history. The feeling of lapsed morality struck a nerve in Americans, still reeling from the tumultuous conflicts of the 1960s and 1970s. People searched for ethical leadership at all levels of society as they sought to right a floundering ship. Could they and their country recover a sense of normalcy? Could the nation once again balance individual political desire with putting democracy first?

The severity of the crisis led many Americans to their religious in-stitutions. Throughout human history, societies have structured them-selves around faith-driven constructs that inculcated cultures with the very moral and ethical foundations needed to coexist and overcome human depravity. For a majority of Americans during Watergate, Chris-tian churches served this purpose. Christianity stepped into the void and asserted a moral authority for their constituents that allayed fears and helped the country heal. In the process, Christians learned anew the power of their political voice in America.

Much ink has been spilled analyzing the events of Watergate. We know a lot about what happened, and the political fallout. Yet for all the books and articles and journalistic probing, relatively little research has

1

investigated popular reactions to the incident. We know very little about either average American opinions or even the thoughts of national leaders outside of the political and media arenas. The events surrounding Watergate shook the very foundations of American democracy. They evinced a moral and ethical collapse that engulfed the nation in crisis. How did Americans respond? What did they see as their role in trying to address the political emergency?[1]

Research remains to be done to provide a broad sense of how everyday citizens across all walks of life viewed and engaged with Watergate. This book looks at one significant slice of the American public, Protestant Christians, to both uncover their reactions and trace the long-term effects on the American political landscape. True, a focus on Protestants leaves much as yet uncovered. But in the 1970s, Christians made up well over 85 percent of the nation's population according to various polls, at least 60 percent of whom were Protestant. Moreover, as we will see, there was much diversity within this large sample of the American populace. Within Protestant Christianity there were significant variations in responses to the proceedings, offering an important step in surfacing the opinions of everyday Americans to the Watergate controversy. Moreover, the engagement of Protestants in the political crisis had particularly important ramifications for Americans politics, which persist to this day. Protestants engaged Watergate in order to solve the moral catastrophe and, as a result, intensified their political activities. In inching into this realm, they became accustomed to having political influence.[2]

In recent years, Watergate and its legacy have again become prominent in American life. The political world ushered in by the presidency of Donald J. Trump was built on the past, and as many scholars and commentators have noted, nothing gets discussed today without a Watergate lens. The Trump presidency propelled the nation once more into critical conversations about morality and ethics in politics, and what they mean for the future of the nation. Grasping more fully the dynamics of Christian responses to Watergate enables us to comprehend more completely that volatile moment in US history, providing important context to make sense of reactions to our more recent political turmoil.

President Richard M. Nixon resigned on August 8, 1974. The impeachment inquiry that precipitated his fall began with a botched burglary at the Watergate offices of the Democratic National Committee in Washington, DC. Judicial, legislative, and journalistic investigations not only uncovered illegal activities by people serving under the president both in the White House and in his campaign but also ultimately proved the president's own attempts to cover up the crimes. Nixon resigned after the House of Representatives initiated impeachment proceedings that were almost certain to result in a Senate trial. The episode became so notorious that the very mention of "Watergate" with no other context provokes images of government corruption, abuse of power, and threats to the rule of law if not checked by the balance of powers embedded in the Constitution. Almost every subsequent political scandal has borne the "gate" moniker, such as "Irangate" during Ronald Reagan's term in office. The references extend all the way to more mundane controversies in professional sports, including the infamous "Spygate," when the New England Patriots filmed their opponents from the sidelines, against National Football League rules. "Watergate" as an idea ushered in mistrust of the government and investigations of almost every subsequent presidency.[3]

Obviously a major turning point in American political history, these events also brought about a key shift in the commingling of faith and politics. In two short years, from 1972 to 1974, the moral and ethical breach manifest in this constitutional crisis sharpened the ways in which Christians addressed politics, bringing them more forcefully into the political arena. Coming amid a decade of intense political instability and shifts, marked in part by political party affiliations and political factions moving around and reorganizing, Watergate proved a ripe time for Christians to assert where they stood in this changing landscape. This book investigates Protestant reactions, in all their dramatic richness, to the Watergate controversy. It argues that the episode formed a pivotal moment of change for the mixing of politics and religion in America. And it makes the case that we can learn much about the nation's contemporary political and religious climate by looking at Watergate through a Protestant lens. As most historians of American religions agree, despite the constitutional separation of church and state, Christianity has shaped politics from the United States' founding to the present day. When the founders legally separated the institutions, they knew full well that humans lived in and easily moved between the two; the founders even wrote about their own reliance on moral and ethical reasoning in the public square. They also recognized that the diversity of beliefs and religious organizations would create debate about faith's influence in the country and allowed for such disagreements to abound.

American history reflects a waxing and waning of religion entering the political arena as a major force. Certain moments have brought heightened religious passions to the fore, demonstrating how religion and American politics interacted at a high level, particularly in moments of crisis. No period embodies this truth better than the abolitionist push to eradicate slavery that helped drive the nation into civil war, as well as the counterspiritual argument by southern and proslavery religious leaders. Urbanization, industrialization, and expectations for mutual benefit were swayed by the Social Gospel in the late 1800s and into the early twentieth century. Religious believers led these reform efforts, hoping their Christian influence would improve the plight of immigrants and the impoverished. Religious zeal also fueled the prohibition of alcohol with the Eighteenth Amendment to the Constitution and fired up intense social debate about Darwinian theory, as Christian principles from a particular point of view flooded into secular politics. Arguments over the theory of evolution entered local politics about what was taught in public schools. Farther into the twentieth century, religion became a central component of the Cold War, often prompting Americans to cast it as a holy war, with US Christianity standing against the forces of Soviet atheism. In the twenty-first century, a presidential candidate's faith has come under more scrutiny than ever, and the Religious Right has become a fierce component of the Republican Party. The spillover of religion into politics in America has a long history, requiring us to recognize not only that it happens but also why it has happened, and what it has meant for the United States. What has brought religion to the forefront at certain times? Watergate presents one of those intensified moments of change, and its legacy continues today.[4]

Of course, some periods have experienced more waning of religion in politics, with faith becoming more of a background issue than a major political influencer. To be sure, religion never disappeared completely, but it sometimes slipped into a quieter role. American history saw a lull in religion and politics during the American Revolution and the Federalist period, all the way to the 1840s and the beginnings of the intensified debates over slavery. The post–Civil War period witnessed a quieting of religion and politics until the Social Gospel gained steam. And religion lost some traction in politics in the 1930s and 1940s, first because evangelicals retreated after the embarrassing loss of public support in the wake of the Scopes Trial and then as Americans concentrated their energy on first solving the Great Depression and then fighting World War II. While the 1950s and 1960s brought Christianity into the Cold War, this intersection of faith and politics did not result in much debate because Americans largely agreed about being a Christian nation fighting atheist communism.[5]

Yet even in the 1950s, 1960s, and early 1970s, there were hints that a new era of religion merging with American politics was about to begin. In part, this process stemmed from an overall era of political instability and shifting currents, with religious currents mirroring the political landscape as a whole. During this time mainline Protestant churches and liberal Catholic priests became active participants in the civil rights movement, working to fight the immoral force of segregation and racial prejudice in America. The country debated the importance of John F. Kennedy's Catholicism during the 1960 presidential election. Cold War religious consensus broke down during the Vietnam War, with Christians debating the United States' involvement in Southeast Asia and whether the conflict met the criteria for a just war. Other social concerns from the 1960s heightened Christian awareness in American society writ large, including the philosophical question of whether "God is dead"; the loosening of sexual mores; and protests over war, race, and poverty. Then Richard Nixon became president of the United States, and Watergate slammed American religion into the start of another heightened era of political involvement. Watergate tipped the scales from religion influencing social topics to its more assertively marching into the political fray.

Watergate demanded the attention of religious institutions, impelling them to assert their moral authority. This major moment that so changed American history prompted Protestant institutions of all types to act to meet the political emergency by infusing their various belief systems into politics. In the process, they began to operate more vigorously and comfortably in the political sphere, establishing a precedent that continued after Watergate ended with Nixon's resignation and laying the foundations for their very strong influence on politics today.[6]

Though the June 1972 break-in at the Watergate complex in Washington, DC, initiated the moral and ethical crisis, as initial reports appeared in the media, not everyone agreed about Nixon's guilt or the extent to which Americans should concern themselves with the matter. By exploring a diverse sampling of Protestant reactions, this book seeks to uncover how various religious institutions understood Watergate with regard to their perception about Christianity's role in politics. What theology did they employ to guide their reactions to this crisis? Did their perceptions of Nixon and/or general politics, before and after the scandal, affect them? How did they believe they could act to help save the nation from immorality in secular politics? And how did Watergate shift their behavior moving forward after Nixon's resignation?

The Protestants whose views are analyzed in this book offer a broad spectrum of political and theological beliefs, ranging from evangelicals and conservatives to mainline Protestant and liberal entities, plus those standing in the middle. This sampling includes the spectrum of right to left to moderate leanings, both theologically and politically. It provides a solid cross section of opinions and points of view, despite its limitations in terms of representing all of American "Christianity," a broad category with numerous points of view, adherents, and representatives. It focuses on Protestantism, still the dominant category of believers at the time. While wider inclusion might have been more holistic, it was also prohibitive in terms of length and amount of coverage needed for complete analysis. That said, at times I use a generic label of "Christian" to reference responses to Watergate in this book in order to vary wording and not bog down the narrative with constant reminders about its Protestant concentration. A note about my usage of "conservative," "liberal," and "moderate" is also in order.

Unless otherwise noted, by "conservative" I mean Christians who leaned rightward regarding both politics and religion. This reflects a neoconservative outlook that sought limited government influence on society and laissez-faire economics, and yet advocated a strong military and a staunch anticommunist Cold Warriorism. They typically supported the Republican Party. Religiously, conservatives tended toward biblical literalism, missionary outreach, and revivalism grounded in pietism.

"Liberals," too, usually applied their leftist philosophy to both their politics and their faith. Politically, they favored social justice movements, especially the civil rights movement and women's rights movement, and they distrusted the Cold War outlook as warlike and dangerous. They sought instead détente with communist nations: disarmament and reduced global tension. A theology of human improvement guided most liberals, whereby they advocated programs and initiatives that bettered the human condition regardless of religious affiliation. Their politics leaned toward the Democratic Party, and they by and large disdained Nixon long before he became president.

"Moderates" fell somewhere between these polar opposites, and they are described individually throughout the text, as each had unique circumstances and blendings of conservative and liberal politics and/or theologies. American Protestants of this era contributed to the Christian history of contentious debate about theology, while paralleling one another in their drive to add religious values to everyday life. Being a good Christian and a good citizen blended together, with democracy allowing believers to try to influence government, even as they debated exactly what values a godly society should adopt.

Across the spectrum, Protestantism thus sought to interject itself into the national debate about politics as related to Watergate in order to assert its moral authority and to save the nation from collapse. Yet the wide range of theologies, political viewpoints, and perceptions of church actions in politics meant that Christians held diverse opinions about these matters. Recognizing the role that religious institutions played in this political watershed contributes much to understandings of how Americans reacted to Watergate and post-Watergate efforts to heal the nation. It pinpoints a moment when religion became more comfortable operating within politics, at least since the nineteenth and early twentieth centuries. Today we see such institutions behaving in intensely partisan ways, to the point that many identify with one political party over another. The line between religion and politics that Watergate blurred has in many respects become invisible.

Time Period and Historic Context

This study begins in June 1972 for two reasons. First, that moment offers a glimpse into how the various entities viewed Nixon during the presidential election but before the Watergate scandal began to intensify or in some way shape their perceptions of him. It thus establishes a sort of baseline perception or starting point from which people reacted as the political crisis came to light. It also showcases the level of religious involvement in politics before Watergate. Second, the break-in at Watergate by Nixon operatives occurred in June, and the reporting of it started shortly thereafter. The timeline then ventures through the next two years of White House obstruction, judicial investigation, congressional inquiry, and media scrutiny, with Protestant conversations about political ethics and public morality woven throughout. This process allowed Protestants to become more comfortable than previously in the twentieth century with adding a partisan voice to political discourse. It ends with an examination of how Christians handled Nixon's resignation based on their constructions of Watergate to that point.

This two-year period provided ample opportunity for periodicals, Christian leaders, denominations, and various individuals and committees to articulate their responses to Watergate, as well as how they wanted to ameliorate the national moral and ethical crisis. Periodicals, whether published weekly, biweekly, or monthly, utilized traditional reporting, letters to the editor, and editorials to comment on a myriad of issues, including Watergate. Pastors and other leaders inserted their voices where they thought appropriate, through sermons, public statements, letters, or addresses to national assemblies. Each denomination's national assembly met at some point during this two-year period, allowing us to view how these collective bodies framed Watergate. These gatherings provide a sampling of lay opinions, as do many letters to the editor and sundry other materials. Some denominations met yearly for national assemblies, others every other year, and all of them had various committees and task forces that made comment between the assemblies. Collectively, these sources offer us the clearest view of Protestant politics in this period that we are likely to find.

Nixon stormed onto the national political stage in the late 1940s by establishing himself as one of the foremost investigators of communist infiltrations in America during the Cold War. After gaining special notoriety during his successful prosecution of former State Department employee Alger Hiss, he went from the House of Representatives to the Senate, and became vice president of the United States under Dwight D. Eisenhower in 1953. His staunch anticommunist credentials gained him many admirers, but from the beginning of his first congressional campaign he displayed a penchant for dirty campaign tricks as a tactic in his win-at-all-cost strategy. In both his House and Senate campaigns, for example, he falsely labeled his opponents as communist sympathizers and created dummy organizations to spread malicious rumors about his foes. His own reputation and a telegenic John F. Kennedy stymied his career in 1960, but Nixon patiently and methodically rebuilt his reputation and launched a triumphant bid for the presidency in 1968. Once again, he employed a combination of shrewd political skills, savvy public relations, and behind-the-scenes illegal and unethical tactics to win the election. Most infamously, he interfered in the peace negotiations undertaken by Lyndon B. Johnson to try to end the Vietnam War in order to avoid the Democrats claiming victory with an end to the war. Some historians have since labeled his action treasonous. Nixon's background as a master politician and sharp diplomat, but also as a devious and underhanded mastermind in his quest for power, set the stage for Watergate amid the 1972 presidential election. By that time, he had developed a complicated public image, with scores who backed him and seemingly as many who mistrusted or even despised him. His temperament and legacy fit well with a decade rife with political instability and change. As with the rest of Americans, Christian reactions were just as conflicted. One may see similar dynamics at play with the reaction to President Trump approximately half a century later, with many on the left decrying outright lies and misdeeds even as others embrace his rhetoric about placing America first and his stance against abortion.[7]

Nixon's journey from Congress to the White House thus nurtured the mentality that led to the actual break-in at the Democratic National Headquarters at the Watergate complex in June 1972. Not surprisingly, then, from the beginning of his first term in office, he contemplated wiretapping his enemies, attacking those who disagreed with him using the Internal Revenue Service, and in general creating an atmosphere that prized victory above all else. The *New York Times'* publication of the Pentagon Papers, a secret Defense Department history of the Vietnam War that highlighted the Johnson administration's mishandling of it, set in motion the specific activities that led to Watergate. While the report condemned Lyndon B. Johnson, and thus a Democratic president, Nixon and some of his associates fumed about the leak, in part worried about what might slip out regarding their own operations. In response, White House operatives created "the plumbers" unit, charged with ending leaks and exposing the leakers. The plumbers burglarized the offices of a psychiatrist who treated Daniel Ellsberg, the man who gave the Pentagon Papers to the press, and attempted to orchestrate other illegal and covert actions on behalf of the president.[8]

While the Nixon administration set course for its second term and, most notably, negotiated a settlement to retract the United States from the Vietnam War, the investigation into the burglars of the Watergate complex continued apace. Former White House aides G. Gordon Liddy and James W. McCord were convicted of conspiracy, burglary, and wiretapping, along with five other men who plead guilty in January 1973. In response to these events, the Senate that February created the Select Committee on Presidential Campaign Activities, chaired by North Carolina Democrat Sam Ervin. Next, McCord flipped from remaining silent about what he knew to informing federal judge John Sirica that those who plead guilty had perjured themselves. Further investigation linked the scandal to the president's chief of staff, H. R. Haldeman, and White House counsel John Ehrlichman, both of whom resigned under pressure in April 1973, as did Attorney General Richard Kleindienst. By May, the Senate Watergate Committee began holding public hearings that captivated the entire nation's attention. John Dean's testimony at these hearings became one of the most notable turning points in Watergate. The former White House lawyer, who started cooperating with prosecutors in April in exchange for a lighter sentence, rocked the nation when he reported that he had discussed Watergate with the president. New attorney general Elliot Richardson appointed Archibald Cox, a former solicitor general, as the Justice Department's special prosecutor in May, largely in response to pressure applied by the other investigations. Another bombshell hit that July, when Alexander Butterfield, a White House aide, revealed under oath that the White House operated a secret taping system of phone and face-to-face conversations. Nixon promptly shut the system down but kept all previous recordings to assist himself in later writing a history of his administration, a decision that would help link him directly to Watergate. Nixon stubbornly refused to turn the tapes over to prosecutors and on October 20, 1973, fired Cox and abolished the special prosecutor's office. With Cox went Richardson and Deputy Attorney General William D. Ruckelshaus, who both resigned after refusing to fire Cox. After a series of court challenges, Nixon handed over some of the sought-after tapes to Leon Jaworski, the newly appointed special prosecutor. The combination of judicial and congressional investigations, along with journalistic research and other testimonies, increased the calls for the president to resign by late 1973. But the president insisted on his innocence and lied that he knew nothing about the break-in.

Inquiries, pressure, and investigations escalated throughout early 1974, prompting the House of Representatives to authorize the House Judiciary Committee to probe into Watergate in February, a prelude to impeachment. Perhaps the climax of the year and the moment that Watergate sealed Nixon's demise came with the forced release in April 1974 of transcripts of the White House tapes to the public. Jaworski had subpoenaed all of the tapes, but Nixon refused, instead agreeing to provide edited transcripts to the Judiciary Committee. The demeanor of the president and his associates as revealed in the tapes shocked Americans. This moment accelerated a decline in Nixon's support and, despite his attempts to thwart it, the House Judiciary Committee began impeachment hearings and pressed to obtain the actual tapes, which the Supreme Court ultimately ordered in July. The endgame came rather quickly thereafter, with the House Judiciary Committee passing articles of impeachment between July 27 and 30, charging Nixon with obstruction of justice, misuse of power, and violations of his oath of office. In early August, Nixon released tapes that provided "the smoking gun," as it came to be called: evidence that Nixon had, indeed, attempted to stop the FBI investigation and participated in the attempted cover-up, as early as June 23, 1972. On August 8, 1974, Richard M. Nixon became the first president in US history to resign from office. The result was a nation that viewed its political system in a turmoil of lapsed moral and ethical standards and that sought resolution in part from Christian institutions engaging the political realm.

Reactions to Watergate

As noted, while ample attention has been given to the people directly involved in the controversy, far less is known about American reactions writ large. Yet without knowing how citizens responded, our comprehension of this vital moment in US history lacks context. Studying Protestant reactions to Watergate increases our understandings of how Americans reacted to Nixon and Watergate and gives clues into how they sought to use their faith to solve the crisis. This fact subsequently made it more comfortable for them to affect politics after 1974, to the point they almost all do so with comfortable regularity today.

This book serves as a biography of sorts of the Protestant entities it considers, showcasing how they commented on Watergate as spiritual leaders of the nation at a time of great public crisis. Protestants struggled to reconcile their hope for a moral government based on Christian ethics against evidence of individuals within it whose character and actions failed to align with this ideal. While the Christians discussed here shared a belief that they held a responsibility to shape the nation's reaction to Watergate, they hardly agreed on what to believe, how to respond, or what remedy to enact.

On the left, a theology that valued social justice and a broad coalition of believers and nonbelievers proactively working for society's greater good combined with a long-standing dislike of Nixon. The perpetrators of Watergate, and especially the president, confirmed their perception that the sin of American individualism lay at the root of the problem and needed to be eradicated from each person, society in general, the church, and, of course, the government. Moderate voices at first avoided the left's harsh language, but as evidence grew against the Nixon administration, they merged gradually with the left to cry out to oust the president. Others brought a leftist view of politics but a more pietistic theology, thus bridging ideologies between liberal politics and conservative theology. To them, Nixon represented the obvious evil, but the theology they employed called for individual conversions that would lead to massive national conversions, thereby inculcating the United States with a Christian spirit to overcome the demon infecting its federal government. In that way, they matched the right, in which conservative Christians espoused what political scientist Benjamin T. Lynerd has accurately labeled "Republican Theology."

The conservative Protestants discussed in this book leaned right both politically and theologically, and very much conformed to Lynerd's Republican Theology. Conservatives shaped a political/religious ideology that demanded limited government and focused on the separation of church and state while simultaneously decreeing a public morality based on their Christian principles. Regarding Watergate, this meant that the only acceptable Christian response came through prayer and through the campaigning for individual conversion experiences, which it was believed would lead to a wave of Christian changes across the nation. Their prayers related closely to a belief that Christ's return was imminent, perhaps within their own lifetimes, and thus the saving of people and by extension the nation was an urgent matter. Indeed, a large percentage of religious conservatives believed that a literal apocalypse was close at hand, and they therefore dedicated their righteous works to saving people. Such piety would please God and thereby gain divine favor for the United States. The theological differences within Christianity were as profound as ever, even as Christians at times worked of one accord to use their platforms, leadership, and influences to fix a nation on the brink of complete moral collapse.[9]

A related strand woven into these political and theological discussions was a debate about whether the United States was a uniquely Christian nation. Conservatives often framed the Watergate debate in the context of America being a favored nation, thus necessitating that they fight to maintain God's favor or, in the case of Watergate's ethical and moral collapse, to regain it in order to save democracy. Liberal counterparts found this rationale specious when it asserted that God sanctioned US policies and deeds; became preoccupied with national strength, progress, and power; and prompted the United States to superimpose its political philosophy on other nations. In explaining their political activities regarding Watergate, conservatives espoused that the United States was uniquely Christian and chosen by God, while liberals derided that perspective as worshipping a false idol and therefore part of the problem.

One study of a cross section of Protestant America hardly fills in all of the gaps in scholarly understandings of how Americans addressed Watergate as it unfolded. But it starts this important conversation. Examining the religious entities that many—perhaps a majority of?—Americans looked to for ethical guidance, this book reveals how the churches sought to shape a country that had spiraled so far out of control, whether in truth or in perception. And in scrutinizing the ways that these churches applied their theology to Watergate, it uncovers the moral framework that at least a significant segment of the American populace utilized to inform their reactions. Christianity sought to save the country as part of its calling to save souls, an activity that became more pronounced than ever during Watergate. This evolution toward comfort in politics persisted to the point that it seems natural today to see partisan religious currents as part of the political process. Watergate ushered in this reality.

Methodology

To research this book I examined five denominations and two periodicals: the Southern Baptist Convention (SBC), the Lutheran Church in America (LCA), the Lutheran Church—Missouri Synod (LCMS), the African Methodist Episcopal Church (AME), and the United Church of Christ (UCC), as well as the evangelical and conservative magazine *Christianity Today* and the mainline Protestant and liberal *Christian Century*. This spectral sampling surveys how Protestants both responded to Watergate and contributed to conversations about its moral and ethical meanings for America. It provides a variety of viewpoints, including of conservative evangelicals, Protestant moderates, and liberal mainline Protestants, and from within those broad categories a myriad of subtle and profoundly different religious and political perspectives. These Christians reveal a sense of the many religious responses to Watergate, both in how Protestants framed their political points of view and in how they applied their theologies to a national spiritual crisis. These responses enable us to develop a more complete understanding of how all Americans understood Watergate as it unfolded before their eyes, and how it brought them to expect the mixing of religion and politics after the controversy ended.

Christianity Today provided a nationally respected voice for evangelical Americans with a broad readership, and its reach extended beyond any one particular denomination. Though it was affiliated with a number of Southern Baptist Convention members, the periodical's link to the Reverend Billy Graham and other evangelical leaders who transcended particular denominational affiliations gave it an even greater impact. For a Christian periodical, too, it had a large circulation of 253,579 in 1968, with a number of Americans and institutions looking to it as a news source on political, international, and social affairs from a conservative Christian theological viewpoint.[10]

Furthermore, *Christianity Today* was enmeshed in both theological and political conservatism. As such, it conformed well to the Republican Theology of limited government interference, increased oversight of American morality, and greater US influence around the world. These policies aligned with Richard Nixon's public stances on a number of issues and therefore endeared him to the periodical. Moreover, the publication's editors supported his foreign policy, including in Southeast Asia, because of their staunch anticommunism and support of Christian missions around the world, which they felt also thwarted communism. The newsmagazine's support of Nixon was increased by its reverence for Billy Graham, who also publicly backed Nixon. Thus, throughout much of the Watergate scandal, *Christianity Today* attempted to back the president and demanded that Americans withhold judgment until a fair trial had occurred. The magazine's evangelical audience and writers believed Nixon until the summer of 1974, when the evidence against him became decisive. Only then did the editors and most writers reluctantly deal with the truth and depth of the scandal.

This response makes sense given the periodical's history. Created in 1956 as a journal for evangelical outreach and opinion making to counter more liberal mainline Protestant journals, *Christianity Today* grew rapidly, again in part because of its affiliation with Graham, a founder who maintained an active role with the periodical. Throughout its history, the journal proclaimed a conservative theology that warned of

God's impending judgment and emphasized the need for evangelical outreach. It was the first newsmagazine dedicated to fostering the evangelical message to a wide US audience. As historian D. G. Hart states, the periodical "by the 1960s had emerged as the magazine of record for evangelical Protestantism."[11]

One of the theologically and politically liberal periodicals that *Christianity Today* was meant to counter was the *Christian Century*. The *Christian Century* sheds light on the elite intellectual perspective of mainline Protestantism. While hardly indicative of the entire population, it represents the liberal political thought of an influential group of thinkers who often had the ears of political leaders and could sway their readership with carefully argued and well-documented analysis. Again, the use of this periodical by numerous historians attempting to ascertain public opinion about various issues throughout the twentieth century testifies to its importance. Admittedly, it had a smaller circulation than *Christianity Today*, with only forty-five thousand subscribers in 1968. However, it also competed with other liberally and intellectually minded Christian periodicals such as *Christianity and Crisis*, whereas *Christianity Today* stood virtually alone on the right. As the liberal leadership of mainline Protestantism struggled to find a voice in the secularizing world, they nonetheless built bridges for Americans who listened to them between an older, isolationist individualism and a more evolved notion of other truths existing. This notion extended both into academic/intellectual arguments and toward acceptance and understanding of a broad array of peoples, races, and cultures. While this caused the *Christian Century* to lose constituents during the 1970s because people went to more conservative realms, it emboldened a profound ecumenism and a theology of human improvement that brought much good to the world. Adding a liberal intellectual perspective to this study through the *Christian Century* balances the lay opinions that appear elsewhere and which often paralleled those found in its pages.[12]

By the 1960s, the *Christian Century* had become the leading voice of liberal intellectual thought within American Protestantism. It persistently campaigned on behalf of the civil rights and women's rights movements, welfare programs, and interreligious dialogue. The *Christian Century* strove to assess academically various issues with the goal of uniting people in an effort to live together peacefully, whether within the

United States or the larger global community. Interdenominational in nature, it championed human rights issues and discarded a 1950s Cold Warrior mentality to instead back arms reduction and peaceful coexistence with communism. Yet in the process it began to lose constituents, as its increasing liberalism fell out of favor with more moderate readers.[13]

This overall liberal political and theological outlook pitted the *Christian Century* against Richard Nixon almost from the onset of his administration. While editors, writers, and readers at first hoped that he truly wanted to unite America, as he promised in 1968, his continued prosecution of the Vietnam War, his often racist policies, and his affront to welfare programs quickly disabused them of this optimism. These facts combined with a long-held mistrust of Nixon by the left, dating back to his campaigns of the 1950s and 1960s. *Christian Century* writers questioned his character publicly long before Watergate became a household name, and so hardly appeared shocked at revelations of White House misdeeds and crimes. The *Christian Century* was therefore on the forefront of the Christian opposition to Nixon from beginning to end.

Turning toward denominations, I explore here two Lutheran entities. While American Lutherans represent a broad spectrum of political, religious, and social ideologies, these two denominations add moderate voices to the chorus. The Lutheran Church in America embodied a more left-leaning and mainline leadership but much more moderate laity, while the Lutheran Church—Missouri Synod presented a right-thinking leadership with a more middle-ground church body overall. Most studies suggest that Lutherans primarily belong to a middle-class group of predominantly white Americans. They lived in every region of the United States, though a majority in the LCA and LCMS resided in the Midwest. Furthermore, Lutheran denominations had a fairly high level of lay participation. While the clergy held most leadership positions, laypeople had strong voices through the various denominational conventions, control of their local congregations, and economic support of their church bodies. Additionally, Lutherans historically belonged to a group of Americans who seldom pronounced their views in loud and demonstrative ways despite having strong convictions about politics. They participated in such debates through traditional means that affected political leaders with petitions, letters, and voting. They openly deliberated in their periodicals, with letters to the editor and to church leaders, at churchwide assemblies, and in official and private correspondence. Seldom did their discourses, however, appear in secular newspapers or on television. Lutherans therefore functioned as part of the silent majority; they affected perceptions of Watergate but did so in a somewhat covert way. In the end, Lutherans represent a microcosm of average Americans in how they viewed Watergate.[14]

Specifically, the Lutheran Church in America was the largest Lutheran denomination and generally espoused a mainline Protestant viewpoint that advocated moderate to liberal positions on theology, foreign policy, and domestic politics. Its membership stood around three million in the early 1970s. Four Lutheran denominations had merged in 1962 to form the LCA, including the United Lutheran Church in America, which traced its history to the pre-Revolutionary period and included the first quasi-national Lutheran body, the General Synod, formed in 1820. This long history Americanized the LCA more than the other Lutheran churches; it also meant that the LCA more closely reflected a "typical" mainline Protestant viewpoint because it and its predecessor denominations had joined in alliances with other Protestants. For example, this was the only Lutheran church that belonged to the National Council of the Churches of Christ in the USA (NCC), an interdenominational body that lobbied on behalf of shared beliefs around the nation and orchestrated national and global relief efforts to more effectively utilize the resources offered by a variety of denominations. The LCA president during this period, Dr. Robert J. Marshall (1968–78), embodied mainline ideologies, with a moderate religious outlook aligned with more progressive views on social, political, and foreign policy matters. He privately disliked Nixon's policies but seldom voiced this disdain publicly, and only sought to effect change through traditional political channels, such as urging the laity to speak out when voting. The LCA, too, mirrors other mainline Protestant denominations in that the clerical leadership often took more liberal positions regarding theology and politics than did the laity. For example, while a majority of his fellow clergy echoed Marshall's views, as well as his behavior in seeking change, more laypeople backed Nixon to varying degrees throughout the controversy, some even up to and after his resignation. LCA seminaries trained pastors in biblical criticism, and the LCA regularly dialogued with other

Lutherans, Protestants, and Catholics to seek common interests and reduce previous hostilities between Christian groups. The largest Lutheran denomination embodied a predominantly moderate position and gave these common Americans an outlet to voice their opinions without vocally protesting or publicly demonstrating for various causes.[15]

The LCMS followed a much different ideological path than that of the LCA by espousing politically and theologically conservative points of view. Its membership stood at 2.8 million in 1974, making it the second-largest Lutheran body in the nation. Established in 1847, the LCMS had a staunchly German background and experienced no significant mergers to seriously alter its tradition. By the early 1970s, the LCMS advocated biblical inerrancy by disputing historical criticism. Significantly for the LCMS during this period, this position caused a major rift within the denomination because some fought this conservative viewpoint. For example, a faction broke away from the LCMS in the mid-1970s because of a dispute over teaching biblical criticism at Concordia Lutheran Seminary in St. Louis. President Jacob Aall Ottesen Preus (1969–81) epitomized LCMS conservative thought regarding this controversy and when considering political topics. He argued in favor of US policy in Vietnam and the Cold War in general, leaned toward the right on social issues, and backed Nixon throughout Watergate. He continued this support of the president even after Nixon's resignation, minimizing the scandal as political theater. And, in general, LCMS leaders and a majority of the laity concurred with this viewpoint on Watergate, though a moderate faction in the denomination voiced more qualms about the ethical behavior of their government. Furthermore, Preus visited Nixon in the White House and aided government efforts to free US prisoners of war held in North Vietnam. Also of note, the LCMS was an insular denomination that harbored suspicions against anyone who participated in interfaith dialogues and condemned those who prayed with non-LCMS Lutherans. Its political and theological outlooks aligned it with a broad segment of conservative America even as its leaders insisted it maintained its own unique position among the country's religions.[16]

Another conservative Protestant denomination, the Southern Baptist Convention, regarded the president highly and attempted to minimize the meaning of Watergate. The SBC espoused an evangelical point of view that encompassed the largest Protestant denomination in America, having 11,140,000 members in 1967. This denomination offers an interesting comparison to *Christianity Today*, especially with more Baptist lay opinions represented in the sources. With a fiercely decentralized polity, no denomination more adamantly protected local congregational rights. It also provided a mix of patriotic/conservative backing of the government with a staunch stand in support of the separation of church and state, which prompted unique ruminations during Watergate. Finally, the SBC reflects an interesting regional perspective in that it predominantly represents the southern United States, a useful contrast to Midwestern Lutherans.[17]

Southern Baptist Convention history indicates that this predominantly white church body, headquartered in and having a vast majority of members from the South, incorporated a conservative political and diplomatic agenda by the 1970s in all aspects of its church life. Founded in 1845, in part as a theological bulwark in defense of slavery, it broke from northern antislavery Baptists. It instituted a polity that defended local congregational control, followed by subsidiary state conventions and a national church office, a structure that held true for the 1970s. The twentieth century brought with it a retrenchment of Baptist conservatism, particularly in relation to the fundamentalist/modernist controversy. This eventually led to the ouster of even moderate Southern Baptists from power in the 1980s, including, for example, Foy Valentine, the leader of the Christian Life Commission, who offered a moderate political point of view with an antiwar stance and who sometimes questioned Nixon. Furthermore, the denomination lived with an interesting dichotomy regarding its view of the nation. On the one hand, it maintained the strong Baptist legacy of championing the separation of church and state, because of historic persecutions of Baptists by governments. Even before the SBC existed, Baptists somewhat ironically utilized this emphasis to insert themselves in politics by urging members to support candidates and government policies that ensured this separation. Thus, on the other hand, the SBC often sounded patriotic in its portrayal of American democracy and values, becoming defensive when people questioned the federal government. In other words, this denomination embodied Republican Theology more than any other. The SBC by and large supported Nixon, viewed Watergate as merely another example of sin in America to heal through mass conversion, and only became alarmed about the scandal in the summer of 1974 when too much evidence pointed to a major problem. SBC convention resolutions, periodicals, official papers, and lay sources thus contribute an important denominational voice with a southern, white, and evangelical outlook that paralleled that of fellow evangelicals at *Christianity Today*.[18]

To include voices other than predominantly white American Christians, I also engage with the African Methodist Episcopal Church, which had a membership of 1,166,000 in 1951. Though often less studied than its black Baptist counterparts, the AME contributes a Methodist voice to this study along with a willingness to engage in political, social issues in a public way. AME members, however, were generally more theologically conservative than many black Baptists, except when it came to the civil rights movement.[19]

Founded in 1816, the African Methodist Episcopal Church came about because of racism within the Methodist church that segregated congregations and made black leaders such as Richard Allen, its founder, a subordinate to white clergy. Theologically, therefore, the AME paralleled Methodism in general with an emphasis on living a strict moral life, temperance, and spreading the gospel through mission work and revivals. But it diverged from white Methodism and the white churches due to race. Because its inception came about as the result of a social issue rather than a theological dispute, the AME matched the history of other black churches with regular commentary on race relations and social activism first on behalf of the antislavery movement, then education and literacy for black people, desegregation, and civil rights. The ability to congregate and thereby discuss race issues prompted African Americans in all denominations to utilize the church as a bully pulpit and to fight for equality from the early 1800s to the present. This propensity to mix religion and politics differed sharply from many white Protestant denominations that avoided such activism for fear of alienating members or creating dissension. The very safety and livelihoods of black church members demanded social justice participation from their congregations. AME leaders and members alike therefore had few qualms about bringing social issues into the church. The AME elected leaders to local and national offices, thus further intensifying dialogue within the denomination about a range of social issues. When bishops, especially at the national level, spoke contrary to the will of an individual, congregation, or district, they found it necessary to defend themselves from attack and struggled for reelection. The division into districts that held annual meetings also fostered debate about current issues, including Watergate, because each could pass its own resolutions, and a vast majority in the denomination disliked Nixon. While the AME attempted to steer a moderate course politically and wanted to back the president, Nixon's poor record on race relations compelled black Methodists to oppose him. Their public denunciations meant that the president, in turn, ignored and disliked them. They parallel the other evangelical conservatives with a pietist solution to Watergate, but contrasted with them in their denunciations of the president and eventual calls for impeachment. Nixon's racist policies, in other words, allowed them to move quickly toward belief that he and his compatriots did something wrong, even while they clung to conservative theological solutions.[20]

Finally, the 2,053,000-member (1967) United Church of Christ contributes a unique voice because of its unflinching liberal activism, in terms of both theology and politics. Furthermore, they afford us the viewpoint of a more eastern Christian element, often parallel to the *Christian Century*. The UCC, similarly to the *Christian Century*, gives weight to using a Protestant liberal intellectual voice because of the lay opinions that it included. It therefore contributes another strong voice opposed to the Nixon administration almost from the moment of his inauguration in 1969.[21]

Such a strong position against Nixon should not surprise, coming from a denomination committed to social justice since its founding in 1957 with the merger of the Congregational Christian Churches and the Evangelical and Reformed Church. Because polity had so dominated merger discussions, especially the issue of local congregational control, and because ecumenism and unity were foremost in the minds of leaders, the founders spent little time articulating a firm theological direction for the UCC. Furthermore, the new constitution specifically called the denomination to "Christian action in society." This change left it to the new leaders, and especially the denomination's periodical, *United Church Herald*, to create the United Church of Christ's approach to national and global issues. They focused on human improvement. From its inception, these leaders took up the causes of civil rights, the women's rights movement, poverty, and other social justice issues and made them projects of the church. They also protested against the Vietnam War. Members soon followed, so that, already by the mid-1960s, the UCC became known for its activism on behalf of a liberal Christianity that wanted equality and justice for all people. Almost all of these positions stood in opposition to Nixon policies, and so the denomination and president had little regard for one another, with Watergate worsening the situation. The UCC concluded that Nixon had destroyed America's moral and ethical standing.[22]

In engaging with these various sources, I have aimed to transcend exclusive examinations of intellectuals or denominational leaders by including as much lay and reader opinion as possible. In addition to denominational and print data, I incorporate analyses of letters to the editor and to denominational leaders and committees, voting results at national conventions, and any lay correspondence or materials available in the archival sources. Considering items alongside the opinions of leaders and intellectuals broadens the perspective to offer a more complete sense of American reactions from a variety of levels. Nonetheless, admittedly, a certain amount of "elite" church history remains herein, as it does for many who attempt to research American religious history. The sources on which we are drawing are predominantly, though obviously not exclusively, from white middle- to upper-class citizens with a higher education. The conservative members of this group clearly belonged to the "silent majority" as labeled by Nixon. The denominational sources and periodicals included offer another means for us to view how Americans understood Watergate, particularly from a religious sensibility, a vital component of American life. Much of the material included centers on intellectual elites because they led the churches. Whether lay or clergy, highly educated individuals shaped the course of Christianity during this decade in profound ways. That their voices are heard more than many lay voices is only natural, because they recorded their thoughts and served through elections as the voice of Christianity. To avoid the "gap theory," in which denominational leaders swing more to the left than their lay constituents, I researched as many lay sources as possible and have included them in this book. Additionally, the use of convention minutes and resolutions assisted with this problem, because delegates were elected by congregations for all of the denominations studied herein. The popular vote at national assemblies, especially for the Southern Baptist Convention, indicates that at least this population of elected lay and clergy people agreed with their leadership. Surviving sources make it almost inevitable that a survey of this many institutions will still suffer to some extent from the laity/clergy gap. Yet if we take seriously the lay voices that we do find, and trust in the democratic process that the five denominations in this study employed, then we avoid this becoming a study that *singularly* examines elite church leadership.[23]

And so with this sampling we further the process of understanding reactions to Watergate. We are able to explore a spectrum of belief systems and histories, all of which played into how a particular periodical or denomination shaped its positions. This information better illustrates how Protestant America participated in the political drama that unfolded, asserted opinions publicly, and contributed to American attitudes about the moral crisis. It also provides us with a more accurate sense of US opinions in general at a critical moment of history. Liberal, moderate, and conservative Americans all voiced their opinions and shaped how the United States responded to the Nixon White House. Furthermore, they all employed their unique brands of theology to explain what had happened, to frame an appropriate response, and to offer Americans a way out of the nightmare. While it is virtually impossible to discern how or when Protestants had a decisive influence on American policymakers, public opinion, or the court system, this book demonstrates that Christian debates were a key element in American understandings of Watergate. Moreover, it reveals how they sought to act to make Christianity a living reality in American life, as a way to solve an essentially spiritual crisis. Protestant America voiced its opinion about Watergate in a frantic effort to assert moral authority at a time when it seemed particularly lacking and as people feared the ethical disintegration of their government. This strong response occurred at a time of great political shifting and instability, thereby allowing for a new way of viewing how Christianity contributed to politics. Christians therefore grew satisfied with contributing to political discourse even after Nixon's resignation. Watergate established a more intensified religious commentary in US politics moving forward.

I began this project around 2005, hardly knowing that conversations about Watergate and its legacy would resurface so forcefully in American life. As with Nixon, who propelled himself to power in part by falsely labeling his opponents as communist sympathizers, Donald J. Trump spent a good part of the Obama presidency claiming, falsely, that Barack Obama lacked an American birth certificate, and then establishing a base of supporters around his nationalist Make American Great Again slogan. Trump's shocking number of outright lies has been well documented, and Justice Department, congressional, and media investigations have detailed many instances of apparent obstruction of justice. Yet as with Nixon, many of Trump's white evangelical supporters in particular evinced a strong reluctance to abandon the candidate whom they had helped to take the White House, with religious leaders split between condemning him and his policies or overlooking his transgressions due to their embrace of his socially conservative platforms. Religion has played a key role in the nation's political dialogue of the past several years in great part due to shifts that occurred during Watergate. The United States once again found itself pushed by the actions of a controversial and seemingly dishonest president into critical conversations about morality and ethics in politics, and what they mean for the future of the nation. How and when did Protestants become so enmeshed in partisan politics? Grasping the dynamics of Christian responses to Watergate enables us to comprehend more fully that rancorous moment in US history, and to react amid new ones confronting us today.

1

A Presidential Election and Third-Rate Burglary

Numerous religious periodicals printed forums in the run-up to the November 1972 presidential election, offering a glimpse into perceptions about Nixon before Watergate solidified their political participation. To maintain their tax-exempt status, however, they had to present bipartisan reactions and thus asked a Nixon and a McGovern supporter to respond to a series of questions or write an opinion piece.

A.D., the official periodical of the United Church of Christ, published such a side-by-side piece in early November. Jack Steinman, a member of Christ Church in Fort Thomas, Kentucky, asserted a common Republican perception that McGovern "is a wild radical in his positions on taxes, welfare, and defense" and instead favored the "progressive changes of Nixon." A fellow member of the congregation, Stella Helmbold, countered that she saw McGovern as more "sincere" and principled. These brief comments shine a light on how Christians disagreed about the candidates, based on trustworthiness and capacity to move the nation forward. The Lutheran Church—Missouri Synod's *Lutheran Witness* printed a similar comparison. One side supported Nixon because he "has succeeded in tackling and finding solutions to the great number of problems he inherited when taking office" and offered the best chance to bring peace and prosperity to the nation. This person trusted the president and applauded his record, in contrast to the McGovern champion who asserted Nixon grew the deficit and continued an unnecessary war in Vietnam. The McGovern statement insinuated Nixon misled Americans about his campaign promises in 1968, and therefore "the people want a change of direction." The two Christian sides had already framed their stance on Nixon based on whether or not they trusted him.[1]

Protestants therefore held opinions about Nixon and his administration before Watergate plunged the nation into a constitutional crisis. While few religious bodies or periodicals took much notice of Watergate prior to November 1972, their perceptions of Nixon, conditioned as they were by already existing theologies and political inclinations, foreshadowed how they would confront it. The goals of social justice and concern for the greater good above individual desire endeared liberals to the Democratic candidate, George McGovern, while Republican Theology inclined conservatives toward Nixon's limited government and proclamations of public morality. Moderate Christians avoided political endorsements in 1972 and were more restrained, collectively, in terms of their political dogma than they would be after Watergate.

National events and political issues in 1972 set the stage for how Christians debated Nixon's Republican candidacy over against McGovern's Democratic challenge. Nixon continued his 1968 themes but insisted he had accomplished many of his goals, most important among them the reestablishment of law and order and détente with the Soviet Union and the People's Republic of China. The president also asserted he was on the cusp of bringing peace with honor to the Vietnam War, although in retrospect this was an empty claim. The Republican National Convention in Miami, Florida, highlighted these achievements. Publicly, the convention appeared jubilant and dedicated to a celebration of the sitting president's accomplishments, but behind the scenes, organizers took great pains to conceal protest and discord from those less than pleased with their president. In contrast, George McGovern ran on a leftist platform of ending the Vietnam War, expanding social welfare programs, and offering the nation a softer approach from the federal government.

Protestants reported throughout the summer and fall of 1972 on the presidential election in the restrained way common to much of the twentieth century for Christian involvement in politics. Watergate barely touched the surface of public opinion, especially within Christian institutions. But the way Protestants characterized President Nixon predicted how they would respond to Watergate in the coming months, as they grew increasingly bolder in their claims. The lines between his benefactors and detractors had already been drawn in 1972.

Christian Citizenship

Long before Watergate, conservative denominations and periodicals articulated a vision of what it meant for their churches to participate in American democracy. Whether they advocated a strict institutional separation of church and state or a theology of Christian citizenship, they employed the idea of the United States as a Christian country, one where moral and ethical beliefs from their faith background integrated with public discourse and the nation as a whole. The churches and their leaders demanded that their denominations and individual members engage their Christian convictions when considering political matters. The discourse did not yet address Watergate and was less partisan than after it, but the way conservatives envisioned their role in the public realm later guided how they tackled the approaching crisis.

During and just before Watergate, many Christians viewed participating in the nation's political system as essential service to God. Their faith incorporated a sense of American exceptionalism and a righteous attitude that paralleled the United States' policies, whether domestic or foreign, with God's plan for humanity. While Watergate dampened nationalism temporarily, conservatives invoked God's favor in this crisis to underscore America's exceptionalism. Making the United States a Christian nation provided a moral underpinning to the country, though sometimes it became an idolatrous worship. Both of these notions became manifest in how conservative Protestants addressed Watergate.

The Southern Baptist Convention most adamantly promoted the identification of Christianity with the United States during the Watergate period. While this stance could have contradicted the SBC's staunch backing of the separation of church and state, it fits well with Republican Theology as promoting limited government undergirded by strong public moralism. Individual religious liberty allowed the SBC the freedom to pursue the higher purpose of revivalism and faith building, which in turn created a stronger social morality. As Watergate progressed, the SBC sought to influence the conversation about Christian morality in the public realm in this way. Already in June 1972, the *California Southern Baptist* published a cartoon with a white American male holding an "America" sign, with a banner identifying him with "Our Christian Heritage" on one side and "One Nation Under God" on the other. This cartoon contributed a visual explanation for how Baptists viewed this blend of religious freedom, Christian influence on government, and the SBC role in both. Fred B. Rhodes further illustrated this notion. Rhodes, a previous worker on the Manhattan Project and in the intelligence community, as well as the administrator of the Veterans Administration under Nixon, informed his fellow Baptists that "the responsibility to govern stems from God himself." He maintained faith that a Baptist theology must guide the way he felt about his country and operated as a citizen. For members of the Southern Baptist Convention, God and nation united.[2]

Hudson Baggett, the editor of the *Alabama Baptist*, employed such arguments for his readership, too. While stressing that the paper never endorsed a candidate for public office, he asserted "the President is a key man in bringing" to reality the rule of God over the nation. The presence of faithful people at political conventions and when voting, especially for the president, gave hope to Baggett this truth would become real. He therefore stipulated Christian principles had to guide a person's vote. He wondered, "Why shouldn't Christian principles apply to politics both on the part of voters and the candidates?" Baggett encapsulated the essence of Southern Baptist notions of God and country, essentially that separation of church and state was not incompatible with a Christianity undergirding democracy.[3]

This SBC vision of Americans as naturally devout Christians was common among fellow editors, a guiding principle in print media for many lay and clerical constituents. Donald T. McGregor, editor of the *California Southern Baptist*, provided a classic explanation for how the SBC reconciled support for the separation of church and state with an obligation for Christian participation in politics: "A discussion of a free election has a place in a religious magazine because freedom of religion could well be the first freedom destroyed if elections were taken away." He had earlier emphasized "we are responsible" if things went awry in the United States; therefore Christians needed to voice their opinions through voting and other political operations. Or, as *Arkansas Baptist Newsmagazine* editor J. Everett Sneed commanded, all citizens had the responsibility to vote, but "as Christians, our obligations go much deeper. We should help to shape political opinion" based on Christian ethics and morality. Editor L. H. Moore of the *Ohio Baptist Messenger* grounded this argument even more deeply in a Christian context. After stating it made no difference for whom a Baptist voted, he wrote that Christians nonetheless had a moral duty and responsibility to the government to vote. Indeed, "not to vote is a sin of omission for the Christian." Therein lay the explanation for Southern Baptists who disdained the thought of mixing church and state but clung to a patriotism that drove them to the polls to protect their nation's interests and their own religious freedoms. They crafted a very careful religious platform to guide their political thoughts.[4]

National leaders of the Southern Baptist Convention drove home this balance between demanding autonomy from the government and insisting on a Christian's responsibility to it. Foy Valentine, executive secretary of the Christian Life Commission, conveyed the importance of a citizen "to stir up the spark of patriotism in his breast" while also remaining "absolutely" loyal to God. He called his constituents to discuss the relationship of Christianity to the political campaigns: "Christians can and should seek to be God's instruments of change, loving their country with the kind of responsible and disciplined love which will move it in the direction, under God, in which it ought to be going." At least one lay Baptist took this message to heart. Don Murdock explained that Valentine "challenged me to renew my effort to love my country more adequately by helping her move closer to God's standard of righteousness and justice." The executive director of the Baptist Joint Committee on Public Affairs more pointedly stated, "To moralize about the world while remaining aloof from public affairs, 'keeping one's hands clean,' is incompatible with the church's apostolic mission and a denial of its claim to be the body of Christ." Time and again, Baptists heard about a citizen's obligation to vote combined with a faith to do so according to Christian principles. Phil Strickland, a lobbyist for the Texas Baptist Christian Life Commission, rallied Baptist voters in much the same way. Though he acknowledged politics was fraught with temptation, he reminded people that "Christ walks there before us," and Baptists must venture to "the difficult places of life" to witness.[5]

Southern Baptist leaders had company in voicing this vision of civic duty as a Christian obligation when messengers gathered for the annual Southern Baptist Convention. Meeting in Philadelphia in 1972, "the birthplace of the Constitution of the United States," messengers resolved to uphold the Bill of Rights and its protection of liberties while urging "all Southern Baptists to work effectively as Christian citizens in support of these rights through appropriate legislative, judicial, and administrative action." Along with this responsibility, messengers affirmed the importance of a strict separation of church and state. In defining Christian citizenship, messengers decreed they "urgently call upon all Southern Baptists to carefully consider the vital moral issues in this year's campaigns, examine the moral positions of the candidates, scrutinize the platforms of the political parties, and the economic interests supporting the candidates, apply Bible truths and Christian insights in arriving at decisions related to politics, and prayerfully work for those who seem nearest to a responsible Christian position."[6]

The Southern Baptist Convention defined its blend of Christianity with the American political process in what it called Christian citizenship. While advocating the separation of church and state, SBC leaders and messengers explained that infusing the political process with Christian values created the godly bedrock to sustain freedom. They further based these ideas on their pietist theology of individual conversion and sweeping revivalism. Little did messengers know the extent to which events unfolding in Washington, DC, would test this very Christian citizenship and compel them to proclaim its importance even more urgently.

Compared with the Southern Baptist Convention, no Protestant group gave such a detailed articulation of nation and religion mixing. Nonetheless, glimpses into this concept appeared in various ways, especially among other conservative evangelicals. For example, *Christianity Today*'s editor reiterated this type of thinking in a letter to Senator Mark O. Hatfield of Oregon. Harold Lindsell requested an essay to encourage evangelicals to seek public office to further their message and to influence the government. Hatfield's success as a Republican senator and outspoken evangelical made him a living example. Gary Heikkila, the pastor of Mission Evangelical Congregational Church in Maynard, Massachusetts, stated his congregation's Fifth Annual Service of Patriotism garnered vast attention to "dedicated Americans who love this country" and would witness to God and country together. The service highlighted prayers for the president, others in authority, and service personnel as it echoed the SBC's call to vote with religious convictions. Of the various groups studied herein, those leaning toward a theological conservatism most often relied on Republican Theology because they combined love of limited government and liberty with public moralism, and individual pietism in the service of American power and greatness.[7]

Although it later broke from white conservative voices regarding Richard Nixon and Watergate, the African Methodist Episcopal Church had a similar message to its constituents, as voiced by the *Christian Recorder* editor B. J. Nolen. In asserting the presidential election year of 1972 brought "a burgeoning interest in spiritual vitality," Nolen offered that religion and politics interacted despite being seemingly at odds because "these themes are not mutually exclusive." Rather, he asserted that the current age of "personal anxiety and personal uncertainty" called for religious principles in all areas of the nation. Even before Watergate, the AME acknowledged the dissent that framed the previous decade regarding war, race relations, and women's equality. This viewpoint paved the way to begin thinking about the intersection of Christianity and government, from a denomination that since World War II grew comfortable with the mixture of politics and religion because of participation in the civil rights movement. The AME moved more slowly into politics during the twentieth century but by the late 1960s and into the 1970s had become comfortable with mixing faith and politics. Thus, unlike its white Protestant counterparts, the AME blended politics and church in a profound way by the Watergate era. AME leaders "announced a national voter registration drive," hoping to get two million more African American, and presumably Christian, voters to the polls in 1972. While not offering as deliberate a message as the SBC, the AME just as strongly voiced the concept of lay responsibility to the nation.[8]

Two Lutheran denominations also articulated some sense of the individual Christian's responsibility toward the American government. Both the Lutheran Church in America and the Lutheran Church—Missouri Synod came from a long American Lutheran tradition of quietism, avoiding controversial political topics within the denominations in order to maintain harmony and avoid uncomfortable dissension. They each, for example, refrained from even appearing to endorse one of the presidential candidates, especially within their official periodicals, the *Lutheran* and the *Lutheran Witness*. Even so, neither denomination completely shied away from crafting a sort of outlook regarding Lutheranism and country. The Lutheran Council U.S.A. (LCUSA), a joint venture of the LCA, LCMS, and American Lutheran Church, reported this exact sentiment in its *Focus on Public Affairs*. Robert E. Van Deusen, the LCUSA director of the Office of Public Affairs, wrote "churches could well provide facilities and encouragement for the discussion of basic issues. Individual Christians, whichever candidate they favor, face an important choice: to be active participants in the democratic process, or to observe it from the sidelines. The decision should be an easy one." Thus, Lutherans tended toward a more passive version of blending their faith and politics, though they certainly engaged the topic.[9]

Lutheran editor Albert P. Stauderman explained this same principle in a letter to one reader who complained he felt the periodical leaned toward a liberal point of view. Stauderman defended the magazine, pointing out its 142-year history of not engaging in partisan politics and emphasizing that it never supported specific candidates for office. Yet, he continued, "We do, however, have a responsibility to indicate the moral or doctrinal aspects of political questions." In this way, he and other LCA officials developed a Christian politics of linking faith to politics. His August 1972 editorial about the upcoming election more forcefully explained, "Our assignment, like that of every Christian, is to try to see through the shouting and slogans to the important questions facing the nation. There are moral issues that affect us all. The outcome of a presidential election can set the course for action on such issues for at least four years." While such words never endorsed Nixon or McGovern, Stauderman pled with readers to consider their Christianity when voting. In a more subtle way, the calendar of intercessory prayer issued by *Lutheran Women* asked all constituents to pray "we may have God's guidance to make responsible political decisions." A heritage of quietism did not signal a divorcing of Lutheranism from US politics, a point that would become more and more important as the Watergate investigation developed.[10]

Despite the LCA leaning toward a more moderate to liberal point of view on most issues and the LCMS becoming increasingly conservative throughout the 1970s, the two Lutheran denominations mirrored one another regarding politics and their faith. Citing the dangers of war, pollution, poverty, and other travails, LCMS *Lutheran Witness* associate editor Frank D. Starr warned, "Christians dare not be content to be *spectator citizens*." It was imperative for him that Lutherans directly involve themselves in world history and politics. He further prophesied, "It is not enough to sit in our comfortable houses of God and lament the breakdown of the family, corruption of government, or failure of church and school to change the hearts of man." Rather, Christians had a responsibility to act. LCMS president J. A. O. Preus sent the same message to fellow pastors. The presidential election offered the opportunity to ask for God's blessing on the nation and all elected officials, and such prayers could "give us pious and faithful rulers." LCMS leaders refrained from endorsing any candidates, but such nonpartisan rhetoric must not divert historians from understanding that Lutherans, too, felt an obligation toward the United States. A conference in which both LCA and LCMS members participated made this point clear when it decided "Christians are not political enough. The alternative to involvement in national priorities is an atrophied church which exhibits the image of a museum or mausoleum. The church can identify where its message and value commitments intersect with the political arena and it can inform its own members and the wider society of this interaction." Lutheran quietism, in other words, was not the same as inaction or indifference.[11]

Compared with evangelical and moderate Protestants, Christians from the left tended to endorse Christian commentary on the public sphere while also condemning anything smacking of framing America as a "Christian nation." Liberals avoided identifying Christianity or its theology with the United States and its government. United Church of Christ editor of *Social Action*, Huber F. Klemme, complained about Richard Nixon's "bad foreign policy," his lack of integrity on economic justice, and his avoidance of race matters. He added, "Any citizen who fails to vote, who votes without weighing the issues discussed in these pages, or who having voted fails to continue working for the realization of these objectives, deserves four more years of frustrated hope." This opinion bordered on taking Christianity into the voting booth, but otherwise neither the UCC nor the *Christian Century* framed the election year in any Christian context. Both entities voiced strong political opinions and wanted people to adhere to Christian values in public, but they did not see such activity as having special implications for the United States as a Christian nation. They in part shied away from this concept because they denounced America's racism, sexism, and other discriminations, prejudices that hardly aligned the nation with God's vision. Their stance against "idolatry" became more and more evident in the coming months, when they would in part blame this mixing of theology and politics for the Watergate affair and Nixon's behavior. It represented a dangerous form of nation worship that undermined both the government and Christianity.[12]

Little of what Protestant entities knew by November 1972 pointed toward the crisis that would engulf the nation over the next couple of years. Nonetheless, the national election offered Christians the opportunity to explain their perception of faith and the public world. Most Christians asserted they had a moral obligation stemming from their faith life to vote according to these convictions. The separation of church and state did not divorce individuals and even their institutions from the public sphere. At the same time, all Protestants were relatively cautious to avoid being too partisan or one-sided, instead urging that a blending of Christianity and politics guide an individual's voting choice regardless of political leaning. This caution mirrored much of the twentieth century in how American Christianity remained on the outskirts of partisanship. And it shows how a foundation already existed that justified Christian action in politics, making it easier to launch into politics as Watergate materialized. As the moral failings of the Nixon administration came to light, combining faith and politics would become increasingly important to them, even for those liberal voices who criticized the idea of America being a Christian enterprise.

Opinions about Nixon

Understanding the points of view about Nixon also laid a foundation for later Christian reactions to Watergate, because of course not all Christians viewed the president in the same light during the 1972 election. Lining up in conservative to liberal theological lines paralleling national political trends, more conservatives endorsed the president, while the left tended to castigate him. Only the quietist Lutherans avoided any explicit public statements about either candidate. Protestant opinions about Nixon stirred in 1972 despite the restrained twentieth-century behavior of American Christianity, attitudes that played a vital role in how factions later conceptualized Watergate and moved more assertively into politics.

Richard Nixon and his staff courted the conservative Christian vote throughout his presidency. Scholars have traced the rise of conservative religion into the political realm, and particularly toward the Republican

Party, from a slow movement at least dating from the 1930s, if not before, and building throughout the 1960s. Nixon and his advisers looked to take advantage of this phenomenon, showing the strength of this movement already in 1972.[13] And, ironically, it would be Watergate that propelled them even further into politics. Of the Christian endorsements for Nixon's reelection, most emanated from the evangelical right. A fall survey of Louisiana Baptist pastors showed a stunning seventy-three out of seventy-five pastors stated they would vote for Nixon. Surprisingly, given other black churches more often criticized Nixon, Joseph A. Jackson, president of the National Baptist Convention, U.S.A., angered his delegates by also supporting the current president. Perhaps Harold Lindsell, editor of *Christianity Today*, most succinctly proclaimed, "I will be in Europe on Election Day, but before I go I will cast a vote for Mr. Nixon." A plethora of examples prove Christian evangelicals backed Nixon, and other statements give substance to this kind of pro-Nixon rhetoric.[14]

Quite often, these conservative Christians voiced appreciation for Nixon's foreign policy as the reason for endorsing him. They especially gravitated toward his détente efforts and believed he was bringing the Vietnam War to a conclusion "with honor." My study of evangelical reactions to the Cold War and the Vietnam War demonstrates conservative Christians often applauded any work against communism as in line with maintaining their global missionary efforts. Regarding the Soviet Union and the People's Republic of China, this meant improving relations might open new doors to missionary work, while protecting South Vietnam from defeat allowed missions to work there. Thus, people such as David E. Kucharsky, one of the editors at *Christianity Today*, proclaimed, "Nixon is characteristically a disciplined man who makes the most of his opportunities, and this one [his visit to the Soviet Union] might well be his greatest." Even the usually quiet Lutherans of the LCA Ohio Synod resolved to give their "wholehearted support to President Nixon in his peaceful efforts to bring an end to U.S. military involvement in Southeast Asia." Though a private sentiment, *Lutheran* editor Albert P. Stauderman combined these ideas when he stated Nixon's foreign policy brought an "overwhelming feeling of relief among most Americans that there may be a way out of the cold war." Conservatives absorbed Nixon's self-image as a peacemaker, thus aligning their Christian principles with his perceived actions, which in turn spurred them to vote for him in 1972.[15]

Harold Lindsell, who later committed to voting for Nixon, used his association with Billy Graham to gain access to the president. In March 1972, Graham orchestrated for Lindsell and other religious leaders to meet with Henry Kissinger, Nixon's national security adviser and main diplomatic operative. Graham took such initiatives on behalf of the president to help secure favor among the evangelical voters in the upcoming election. This work certainly had a favorable outcome for Lindsell, who wrote a thank-you to the president for allowing him to learn about foreign issues from prominent government officials. He declared, "Dr. Kissinger performed superbly, exhibiting not only his extreme knowledge of past history but his ability to relate the lessons of the past to contemporary problems of national policy." To Kissinger, Lindsell explained, "As one who is committed to the Christian faith I am deeply persuaded that the larger and the long-range interests of any nation depend in great measure upon policies forged within the framework of a life and world view based upon a Judeo-Christian heritage. I am sure you have a full understanding of what I have in mind." Meeting with Kissinger quite possibly sealed the deal regarding not only Lindsell's vote but also his public backing of Nixon. While he would most likely have voted that way regardless, such behind-the-scenes contact greased the wheels for some evangelical leaders. A combination of Nixon's reaching out to evangelical voters and their own conservative political/theological leanings brought the two together in 1972.[16]

Yet the battle lines remained somewhat fluid at this early stage of the Watergate era, as evidenced by the fact even the *Christian Century*, which proved resolutely antagonistic to all things Nixon, published an article advocating the president's reelection because of his foreign policy. The periodical had to print such a piece in its election issue in order to maintain its tax-exempt status. Editors chose Thomas J. Houser, the chairman of the Illinois Committee for the Re-election of the President, to write the piece. He summarized his view as follows:

> When I am asked what, in my opinion, is President Nixon's most significant accomplishment during his first term in the White House, my initial response is always: which *one*? For I believe—rather immodestly

perhaps—that a number of President Nixon's accomplishments could be labeled "most significant": His initiatives to end the Vietnam war. His peace-keeping efforts in the Middle East. His moves to put a halt to the arms race and to open relations with the Soviet Union and the People's Republic of China. His efforts to bring about stable economic growth without inflation or unemployment. His government reorganization and revenue-sharing programs. His landmark proposals for environmental protection, drug abuse and crime control, welfare reform, minority business enterprise, pension security and national health care. Any of these could be labeled President Nixon's "most significant" accomplishment.

Not many of the writers or editors for the magazine concurred with this sentiment. Still, it demonstrates how Nixon's flare for dramatic image making influenced many Christian voters.[17]

Furthermore, conservative Christians listed more than Nixon's foreign policy among their religious motivations for backing him. His opposition to busing to solve the blight of segregation drew numerous people into his camp, including racist Christians who feared what integration might do to their cities and children. Though not a Nixon enthusiast, Robert E. Van Deusen of the Lutheran Council U.S.A. acknowledged how Nixon's deliberate handling of key racial matters helped the president gain constituents, even among the Christian community. Nixon intentionally walked a fine line between enforcing civil rights laws and Supreme Court mandates while simultaneously pulling back on rigid enforcement of such things as investigations into university admissions policies. In this way he claimed to demand respect for the law while endearing himself to the growing block of white southern Republicans and other Americans distressed by changing race relations. Finally, his law-and-order platform squared with many conservative Christian points of view. Nixon campaigned in 1968 on law and order to appeal to Americans who had grown weary of the 1960s unrest. He promised to restore order and obedience to the law, blaming lax enforcement on the Democrats and on liberal "permissiveness," and subsequently kept up this fight as president. In opposition to antiwar demonstrators, assassinations, the Black Power movement, race riots, and general disorder, conservative Christians maintained obeying the law lived out their religious convictions. Nixon's law enforcement therefore brought him in line with them.[18]

For any or all of these reasons, Nixon found support among conservative Christians. These Christians found reason to think the president best represented their convictions for the future of the United States, a point of view that often softened criticisms about Watergate and led many of them to believe in the president's innocence through much of the turmoil.

In contrast, most Christians from the theological left denounced Nixon and worked to defeat him. Nixon had many liberal detractors regarding his foreign policy, especially as it related to the Vietnam War. A vast majority of liberals did not see him as a peacemaker and instead accused him of deliberately prolonging an immoral war. Liberal mainline Protestants accepted Nixon's election and promise to work for peace in 1968 but quickly grew disenchanted as the months and years passed with no sign of an end to the war. Their antiwar platform and Nixon's continued fighting of it turned them against his reelection campaign before it even started.[19]

Richard Nixon and Henry Kissinger repeatedly stressed they could only accept peace with honor under Vietnamization. Privately they hoped South Vietnam's collapse would take place a couple of years after the US withdrawal to avoid it looking like an American failure. Christians who opposed Nixon's 1972 campaign often cited this as their number one reason for doing so. Even while admiring Nixon's détente with the Soviet Union and the People's Republic of China, *Christian Century* editor Alan Geyer proclaimed, "It is beyond our belief that recent U.S. actions in North Vietnam contribute to peace." Roger L. Shinn, the Reinhold Niebuhr Professor of Social Ethics at Union Theological Seminary, had harsher words: "But not everyone admits that this has been an *immoral* war. 'We will never stain the honor of the United States of America,' said President Nixon to the Republicans at Miami Beach [the location of the 1972 Republican National Convention]—with no mention of My Lai, burned villages and napalmed children. The President's stance was that expediency might commend withdrawal, but that morality required the courageous decision to persist." Shinn disagreed, as did Dr. James R. Smucker, the chief executive officer of the New York State Conference of the United

Church of Christ. He decried US leaders for basing their thinking on an "eighteenth century" philosophy: "Blood and thunder nationalism produce national honor." He asked, "Whose honor has been tarnished by the death and destruction, the homeless, the fatherless and the despairing people of Vietnam?" The entire UCC Council of Instrumentality Executives, including UCC president Robert V. Moss, worked publicly and behind the scenes to end the war. Moss and others described the war as having been "provoked by Mr. Nixon," and therefore shaped much of their opposition to him.[20]

Denunciations of Nixon's Vietnam policies also led to direct calls to vote for McGovern. Virginia Toth, who regularly wrote letters to the editor of the *Lutheran*, asserted, "People wonder how Hitler got so powerful, well that is not so hard to understand, Nixon is going down the same road. He is rattling his sabers and threatening to destroy Vietnam with bombing and mining." She therefore wanted her church leaders to more publicly denounce the war and advocate for McGovern. The bishop of the United Methodist Church for the Dakotas, James Armstrong, forcefully agreed with her: "Senator McGovern has been right about Vietnam. Richard Nixon was part of the mind-set that brought about the tragedy in Southeast Asia" and continues as part of the problem. Since Nixon's 1968 pledge to end the war, Armstrong pointed out, "20,000 American men have died; more bomb tonnage has been dropped than the total during the preceding 15 years; more American tax dollars have been spent than during all of those 15 years. And the war has been expanded into Cambodia."[21]

No Christian campaigned against Nixon more forcefully than Martin E. Marty, the Lutheran pastor, church historian, and columnist for the *Christian Century*. Mocking that the Republican National Convention appeared as more a coronation than political activity, Marty pointed out its careful orchestration and avoidance of controversy. He said, "Most of the time a yawn had been the appropriate response of the public." Turning his attention to the Vietnam War, Marty complimented Nixon's announced meeting with China but added, "Maybe it will occur to him to stop that bombing [of Vietnam] one of these days or years. If that should happen, no one would yawn." But it was the president's daughter who especially rankled Marty and linked his opposition to Nixon to his antiwar platform:

most campaign rhetoric has not been worth listening to this year. But one phrase did catch on. In an effort to keep us all whipped up about bombing the Vietnamese, the President's daughter sweetly offered herself for the cause. Everyone knows: Julie Nixon Eisenhower would willingly die that the Thieu government in South Vietnam might live.

That statement made me mad; were I not nonviolent it would be necessary to say *damn* mad. How better to trivialize the lives of the hundreds of thousands *they* killed and the hundreds of thousands *we* killed than to announce, from the sanctuary of the White House, that one would join them in suffering and sacrifice and even in death. Greater love for corruption hath no one than this, that she would die for Thieu.

Antiwar Christians did not believe Nixon regarding his promises to work to end the war, which led to defiant words against him during the campaign.[22]

Other domestic policies brought about Christian opposition to Nixon. As mentioned previously, the United Church of Christ disliked his economic policies and track record on race relations, which also drew comment in the *Christian Century*. But there was no harsher condemnation of Nixon and his lack of support for civil rights than from African American denominations. Though lackluster in their support for McGovern, the two thousand delegates to the National Baptist Convention of America, meeting in Dallas, Texas, unanimously approved a resolution to condemn the Nixon administration in part because it "consistently acts against the best interest of poor minority citizens" and thus "threatens progress toward full citizenship of all citizens which this nation has made over the last two decades." Reading the literature from the African Methodist Episcopal Church throughout 1972 gives the same sense of unease about Nixon's commitment to equality. In August 1972, delegates to an AME convention resolved, "Blacks and the poor have been left out of everything during the administration of President Richard M. Nixon, who has exhibited an attitude which is anti-Negro, anti-poor, anti-humanity, and consequently, anti-Christian." The convention, however, did not avoid controversy. There were pockets of AME leaders who tried to remain more neutral, and though they did not endorse Nixon, they did not want to publicly denounce him. This led to a debate when the General Conference Commission invited Nixon to speak to the quadrennial conference. New York bishop D. Ward Nichols explained that they invited him out of "citizenship" and respect for him as president of all the people, "white or black." Nixon declined to attend but sent one of his brothers. A protest ensued, leading the brother to leave out a back exit. Despite the gesture toward Nixon and evident in the forces that removed his brother safely from the auditorium, most members of the AME opposed Nixon's reelection because of his domestic policy agenda.[23]

Nothing about these pro- or anti-Nixon reelection statements deals with Watergate. Long before they registered their opinions about Watergate, they had formed opinions about the president and shared them publicly. The periodicals, denominations, and people who here supported Nixon believed his public rhetoric about Watergate throughout most of the crisis and handled the controversy more delicately, while those who worked against his presidency more quickly linked him to Watergate and castigated his actions. Yet the political involvement of these entities was limited in volume except for louder liberal voices, and thus reflected the muted Christian partisanship of the twentieth century. But Protestant opinions of Nixon in 1972 made their Watergate stances more or less vehement in the coming years as they also became more assertive political operatives.

Watergate

While most said little or nothing about Watergate, some Christians did take notice. Theologically and politically liberal Protestant voices commented the most on Watergate prior to November 1972. *Christian Century* editors and writers unsurprisingly led the charge, given their general disdain for Nixon policies even before he became president. Even in its early stages, Watergate gave them one more reason to distrust the president and work against him. In the article they published advocating a vote for McGovern, part of it prophetically explained that Watergate and other Nixonian shenanigans would "challenge the Teapot Dome scandals for their place in the sun of political notoriety." James Armstrong, the bishop of the United Methodist Church for the Dakotas, then complained, "yet, again, the American conscience seems anesthetized" to the problem. So he asked, "If lieutenants of George

McGovern had been caught red-handed bugging the Republican National Headquarters, would the press have been so kind? The judge so accommodating? The public so apathetic?" The liberal Protestant periodical also published a political cartoon that depicts two pastors; one of them is sitting at a desk, and the other one speaks as he walks into the room: "There's a person outside here who would like to make a Confession—provided he's given limited immunity," a clear reference to the Watergate proceedings. In other words, the *Christian Century* suspected from the beginning that Watergate represented more than a "third-rate burglary," used it as further fodder against the president, and spearheaded Christian criticism of the administration as more details became available. The lack of respect for Nixon's past laid the foundation for future rebukes.[24]

Social Action, the official periodical of the Council for Christian Social Action of the United Church of Christ, articulated its misgivings about the Nixon White House before the burglary even took place. In May 1972, the periodical published two stories referencing the Pentagon Papers. Historians now understand the release of those reports set in motion what later became the plumbers operation, which ultimately bungled the Democratic National Committee break-in. This UCC publication had an inclination that just such a thing might happen. Mike Gravel, a US senator from Alaska, criticized the administration's attempt to thwart the release of the papers and wrote, "The elaborate secrecy precautions clearly were designed to deceive, not the enemy, but the American people." Editor Huber F. Klemme pointed out the Pentagon Papers release had prompted the United Church of Christ to ask the president "to stop efforts to impose prior restraint on the publication of political information and opinions" and asked "what possible justification can there be for a democratic government to keep its citizens *un*informed— let alone deliberately *mis*informed—and then pillory those who throw the light of truth on those who have betrayed their larger trust?" As with the *Christian Century*, many within the UCC and especially those at *Social Action* were suspicious about the Nixon administration long before Watergate.[25]

Some moderates to conservatives took notice of Watergate. A reader of the Lutheran Church in America's official periodical, the *Lutheran*, cautioned that national leaders could no longer "hoodwink us with untruth." After the "highest officers in the land" lied to the American people, he wanted Christians to monitor the national scene for further problems and bear witness against them when needed. Even *Christianity Today*, which generally supported Nixon, understood the Republicans "have their fair share of problems," including "the bugging of the Democratic headquarters in Washington." This further proved the importance of Christians participating in politics in order to inculcate it with civility. These two examples represent the more muted exposure other Christian entities gave to Watergate. They referenced it, but like many Americans did not yet grasp the full extent of the problem and where it would lead the nation. Still, the fact that it appeared on their radar meant Protestants would watch in the coming months with close interest as events developed further.[26]

Overall, few Christian denominations or periodicals referenced Watergate in much detail prior to the presidential election in November 1972 because it remained an event of little importance for most Americans. The scarcity of comment demonstrates how well the Committee to Re-elect the President (CREEP) and the White House clamped down on information and kept it from leaking to the public and marring the president's bid for a second term. As historians have uncovered in the legislative branch, the judicial branch, the US media, and eventually the wider public, suppression would slowly unravel for the Christian community over the next two years and bring its members forcefully into politics.

Conclusion

The early months of the Watergate scandal found limited Christian reaction, mirroring the whole nation because investigations had only begun and because Christians at this point in the twentieth century were more politically cautious than they would be after Watergate. Nonetheless, information from June 1972 to the November election provides important clues about how various institutions later reacted based on their theological and political tendencies. Christianity framed much of its narrative in the context of Christian obligation in the public sphere, especially among conservatives. The Southern Baptist Convention, *Christianity Today*, the African Methodist Episcopal Church, and to a lesser extent Lutheranism espoused a doctrine that celebrated American democracy and freedom as mutually supportive of their Christian convictions, if not derived from them. Such patriotism led to support for the president based on his law-and-order platform and strong foreign policy. However, liberal Christians held a more secular view of the government, divorcing the entity itself from Christianity and instead examining individual morality and behavior to see how they affected the officeholder's effectiveness. This stance merged with their already strong sense for social justice and equality. Liberals therefore became more likely to criticize Nixon in these early stages of Watergate.

American Christianity held entrenched beliefs about morality and ethics long before Watergate took center stage, and they paid attention to politics despite being more cautious and nonpartisan throughout much of the twentieth century. The left espoused a strong inclination toward social justice and dislike for Nixon, and labeled nation worship a form of idolatry. The right advocated Republican Theology and applauded America as uniquely Christian through limited government and high public moralism. And the African Methodist Episcopal Church sat somewhere between these views, with a strong sense of piety but left-leaning platforms regarding race and attitudes toward Nixon. Taken with what all of them said about the president and what little they outlined regarding Watergate, this laid the foundation for the debate and turmoil about to set into Christian America as the scandal boiled into a crisis in the coming months. The muted tones and bipartisan efforts would increasingly tilt toward greater Protestant participation in politics as Watergate festered.

2

A Fading Issue or Sinister Plot?

Christian concern about Watergate gradually built from the time of Nixon's reelection in November 1972 through summer 1973, as Protestants became a little more involved in political commentary. Previously held but divergent convictions about him shaped these responses even as a consensus emerged that misbehavior had occurred. As the moral and spiritual leaders of society, Protestants reacted in ways that illustrate their own belief systems and understanding of how to assert their authority amid the growing political crisis. But a nation founded on religious liberty and accepting of most points of view found a Christian community divided over how and where to profess that power as Watergate unfolded.

Key developments in the Watergate investigation made it impossible for anyone to ignore the crisis. First, figures involved in the Nixon campaign pled guilty to or were convicted of conspiracy, burglary, or wiretapping, including G. Gordon Liddy and James W. McCord Jr. By April 1973, pressure forced White House chief of staff H. R. Haldeman and the president's White House counsel John Ehrlichman to resign, followed by Attorney General Richard Kleindienst. Then, in May, Senate committee hearings about Watergate began and were broadcast live on television. The crisis deepened in June, when fired White House lawyer John W. Dean testified the president was involved in the cover-up. In short, Watergate consumed the Nixon presidency in increasing public scandal. Conservative, moderate, and liberal Christians had to voice their opinions or risk being rendered irrelevant in the face of the nation's greatest contemporary crisis.

A poem in the *Christian Century* summarized the liberal point of view, describing a world in which "Illusion" about American ideology died because of the Vietnam War and Watergate. Americans could no longer trust the nation to uphold right against wrong because of too much militarization and political corruption. The "scales are fallin from our eyes" to reveal "Babylon is falling," and Christian prophecy exposes immorality in the highest places. In other words, Christians faced an emergency of nearly apocalyptic proportions and needed to act to save the nation. While moderate to conservative counterparts did not ignore the serious issue, they approached it more circumspectly. *Christianity Today* admitted the Watergate affair was "sordid" and the president must "see that the matter is thoroughly and fully investigated." But the editors still accepted "at face value the claim of the President that he was not personally involved." They inched into the conversation about Watergate cautiously, wanting "to bring the culprits to justice" but not yet seeing a calamity. Still, the conversation about morality in politics brought them an opportunity to again call for individual conversion and greater dedication to Christ, which could became a way to save the country as more and more people gained God's favor.[1]

Through remarks about the president, general commentaries about politics, and a debate about Christianity and the public realm, Protestant America conversed about Watergate at a time it grew into an urgent matter and taught them the importance of their political voice. These months saw a slow shift from the relative nonpartisan nature of American Christianity in the mid-twentieth century to the more overt politics of the twenty-first century.

Liberal and Conservatives Split over Nixon

As throughout the previous presidential election year, conservative, moderate, and liberal Christians approached the Nixon White House with entirely different points of view. Their perceptions in many ways mirrored the polarized opinions of the general population. In the period immediately following Nixon's reelection until summer 1973, those perceptions proved resistant to change even as these Christians all became more comfortable with voicing them.

Conservative Protestant opinions about Richard Nixon stemmed in part from the president's outreach to them as one of his important constituencies. Nixon relied on evangelical leaders, especially Billy Graham, to court right-leaning Christians for his campaign and continued to embrace them after his second election. For example, Graham got Nixon in touch with a number of conservative religious leaders for one-on-

one interactions, organized meetings with groups of them in which the president shared his opinions, garnered them invitations to lead White House religious services, and generally rallied his right-leaning colleagues to support Nixon.[2] Nixon staged numerous White House worship services and enacted such Christian observances as National Bible Week, to make the scriptures "the touchstone of [Americans'] lives." Such ploys endeared him to the Religious Right and particularly evangelical voters. A form letter Nixon sent to numerous constituents further made this point. He often included the line "These are challenging times, and I believe as you do that we need a deeper understanding and application of basic principles of our great tradition in religion to help us solve some of our problems." Conservative backers of the president had little to say about the Watergate affair during this early period of the investigation, in part because they trusted the man and the convictions he conveyed to them. His public display of moralism catered to their longing for Republican Theology, and they were slow to believe any Watergate evidence damaged the image of the man whose rhetoric matched their desire for a godly America.[3]

Leaders such as J. A. O. Preus, president of the Lutheran Church—Missouri Synod, applauded Nixon in a variety of ways. After receiving an invitation to an inaugural event, Preus declined because of a prior commitment overseas but added, "I trust that you will convey to President Nixon my sincere best wishes on this historic occasion and assure him of my continued backing for him and his administration." Nixon not only earned Preus's vote but also enjoyed continued loyalty afterward. Liberal Christian periodicals that criticized the president also heard from rightist Christians, another sign they appreciated his presidency. A United Church of Christ layperson from Illinois blasted *A.D.* for too much liberalism and insisted the one piece the periodical published in support of Nixon before the election spoke for him, "and most Americans, as the election showed." A reader of the *Christian Century* took similar umbrage. He blasted McGovern for claiming a moral high ground and then turning into a typical politician once he received the Democratic nomination. In addition to "moral fervor," the reader noted "it also takes the sound judgment of seasoned leadership, which is able to take the pressures of campaigning and the Presidency" to lead the nation. He concluded, "Richard Nixon showed that he could do this."

Without mention of Watergate, many conservative Christians advocated for the president at the beginning of his second term.[4]

Nothing endeared Nixon's Christian backers to him more than his brokered peace with North Vietnam. Unlike their liberal counterparts, who detested Nixon's policies in Southeast Asia, these believers trusted the president brought a peace with honor. The view of Nixon as a peace-maker fit well with their Christian convictions. Nixon himself linked the peace initiative to Christianity on numerous occasions, including the National Prayer Breakfast in early 1973. Declaring peace must "begin with each and every one of us in his own heart," Nixon explained to those gathered, "A lasting peace in Vietnam is possible only to the extent that both sides are determined to keep the peace." These words at a re-ligious function provided a link between policy and the Christians who supported the president. Preus again contacted the White House, this time to directly correspond with the president and congratulate him for the end of the Vietnam War. Preus explained, "One of our society's prob-lems today is a quickness to criticize coupled with a reluctance to com-pliment. After the barrage of criticism leveled at him by his detractors, it is only fitting that we honor the leader of our country for this peace with honor." He relayed this message through an official press release and with a report in the *Lutheran Witness*. Messengers to the Southern Baptist Convention's 1973 gathering joined the praise with a resolution to commend Nixon "for his efforts in bringing honorable peace to Vietnam and his continued efforts to insure peace in Southeast Asia." Conserva-tive Protestants did more than merely back the president blindly because of his outreach and own words; they also assessed his record, in this case coming to the conclusion he served the United States well with his Vietnam policies. These sentiments set the tone for their ignoring of Watergate as a major problem for such a trustworthy president.[5]

When conservative Christians mentioned Watergate before July 1973, they often dismissed it as insignificant in language that mirrored White House rhetoric. Charles Colson's note to Patrick Buchanan in July 1973 stated, "Watergate is going to begin to fade. People are tired of it, most of the sensationalism is gone and now is the time for the President to step forward and really take the initiative where it counts." A number of Christians voiced this very fatigue. Another way conservative Christians echoed White House rhetoric came with a defense that the president and his men simply carried on a time-honored tradition of dirty politics. A layman in the Lutheran Church in America explained as much: "Watergate is something that has gone on for 100 years. Who was hurt? Anyone killed? Any injuries? Read about the bugging of Goldwater in 1964 and Nixon was bugged in 1968—and Democrats stole the election from him in 1960. (and [sic] Bobby bugged Martin Luther King)." Interestingly, conservative Christians avoided comment about public morality here, most likely because they wanted to continue to support his agenda, because they distanced the president from lower-end actors in the political drama, and because they deemed Democratic malfeasance as even more insidious.[6]

Other indications suggest these Protestants believed the president's protestations of innocence and his pledge to conduct a full investigation. They therefore invoked their faith in the American judicial system and pointed out he was innocent until proven guilty. Though the amendment failed, many SBC messengers backed the attempt by Frank E. Breithaupt of Missouri to add to a resolution on morality in American politics: "And at the same time, we respectfully remind the press that the accused are innocent until proven guilty and that they be careful to treat all accused in such light." This motion failed more because many found it irrelevant rather than disagreeing with it in principle. The amendment also hinted at another cue picked up from the Nixon White House. The president and his associates on a regular basis blamed the Watergate problem on a liberal and overzealous press. Or, as Robert Sternloff wrote to the *Lutheran*, "The threat to press freedom comes not from the White House, but from the press itself as it goes on with its bias, conceit, ego and stupidity." Nixon's popularity with conservative Christians held firm up to a year after the Watergate break-ins. He embodied public morality to them, and they admired his conservatism and his many public displays of religion in the White House. Their pleasure with the president also explains their more subdued political involvement because the power brokers already represented conservative Protestantism. The same cannot be said of moderate to liberal Christians.[7]

Indeed, the religious voices who worked unsuccessfully against Nixon's reelection came down hard on the president in the first months of his second term for a variety of reasons, including that his administration had done nothing to heal national divisions in government, society, and the church. Immediately after the election, the *Christian Century* admonished the president to heal divisions and bridge the gap between "class, race and ideology," but it feared this would require "reversing his domestic style" and doubted he would do so. J. Martin Bailey at the UCC's *A.D.* worried the president was too isolated, but Bailey held out a little hope "perhaps now he will acknowledge how badly we are divided and assume the role of a statesmen in leading us out of the doldrums." He especially believed Christians should demand a leader to "help us overcome our limited goals and avoid narrow identities." Yet the tone of his editorial suggested skepticism that Nixon would rise to the challenge given his past record. Even without mention of Watergate, the president faced doubters among the leftist Protestant community from the onset of his second term. And liberal Protestants led the charge in infusing the conversation with their religious convictions.[8]

In late 1972 and into the first half of 1973, liberal to moderate Christians also insisted Nixon and his administration lied about or failed to follow through on key promises: prolonging of the Vietnam War, combating racial inequality, setting the economy adrift, and rolling back Great Society programs.[9] Everett C. Parker, the director of the UCC Office of Communication, explained, "The Nixon administration is trying to deprive women, Blacks, and other minorities of the right to jobs in broadcasting stations." He noted a bill before Congress to protect broadcaster licenses against charges of unfair employment practices. He concluded, "Nothing in current Administration policy for communication is more vicious than this determination to deny minorities and women their hard-won rights to jobs in television and radio." In other words, he accused the presidency of favoring big business over civil rights protections. The African Methodist Episcopal Church often fell on the more liberal side against the administration on the issue of race. The AME bishops gathered in Washington, DC, in early 1973 to register "deep distress" at Nixon's treatment of "Black people and poor people across this land." They accused him of negating social progress from the 1960s and feared he would "plunge us in the direction of a period of social retrogression and despair." The bishop of the First Episcopal District proposed that "Mr. Nixon come to Newark for himself" to see what the government programs he attempted to cut did for minority neighborhoods, before he put the ax to them. These churches worked diligently to improve race relations and against poverty in America, and their theology insisted the church work for social justice.[10]

A minority of evangelicals also criticized Nixon along these lines. Theologian Ronald J. Sider explained, despite McGovern's loss, "if we are listening to all that Biblical revelation says about justice in society, then our politics must reflect a concern not just about pubs, pot, and pornographic literature, but also about racism, poverty, and grossly unjust distribution of wealth here and abroad," which Nixon failed to do. Stephen Charles Mott, an assistant professor of Christianity and urban society at Gordon-Conwell Theological Seminary, explained to a critic of his McGovern support: "I supported Senator McGovern because his position on social questions such as poverty and militarism to me is closer to Christian standards than that of President Nixon." Long before Watergate ramped up, politically liberal Christians and like-minded conservatives lined up against his failure on social justice.[11]

Theological principles also pushed liberal Christians into an opposition to Nixon's foreign policy, especially the Vietnam War. Unlike their conservative counterparts who saw at hand peace with honor, they saw the president's actions as immoral and a lie. A letter to the editors of the *Christian Century* noted the frequent criticism leveled at McGovern for changing his mind about the Vietnam War, even as the president went from Cold Warrior to shaking hands with Mao Zedong and Leonid Brezhnev, or, as the reader put it, becoming "palsy-walsy" with communist leaders. He saw Nixon's foreign policy as mere window dressing, not a true engagement with peace. Editor James M. Wall, in a postelection interview with McGovern, pointed out this hypocrisy and bemoaned, "The public refuses to deal with the Indochina war on moral grounds." McGovern concurred with this "uncomfortable fact" and backed the periodical's condemnation of Nixon's diplomacy. The UCC's *A.D.* printed an article by Erwin D. Canham, the editor in chief for the *Christian Science Monitor*, questioning why the administration "kept so secret" the peace process to end the war. This led to suspicion about motives and realities, not the conservative applause for ending the war seen elsewhere. Nixon's hard-line stance against amnesty for draft evaders was among the reasons to mistrust the president. The Lutheran Church in America's *Lutheran* claimed Nixon led "opposition to forgiveness" because evaders must pay a penalty first. This position failed to account for the moral qualms that led the men to flee and kept the nation divided. Thus, liberal to moderate Christians doubted the president's sincerity and disliked a majority of his policies because they went against the greater good.[12]

Watergate intensified the liberal Christian stand against Nixon. At first the scandal frustrated many anti-Nixon Christians because too many Americans simply overlooked Watergate or dismissed it as politics as usual. Huber Klemme, editor of the UCC's *Engage/Social Action*, stated, "It is not so easy to understand why, in a region that values decency and good morals, the ITT affair, the Pentagon cost overruns, Watergate, and the wheat scandal had so little effect in tipping the scales" away from a Nixon landslide. He referenced the president's dropping of an antitrust suit against International Telephone and Telegraph Company and the Hartford Insurance Company in exchange for a campaign donation and selling of surplus wheat to the Soviet Union. The AME's *Christian Recorder* voiced more intense skepticism when it reprinted an article from the National Association for the Advancement of Colored People's magazine the *Crisis* in which the writer wondered, "Even if this sinister plot was spawned in the White House without his approval or knowledge, how could the process of executing it have escaped his attention?" This led to frustration at voters who "closed their eyes and minds to this stupid activity—clearly criminal at the time of exposure." Coming in July 1973, the report decried it "went little challenged until after the election."[13]

These preliminary thoughts about Watergate gained traction because liberal to moderate Christians sensed the White House's attack on the press. The UCC Board for Homeland Ministries made this link during a December 1972 meeting in Boston. The participants voted unanimously to back the Unitarian Universalist Association "in resisting the government's interference in its internal affairs." This decree came about after the government tried to subpoena financial records and names of members after the association's Beacon Press published portions of the Pentagon Papers. The Board for Homeland Ministries called it a serious threat not only to freedom of the press but also of religion. The White House's hard line against Watergate and its associated matters therefore alarmed the UCC. Karl H. Hertz of the Hamma School of Theology simply explained, "In the age of Watergate we ought to have learned once again the importance of a free press, uncomfortable as its findings may be."[14]

But it was the *Christian Century* in these early Watergate months that brought the most negative commentary to Christian readers and thus Christian action in the political arena. Built on an already established disdain for Nixon policies and behavior, the periodical guessed from the start the depth of problems the nation would soon face. Editors and writers favored congressional hearings, especially those chaired by Senator Sam Ervin set to begin in late spring 1973. Though still hoping in April "this unsavory business does not directly involve the President," editor James M. Wall worried that an anything-goes atmosphere already pervaded the executive branch under Nixon, and "if the scandal is as bad as we fear, we can only hope that Senator Ervin is patient, careful and unbiased in his pursuit of truth in the whole sordid series of events." Franklin H. Littell, professor of religion at Temple University and an expert on Christianity and totalitarianism, more pointedly wrote, "It is bad enough that cabinet members, generals, members of the National Security Council and top administrators in the White House should have actively fostered illegal and criminal actions. Far more serious is that for many of them such conduct was predictable: as members or sympathizers of an organization that should be unconstitutional, such persons did not merit public trust. Under a wise President they would never have been given it." A guest editorial by Reese Cleghorn, a staff writer for the *Charlotte Observer*, pointed out that the surface information alone condemned Nixon with proof the administration "criminally used the CIA, compromised the FBI and ruined its acting director, destroyed evidence, tampered with witnesses and even a federal judge, played games with the State Department's secret cables, made the very words 'Department of Justice' seem a mockery and tried to 'fix' a presidential election by using the same methods that the dictator of a banana republic might have chosen." Cleghorn sounded the alarm that something had gone terribly awry in Washington, DC. The *Christian Century* only escalated its attacks as the months moved ahead.[15]

In the early stages of the Watergate investigation, Nixon's ability to polarize the nation revealed itself in the Protestant community. Conservative Christians continued to trust him because they believed he had nothing to do with Watergate. They praised his accomplishments,

which they saw as aligned with Republican Theology of limited government and with conservative public morality, and warned against a
rush to judgment. Their liberal and moderate counterparts continued
their established line against Nixon's policies, which made it easy for
them to assume the worst regarding Watergate. Nixon had long worked
against their desire for government that placed American individualism
over greater social justice. In both cases, the theology Christians brought
with them into Watergate informed their first reactions before they ventured into stronger political commentaries as it grew in intensity.

Pietism and Revivalism

Despite their support for Nixon and timid forays into the Watergate
matter, conservative Christians entered the national conversation, adding their theological point of view. In addition to moving cautiously,
they emphasized that Watergate revealed a larger national problem, not
something limited to a few people at the top, using the opportunity to
call for a religious awakening throughout the nation to transform the
political system. Their theology turned to the same solution time and
again: individual Americans needed to convert. They believed "genuine
religion extended beyond church activities to all realms of life." In other
words, pietism meant practicing faith in everything a person did, not
simply on Sunday, including in public and political spheres. They also
took aim at liberal theology, with specific denunciations of situational
ethics. In these early theological reflections, conservatives of this type
steered away from specific mention of Nixon and instead attempted to
make the national scandal into a conversion experience.[16]

These believers, as they did with their brief mentions of Watergate,
urged caution and slow judgments. Many lay members of the Lutheran
Church—Missouri Synod, in fact, wanted the church to stay completely
out of the conversation. Five of the printed letters to the editor in the
November 26, 1972, issue of the *Lutheran Witness* said as much. They
asserted Lutheran theology separated the religious and secular realms
almost completely and expected their church to remain true to its heritage. A layperson in the Lutheran Church in America echoed a similar
sentiment in a letter he wrote to *Lutheran* editor Albert P. Stauderman.
He feared the too many "pastors and laymen who have used Watergate as

an emotional diving board to belly-whop into a pool of anti-government or anti-Nixon abuse" and quoted Martin Luther: "No one shall revile the rulers, be they good or evil." These conservatives adopted a typical Lutheran religious response of wanting their denominations to stay away from the political realm, something historians label as "Lutheran quietism." In the context of these early Watergate months, however, they had company.[17]

Adding an evangelical voice, Senator Mark O. Hatfield, the Republican Oregonian and evangelical, cautioned at the Mayor's Prayer Breakfast in Chicago about the burdens that fell upon the president and saw them as "almost inevitably unbearable and corrupting." The president therefore needed "compassion and our fervent prayers" because the American nation as a whole victimized him with "idolatrous expectations." Hatfield trod lightly into Watergate and warned that religious principles contributed to the problem and demanded prayer. Southern Baptist regional newspapers wrote much the same thing in May 1973. While acknowledging that anyone who broke the law must repent and come to justice, the *Capital Baptist* editorialized, "The same system requires that we see each man as being innocent until proven guilty." Only such dispassionate thinking could redeem the system in these editors' eyes. Gaines S. Dobbins for the *Alabama Baptist* quoted the letters of Paul in telling readers how to monitor Watergate. Paul entreated Corinth to "stand firm and steady. Keep busy always in your work for the Lord." To Dobbins, this meant remaining calm and avoiding too much excitement in reacting to news about Watergate. He further reminded readers, "While condemning sin, let's not forget the Christian duty to be compassionate toward the sinner. Jesus warns, 'Judge not, that you be not judged.'" In this way, evangelical conservatives squared their earlier political convictions with a religious message of restraint, compassion, and sobriety.[18]

Christianity Today was a standard-bearer for these types of theological ruminations about Watergate within the evangelical community. A November 1972 editorial set this tone in an earlier mention of the crime than what appeared in most other conservative Protestant entities. Editors admitted a "moral cloud" hung over the White House throughout the election "because of continuing revelations of dirty dealings." The anonymous piece also stressed the "very damaging" nature of the evidence apart from exaggerations from the liberal media. Also troubling them was "the failure of the White House to counter the charges in any substantial way." Still the paper shied away from blaming Nixon or calling for an all-out investigation. Instead, editors trusted the president would investigate and get to the bottom of the problem. Until then, *Christianity Today* counseled coming to terms with the scandal based on prayer and spreading the evangelical message of repentance and hope.[19]

Another reason for moving slowly into divine judgment came from a conviction that political misconduct was not an isolated phenomenon but a manifestation of the sin permeating American society. Several moderate to conservative leaders sounded this chord from the end of the election to July 1973 as a way of theologically explaining the problem. A June editorial by *Lutheran* editor Albert P. Stauderman nicely summarized this reflection: "Watergate alone may not be an earthshaking crime, but it is visible evidence of the spiritual illness that has afflicted our land." Though committed by people in high places who should therefore convey the highest of moral standards, "Watergate is part of an epidemic marked by lower sexual standards, misuse of drugs, marital infidelity, disrespect for law, general condoning of cheating and a philosophy that advocates winning at any price. The idea that the end justifies the means has infected our lives." This expression of a world spiraling into moral decay and in need of saving came over and over again from the mouths of conservative religious leaders whenever they mentioned Watergate.[20]

James E. Wood Jr., director of the Baptist Joint Committee on Public Affairs, a conglomeration of seven Baptist organizations that lobbied and monitored politics in Washington on behalf of the denominations, articulated a similar Baptist theological response in his June contribution to *Report from the Capital*. He noted the seriousness of the allegations that "raw political power" ran rapid in the nation but asserted that Christian Americans could learn vital lessons from the circumstances. He reminded readers, "The problem of evil is no respecter of nations, political parties, or persons." He warned that demonic forces preyed on the United States and both Republicans and Democrats. "Man's inclination to evil" reflected original sin. Despite other aspects of Southern Baptist life sounding a patriotic tone, Wood cautioned against "blind nationalism and political loyalty" as "good for neither the state nor for the church." He also pointed out the irony of Watergate occurring under an administration that had so staked its legacy on a platform of law and order. He declared it was "manifestly symptomatic of a lack of political morality in government." Sin caused the problems, and only a return to Christian ethics would solve them.[21]

Bill Moyers, a former aide to President Lyndon B. Johnson and ordained Baptist minister, spoke to the Southern Baptist Women's Missionary Union during the national Southern Baptist Convention in June 1972. He asserted America faced a "tangled web of deception and scandal" and a first-time abuse of power of this magnitude. However, he also emphasized Baptists should concentrate on preaching righteous judgment and God's word to everyone. So, while he worried that Watergate drew "the nation to the edge of a police state," he laid the blame more on American reluctance to prophesy than on the administration itself. The nation's moral collapse represented the true illness of the mere symptom of Watergate.[22]

Many conservative Christian leaders prior to July 1973 agreed. Harold Lindsell, editor of *Christianity Today*, pronounced, "On every hand there are signs of a pervasive and continuing spiritual decay. For example, sin has eaten deep into the fabric of American political life. The Watergate tragedy is but the tip of the iceberg." Yet, Lindsell added, "Nothing in that situation is unique nor is it an isolated event." The notion of evil and national sin was so prevalent that "whatever has happened in Washington in recent years can be found in every city, large and small." He listed other modern American "evils" demanding attention as much as politics, including pornography, homosexuality, divorce, single parents, racism, lying, drug use, and gambling—a classic litany of social concerns. He then warned, "America may shortly experience the judgment of God upon it for its sins." SBC president Owen Cooper sounded a similar alarm in his 1973 Annual President's Address. He listed a tome of problems before stating Watergate taught Americans "wrongdoing is no respecter of persons" or exalted positions. He feared scientific and technological advances were crushing Christian ethics, and thereby led to Watergate. He held out this much hope, thinking the time had come for a renewal of Christian moral standards, a constant theme for much of the rest of conservative discussions about Watergate.[23]

Moderate to conservative commentators emphasized prayer as a way to revive personal piety and the nation. *Lutheran Women* included in a section on daily prayer a call to pray for "all who govern, that God will enable them to rule wisely." A nation torn apart by war, social unrest, racial strife, and now political turmoil needed Christian entreaties to God if it hoped to move forward. Albert P. Stauderman made this same point on a number of occasions. Whether about politics, diplomacy, or other aspects of the presidency, Stauderman himself prayed for the president to employ God's will in his decision-making. Editor Hudson Baggett informed *Alabama Baptist* readers that Watergate reminded everyone "no human being is exempt from temptation and sin. As a matter of fact, those in high positions of leadership have stronger temptations than most people." So what could a Christian do to solve the problem, when so far removed from the power brokers in Washington, DC? Baggett urged, "We need to pray that citizens of this country as well as government leaders will realize the importance of honesty and openness in a democracy." These prescriptions for prayer focused on the depravity of humankind, assuming only God could fix the spiritual problems. Anything less than reliance on prayer would fail.[24] Pietists commonly added the absolute necessity of personal conversion in order to pull the United States out of sin. These calls for conversion and taking personal responsibility went out to every American, not simply those in Washington, DC, or in powerful positions. All citizens could help save their country through admitting their own sins and turning toward a Christ-centered life. In this regard, Watergate was more of an opportunity to bring people to Christ than a unique constitutional crisis or threat to the government.

Southern Baptists especially took this plea for personal responsibility to heart. J. R. White, the pastor of First Baptist Church in Montgomery, Alabama, wrote for the *Alabama Baptist*, "In this time of national turmoil, when there is evil in high places, we will do well to seek the mercy and grace of God for our nation and commit ourselves personally in repentance and renewed fidelity." Peter McLeod of First Baptist Church in Waco, Texas, spoke at the convention of the Southern Baptist Religious Education Association in Portland, Oregon: he demanded Watergate call Americans "to national repentance" in order to gain God's favor and thus save the nation, too. He explained, "Watergate is not a glass through which we look. It is a mirror in which we see ourselves." This theory drew a line back through American history, in which pietists blamed not the culprits, chance, or various circumstances for problems but rather unrepentant citizens for allowing God's wrath.[25]

Yet these jeremiads could at times align the dire warnings with a message of hope. Asking whether the American people would ever allow a Watergate scandal again, Donald T. McGregor, the editor of *California Southern Baptist*, explained politics, though "not religious," affected everyone and thus "unless people in politics live by such principles as are based on a biblical faith, we are facing days of even more grave consequences." However, he urged readers, "Rather than letting Watergate cast us into despondency let us determine to do something to help bring a fresh breath to the political scene. We are all part of it," and voicing a Christian conviction nationally would alleviate the situation. Seminary professor Joe Davis Heacock similarly argued that "scandals and corruption in high places can be avoided by heeding the Bible." Even if one did not run for office or serve in the government, a Christian vote and demand for ethics might force the change Americans so desired. Ralph H. Langley, pastor at Willow Meadows Baptist Church in Houston, Texas, further cautioned, "*Praying* and *voting* are both Christian acts and Christians had better wake up *both* to responsibilities and privileges." He therefore blamed Christian neglect for Watergate but added that even in "dirty politics" Christians had to contribute "the ethic of Christ into Caesar's domains to shape and mold and make the politics and political institutions serve our Lord."[26]

This brand of Republican Theology rooted itself in the patriotic sentiment that America could return to its founding faith of Christian morality. Nixon even sensed as much when he gave his second inaugural address, in which he asserted, "We shall answer to God." *Christianity Today* applauded him for this, stating, "He commendably asked for our prayers" that God might guide his decision-making. While this editorial cautioned against pride and feared Nixon encouraged such nationalistic hubris, the evangelical periodical construed his words to call for a revival toward "traditional" Christian faith. The *Ohio Baptist Messenger* also linked the nation's future to its faith base, despite the "imperfection of human nature and the arrogance of evil" as manifested in Watergate. Editor L. H. Moore assured readers, "The sense of morality that stresses personal integrity and decries dishonesty comes from the religious heritage of our nation. We are one nation—under God."[27]

And what better way to please God than with the rallying of Americans toward an old-fashioned revival? In the *Arkansas Baptist Newsmagazine*, Daniel R. Grant, president of Ouachita Baptist University, labeled the Watergate travails as tragic yet urged Americans to ask "whether any good can come out of it." He answered affirmatively. In addition to a need for it to lead to more national humility, it should inspire Americans to "pray asking God to forgive us" and therefore get Americans to return to a moral, religious foundation. LCMS president J. A. O. Preus similarly alluded to both the government's ethical lapses and his own church body's internal split. The LCMS divided sharply beginning in the late 1960s over the teaching of historical criticism, which led moderate Lutherans to defect from their denomination. Despite these evidences of government and church discord, Preus sounded a note of optimism that God "is asking us to 'look for the ancient paths.'" A grassroots return to Christianity could heal what threatened both his church body and the country, according to his concept of people mirroring Christ's time on earth and the misinterpreted faith of the Founding Fathers.[28]

The SBC secretary for the Christian Life Commission of the Baptist General Convention of Texas, James M. Dunn, more pointedly stated, first, the nation must return to a hard-line rule of law. In addition to this more secular matter, he decreed, "The ultimate need of society is for a deep and pervasive spiritual awakening. Nothing short of a real revival will change the moral climate of the nation. Nothing short of authentic evangelism issuing in authentic morality can help us." Otherwise the nation risked continuing its historic downturn and "may very well be in mortal peril." Dunn therefore offered up a call familiar in American evangelical history, with its tone and notes echoing preachers from the colonial period onward. When the United States confronted a problem of immense proportion, regardless of the circumstances, the only solution lay in a widespread "return to the Gospel."[29]

One other conservative theological concern bears mentioning. In an accusation that would become more prominent the longer the Watergate scandal persisted, commentators took the opportunity to fire off against liberal situational ethics for the crisis and other tribulations. *Christianity Today* made this argument when it compared Watergate to the

Daniel Ellsberg case of the Pentagon Papers that had precipitated the White House extralegal activities. Even before that fact became common knowledge, the evangelical periodical blasted liberal commentators for harsh condemnations of Watergate participants while simultaneously defending Ellsberg because they agreed with his antiwar platform. According to editors, Ellsberg committed treason against the United States and stole the infamous Pentagon Papers. They wanted consistent denunciations of all illegal activity, not picking and choosing those things on which one agreed. The May editorial also stated, "We do not think that Nixon knew what was going on at Watergate at the time it happened. We do not think he moved fast enough when he did find out. And we do not think he will be impeached." They *did* think liberal situational ethics were painted across American culture and paved the way for this scandal to erupt.[30]

Foy Valentine, the executive secretary of the SBC Christian Life Commission, also blamed situational ethics for creating an American culture in which the "ends justify the means." In "The Moral Word in the Gospel," his address to the commission's annual convention, he accused Madison Avenue of promoting a new climate that "brought poison to our present political pot" because it "rigs its own response, simulates its own support, manufactures its own applause, and steals the other fellow's secrets in order to guard its own." This notion of certain people seeing themselves as above the law in what they did to succeed stemmed from "the bitter fruit of a derelict situationalism unchecked by moral antibodies. Its issue is compromise and corruption in the church and shattering scandal in the government. It sires such aberrations as the muddy Watergate affair with its lies, corruption, distortions, arrogance, self-deception, crime, crime coddling, complicity, perjury, deceit, and lawlessness." Importantly, this denunciation of situational ethics came from a moderate Baptist, indicating how a broader swath of Christians viewed Watergate. And, to these believers, fundamental Christian values included fixed Christian moral precepts, not situational values.[31]

Although conservative Protestant entities shied away from much detailed and specific discussions about Watergate at this point, and despite the fact that many continued to defend the president, they began to craft their argument based on a traditionally conservative theological message. The political crisis stemmed from a lack of Christian morality governing the American scene writ large. To fix the problem, then, Americans as a whole were called to commit more firmly to their own Christian values. This pietist approach might heal the nation by bringing God's favor to it. In a country with a long history of revivalism, to conservatives it naturally stood to reason America must undertake a 1970s-style revival to save individuals and the government at the same time. They were learning to bring this message more forcefully into the political realm.

Liberal Theology Takes Aim at Nixon

In direct opposition to the conservative Christian caution and pietism, moderate to liberal Christians asserted a more activist theology and blasted the administration for its failed moral leadership. Their religious values emphasized the need for Christians to speak out loudly in the public realm against immoral activities and perform the role of prophet whenever possible. They felt called to this action, in the same way conservative evangelicals were called to pietism. In the case of Watergate, it often meant intense discussion about the corrupting influence of power and, specifically, the case of Richard M. Nixon as president. As outlined previously, these Christian thinkers articulated reasons to dislike this presidency long before Watergate became a national nightmare. As the crisis escalated from November 1972 to summer 1973, they applied their religious values to the matter, which only intensified this disdain and political discourse. They were at the forefront of moving into politics during the era.[32]

From across the leftist spectrum first came demands that conscientious Christians had a duty to speak against government corruption and ills. Leaders in the Lutheran Church in America often made this point. An associate professor of theology wrote about the need for such proclamations in a letter to LCA president Robert J. Marshall. While Marshall and others within the church body spoke publicly about Watergate and other social justice issues such as race relations and the Vietnam War, Dr. H. Eberhard wanted a more forceful denominational stance. He explained the war and Watergate revealed a government in turmoil, "the climax of a moral crisis and at this very moment our church is caught in apathy." Perhaps his and other similar voices prompted Lutheran officials to take more note of the problem, as Edgar R. Trexler did in a July *Lutheran* editorial. The associate editor acknowledged Americans desired an honest government, many churches spoke against Watergate, and basic moral principles failed in this instance. He hoped, however, "the virtues taught by the church are now being upheld and reinforced by millions" of Americans because of Watergate. He continued: "Since the church seems to have more influence in hard times than in good, the day is among us not so much to put-down Watergate as to uplift the enduring values that it ignored. The national uproar is a complement for what the church teaches, and indicates that its message is highly desired. The momentum belongs to the church now."[33]

The United Church of Christ argued the same point more forcefully. J. Martin Bailey privately defended his role at *A.D.* in making statements against the government as it related to Watergate because "I am convinced that the Lord who is interested in persons is interested in us in all of our activities and that the Christian ethic applies not only to individuals but to the structures of society in which we as individuals play a part." With this theological reasoning, readers of the official periodical saw regular and harsh commentary about everything taking place in Washington, DC. A June editorial lamented the lack of concern from all citizens about the government's actions, blaming a "complacent attitude" and ignorance regarding how the White House's actions infringed on individual rights. More troubling, the editors felt "it is especially discouraging that our moral and religious leaders have all but abdicated their responsibility to speak out and to organize some effort to preserve our liberties." The UCC Executive Council went further in this regard and reorganized the Council for Christian Social Action into the Center for Social Action, including a presence in Washington, DC, a denominational arm designed to lobby on behalf of the church body to give it a national voice in politics. The people hired must possess "knowledge of how the U.S. government operates," and the center itself received a mandate to "call the United Church of Christ to a ministry for justice and peace." The United Church of Christ's call for prophetic voices against the Watergate climate met with specific action for the denomination.[34]

The Reverend Doctor Gabriel Fackre, professor of theology at Andover Newton Theological Seminary, summarized this point about Christian voices well in a statement at the annual meeting of the UCC Florida

Conference. Watergate served as a call to national repentance for "the arrogance of power and the apathy of the citizenry." More frustrating to Fackre, he perceived that "evangelism" stood silently as the press, not the church, exposed the problems and "proved to be the conscience of the community." Thus, he prayed "never again in this generation will evangelism be tempted to silence the word and deed of justice and truth." Furthermore, he declared, "We believe that the good news of Christ's victory over the powers of evil emboldens us to stand before the powers of our own day to speak the truth in love." Like their LCA counterpart, the UCC and liberal Christians founded their Watergate commentaries on the ideal of the church's obligation to comment publicly about all issues and to work for change when they confronted ethical and moral lapses.[35]

This call to action led to a search for the base problem within Watergate, which to liberal Christians began with corrupted politics. Debased politics also lay at the heart of their theological reflections because it spoke to a core lack of morality in the government. The United Church of Christ insisted the government first and foremost revealed its abuse of power in the way it attacked the freedom of the press. Nixon made an art of vilifying the press as uniquely opposed to him and talked publicly and privately about the press as a personal enemy, especially wanting his followers to ignore anything negative it published about him. The UCC thought this arrogance demonstrated a propensity to quash bad press in an attempt to control what people heard. Denominational leaders asserted in the context of Watergate this led to the continued cover-up. The executive branch possessed too much power, which led to immoral actions because the administration thought it permissible to try to control everything that went against it. And many of these statements came against both parties, showing Christian liberals spared no special interest. Church leaders from four states within the United Methodist Church protested "the irresponsible and dangerous misuse of power by administrations of both political parties for many years" and then entreated their congregations "to become actively involved in political and social issues," thus linking it to the importance of Christian commentary. A political cartoon in the UCC's *Engage/Social Action* criticized both parties for a multitude of problems. It depicted the "seniority system" in Congress as disabling the legislative branch, while a coronated executive branch looks on. In other words, the power of the old guard took privilege over change and effective government, rendering the federal government impotent. For liberal Christians, Watergate symbolized corrupt government but was hardly unique.[36]

Specific case studies better expose how liberal Christians denounced government corruption, as revealed in Robert Jewett's article for the *Christian Century*. Jewett, a theologian-in-residence at the American Church in Paris on leave from his professorship of religious studies at Morningside College, set his scriptural analysis in Luke 12:2–3. The text explains "nothing is covered up that will not be uncovered, and nothing secret that will not become known." It further testifies that things spoken "in the dark" will be brought to light. Jewett said leaders throughout history ignored biblical warning, "perhaps never more shatteringly than in America today." As the "truth is emerging from the darkness," Jewett accused Nixon of an arrogance in his statements that criticized the perpetrators while still concealing what he knew. He also blamed "zealous nationalism" because it led people to protect their political power without feeling guilty, since they believed their actions protected the nation. In turn, "The message to be proclaimed from the housetops may well be that even a President can be misled by zeal, that his decisions directly encouraged the idea that the government is above the law." Jewett postulated the Bible warns of how people attempted to cover up wrongdoing, but truth won out. He likened Watergate to this situation. Jewett also found hope in the theological reflection that, over time, biblical prophecy would reveal the truth to all Americans and restore order.[37]

While these examples discuss a more general notion about the corruption of power, other liberal Christian commentators directly blasted Nixon and his administration. Once again the *Christian Century* was in the forefront. Historian Martin E. Marty avoided comment on Watergate for much of the year, finally explaining to readers in May, "I know myself. Instant response could mean that I would only 'pile on' my *hubris* to the President's own. If the accused Watergate caperers and coverers-up are indicted, tried and sentenced, I will probably simply find confirmation of the fact that the Nixonian moral tone produced such goings-on." He also charged that Nixon never "recognized moral fault, blame or guilt existentially or theologically" for the corrupted power he oversaw in the White House. So, Marty concluded, he shied away from writing about Watergate because "in my frustration and rage, I would probably be no more spiritually probing than he." Readers by and large agreed with Marty's framing of the White House. E. Paul Weaver, pastor of |Union Center Church of the Brethren in Nappanee, Indiana, wrote to the editors that Nixon "gathered around him a gang of ruthless men who determined to assure his re-election" at any cost. It appalled him that they "violated the constitutional rights of the rest of America" under the president's watch. Like Marty, he saw little redeeming value in the current administration.[38]

Voices within the United Church of Christ sounded a similar tone about Nixon. *Washington Report*, the newsletter of the newly established Center for Social Action, informed readers that the US attorney general announced Henry E. Petersen as the investigator into Watergate, and he reported only to the president. Editors sarcastically noted their mistrust of the president by adding, "Some say this is like putting the fox in charge of the hen house," and later, "The top person in the scandals has not been identified to date." Pastor Allan R. Brockway elevated the problem from politics to a theological danger: "No room for doubt remains about the essential evil that lies at the heart of the Nixon administration." He further articulated that "'evil' in the current context means action that is intentionally contrary to the best interests of the American people but done in the name of the best interests of the American people." He regretted even this periodical went too long without identifying the scandal as such for fear readers would accuse it of having become too partisan. In his writing in July, Brockway proclaimed, "We, at this late date, declare that the name of the evil now coming to light in our nation is not 'Watergate' but 'Richard Nixon,'" which he took to mean the president and all of the men around him who committed the crimes. In one of the earliest, if not first, calls for Nixon's resignation or impeachment, he concluded, "So long as the President remains in office, so long will the evil pervade the national government. Like the centipede, it can and will grow new legs and arms when the old ones are exposed and excised." Thus the UCC merged theology and the current political crisis to mandate theological reflection and the involvement of the church to purge the national sin.[39]

In May 1973, Robert V. Moss added a more nuanced theology regarding the Nixon White House. The UCC president spoke at an ecumenical convocation at the Christian Theological Seminary in Indianapolis and aimed his remarks at the notion of a loss of Christian faith among Americans. He first sketched disappointment that so few Americans voted in the November election and "even when the facts about Watergate began to come out few people confessed to being surprised." This led him to believe "from the perspective of the church several things need to be said about Watergate." He blamed the crisis on a "growing concentration of power in one office and in one person" and subsequently on those who sought to "silence opposition, discredit and even jail prophets, and mislead the people." He likened this behavior to biblical stories about the kings of Israel seeing themselves as above the law until the Word of God came through the prophets to rebuke them: "The story of the kings of Israel is the story of power-hungry political leaders today." He also hoped this might teach Americans the hard lesson that "the presidency is not a sacred office." "If we can bear to hear and face the truth," he stated, the crisis may teach the country to once again balance the powers of government in the three branches. He hoped it would further lead politicians and leaders to "help this nation to again become a people of conscience, united in love of God and love of our fellows." Moss had criticized Nixon's administration long before Watergate, but the scandal clearly alarmed him even more than his dislike of its politics. For Moss and others, this behavior bridged the gap between church and state because something immoral had rooted itself in the government. Society therefore needed the church, and especially its religious leaders, to set forth a renewed Christian principle. But unlike their pietist counterparts, liberal theologians saw it more as a collective condition. They did not call on individual prayer and conversion for a solution, but rather outlined a religious/political argument for Christians together to first censure Richard Nixon as the main culprit with his abuse of power and then turn toward fixing the larger concern about corrupt politics.[40]

Left-leaning Christians extended this theological criticism to include the Nixon administration's hyper-fear of the left. *Christian Century* editor James M. Wall contended Americans too easily forgave Nixon's obvious immorality because "they count on [him] to protect them from the dangers of a nation weakened from within by liberal economics and lax law enforcement." Their conservative bent and fear of the left made them susceptible to Nixon's pandering to their interests. Conservative coddling of the president "serves to dilute moral resentment" and left conservatives so partisan they no longer cared about immoral behavior when it benefited them. Wall linked that belief to a Watergate excuse that "well-intentioned" men committed illegal acts to safeguard the White House. He illustrated how this was a specious argument because it centered on the theory "they sensed a threat from the political left. In popular thought, these were not immoral acts, but excessive acts committed for a righteous cause." Therein lay the heart of the ethical problem for Wall, who obviously disagreed with the perpetrators. Moral and ethical behavior existed above politics, and all Christians needed to espouse these universal principles to solve Watergate. Wall's argument proves especially interesting because the right often accused liberals of situational ethics. In truth, Wall and his counterparts were guided by their own sense of right and wrong.[41]

Leaders within the Lutheran Church in America made the same arguments. LCA president Robert J. Marshall sent a letter to all LCA pastors in which he argued Watergate deceived the American people in part because they accepted a culture of secrecy in the name of national security and "would risk the evils of a police state" to safeguard themselves. Marshall demonstrated how this instead allowed officials to convince themselves "there were dangerous tendencies in the opposition" and "decided it was right to weaken the other political party even by illegal means." He called his fellow pastors to bring trust back to institutions by teaching "God's purpose in creating the economic and political orders" did not include leaders upending ethical standards. Where Nixon and his men had failed, Marshall wanted the clergy to succeed. *Lutheran* editor Albert P. Stauderman employed this rationale in a commencement address at Susquehanna University in which he criticized Americans for accepting "corruption and evil in high places" because of media saturation about it. This complacency might lead to people "swallowing the old delusion that the end justifies the means," as had the criminals involved in Watergate. He further feared too many people avoided hearing the truth because they wanted security over freedom, this despite Jesus saying, "You shall know the truth and the truth shall make you free." He continued: "We fail to recognize that there is no security at all unless it is based on sincerity. We need not only to know the truth but to build our lives on it. And that's where religion comes in, with its unique hope for 'newness of life.'" Stauderman inferred an absence of true faith guided the perpetrators, but Christianity could restore order if Americans sought the truth, both politically and theologically. Evidence suggests laypeople agreed, as indicated by a letter Stauderman received from Martha A. Kopra: "His Way creates a tension between freedom and responsibility that would have made a Watergate impossible for a Believer." Christian conviction combined with ethical standards could save the United States from Watergate, if society turned toward a greater moral precept instead of individuals protecting their own interests.[42]

Liberal Christians also applied the theological theme of evil to Watergate, a true and dangerous force, not some nebulous presence. They argued the notion of evil attempted to infiltrate all aspects of human life, and Watergate merely represented its manifestation in the executive branch. Evidence of such theology emerged in a number of ways, such as when the UCC's *Washington Report* communicated to readers about a new election law in June 1973 designed to make it more difficult to create "large secret campaign" funds because "it was just this type of fund which made the activities known collectively as the Watergate scandal financially possible." Congress's bringing of the money for such activities out of the darkness and into the light became a way of preventing future Watergate evils. Raymond A. Heine paralleled this argument in the *Lutheran*, when he detailed a church resolution in Michigan that "instructed synod to communicate to Michigan senators and representatives in Congress 'our concern for the immediate enactment of legislation governing election campaign practices,'" again to force campaigns into the open, preventing hidden agendas and illegal activities. Open accounting of campaign funds brought light to the murky, read evil, world of election finance and would assist the betterment of the nation.[43]

The UCC's *A.D.* created an award for freedom of the press in a similar vein. Called the Freedom of the Press Award and given in honor of the nineteenth-century minister, newspaper editor, and abolitionist Elijah P. Lovejoy, it awarded $1,000 to a journalist who in the past months suffered penalties for simply doing their job. Seeing the press as under attack, and believing its investigative reporting protected Americans and brought the truth into the open, *A.D.* officials felt a "mandate of the church to sensitize the consciences of the people. If freedom of the press in America is severely curtailed, that in itself will be a grievous evil." The announcement continued: "It will create that climate of darkness in which other evils will flourish." Church backing of new legislation on campaign finance and support for freedom of the press did more than communicate a political position; it became a means for the church to assert its moral influence over the nation.[44]

Robert V. Moss also weighed in on this concept of evil during his address to the General Synod Convention on June 22, 1973. The UCC president explained the scandal represented leadership that was too isolated, then did things secretly, while "in our covenant, power is diffused throughout the church. Where it is given to leaders they are expected to use it not to build their own powerbase but to release the power which others have for the common good." He was thus grateful the Senate Select Committee "is providing a dignified way for the truth to come out. This kind of openness it seems to me is part of our national covenant." This method brought truth to the American people and ended any temptation to broker backroom deals or keep illegal activities hidden. The Senate committee's emulation of the church therefore brought about a better way to prevent evil and seek the truth.[45]

The African Methodist Episcopal Church's *Christian Recorder* also referenced hidden activities leading to evil in government, and added a racial dimension. In a speech to the annual Women's Day Conference, Mary Elizabeth Anderson insisted, regarding Watergate, "all sin will be uncovered," regardless of how much people tried to cover it up. She quoted the Bible and then proclaimed Americans should "look to God" because any wrong would "be proclaimed." Furthermore, persisting with the wrong would lead to God proclaiming the truth even louder. Anderson also pointed out "it is the 'white man's mess, the Watergate.' But a Negro found it and told about it." She noted the fact the perpetrators and most of the Nixon White House were all white men, but a black security guard caught the Watergate burglars. This history linked her theological thinking on the matter to that of other liberals who portrayed the problem as living in the darkness and needing light. And, while God would bring to justice the criminals by revealing the truth, she also hinted God was color-blind in the methods and people he utilized in this endeavor, regardless of the prejudice they faced on Earth. Christians who opposed the administration placed the problem in a theology of evil that grew like mold in darkened places; bringing the truth to light offered a religious way to mend what ailed the country's soul.[46]

The United Church of Christ's Ninth General Synod in June 1973 provides a useful forum of liberal commentary as delegates to the convention articulated their understanding of Watergate, one year after the break-in. In advance materials sent to delegates, the Board for Homeland Ministries and the Board for World Ministries introduced a statement about moral breakdown, which the convention later adopted. While not specifically about Watergate, it often alluded to the government crisis and offered solutions the church might enact to help solve the national spiritual problems. For example, the boards explained how integrity "is the cornerstone of morality upon which the whole edifice of society rests. The decline of integrity is obvious everywhere: In personal, corporate and political dishonesty (the current epidemic of shoplifting, evasion on income tax returns, the Watergate affair)." The adopted statement expressed "concern for the moral breakdown in our society, and confesses the deep contrition of our church for its involvement in moral failure." It urged Christians to realize their role in this breakdown and thus get themselves and their church actively involved in solving the problem. Other advance materials from the Board for Homeland Ministries sounded a note of hope by suggesting solutions to America's "faith crisis," such as "recovery of our traditions, revitalization of worship, building trust, developing relevant theological categories to deal with contemporary realities, increasing evangelicalistic effectiveness, and embodying the faith in ways that meet contemporary human needs." It also called for better communities and more work for peace and justice. UCC leaders and convention delegates struggled with Watergate, sought to address the problem at a national event, and worked for the UCC to help solve it. They blamed the church, in part, for allowing Watergate but also held the same church could fix it.[47]

Yet the Ninth General Synod failed to pass a specific statement about Watergate. Clearly the UCC, in spite of its general dislike of the Nixon administration, moved cautiously toward a public judgment at this stage in the investigation. This failure was not from a lack of trying. Prior to the convention, President Moss received complaints that advance materials failed to address Watergate. He therefore asked Dr. Robert Shinn to draft a resolution, which he presented to the Executive Council. The

Executive Council resolved to refer it to "Small Group #15," which already had to address the more generic resolution on moral breakdown.[48]

The Shinn resolution as amended by the Executive Council and sent to Small Group 15 also detailed a number of the liberal Christian themes regarding Watergate. The draft document presented an emphatic statement about the moral corruption facing the nation. It began by quoting Psalm 98:9: "He will judge the world with righteousness, and the peoples with equity." The document asserted, "A society with self-esteem already battered by a war that tried the loyalty of many citizens has taken a second blow to its confidence" in Watergate. It repeated the familiar refrain that the law-and-order executive branch became a "law breaker," and even top law enforcers "described the story as sordid and sleazy." It then declared Christian churches "have a concern for the moral climate of the nation" and needed to step into the debates over Watergate because God "judges nations" and "ordains government for the good of the people." Indeed, it proclaimed, "In times like the present the churches have no right to be silent." In this way, the failed resolution framed a theological call for the UCC to point out the darkness and concealment of truth, as had others, and then went further against the accused in rejecting their Nuremberg-like defense "that they were only obeying orders. Some say that they assumed politics was like that. Most often and from the highest places we hear justification of great wrongs based on loyalty to national security." This thinking left "deep flaws in the national character," a legacy of the last two presidential administrations. The statement insisted on genuine law and order, wanted to hold accountable all people, and sought to uphold the freedom of the press. It reminded people "moral responsibility cannot be evaded by deference to political authority." It thus called for an uplift of politics to an "honorable vocation," supported campaign finance reform, desired to cultivate a more rigorous public morality, and, finally needed to get the churches to insert themselves in bringing about these changes. Despite these efforts, the General Synod never even considered adopting the resolution, for reasons not revealed in the documents. Apparently not all left-leaning Christians completely agreed with the church's prophetic role when it came to direct condemnation of the White House at this juncture.[49]

Another resolution considered by the Executive Council prior to the national convention came from the Clergy and Lay Evangelism Planning

Team. This committee viewed Watergate "as a call to national repentance for the arrogance of power and the apathy of the citizenry." Furthermore, it "is also an urgent mandate for an evangelism that proclaims both the Good News of salvation and the bad news of judgment on wickedness in high places." In other words, the statement's theological reflections mirrored those of other liberal Christians. The resolution also referenced "a White House religion that insulates the leaders of government from the prophetic Word," a "White House ethics of deceit and dishonesty," and called out the church for failing to act more during the crisis. Group 15 also saw this document but failed to advance it, indicating most within the UCC preferred the less specific denunciation of moral breakdown.[50]

Why the General Synod declined a specific statement about Watergate remains elusive. No doubt some felt the statement on moral breakdown they passed was sufficient. Others clearly disliked how procedural moves brought it to a vote and thus blocked it without addressing the content. Robert Moss indicated as much in a 1975 statement, where he blamed procedure, not content, for the failure. Others complained the Small Group lacked enough time in the intense and busy atmosphere of the General Synod to deliberate appropriately. Failure also reflected a lay-clergy divide, wherein the liberal theologians, pastors, and leaders of the UCC met a more moderate laity that put the brakes on more liberal positions. Or perhaps a majority of delegates wished to void any repercussions of a church making political statements.[51] *A.D.* editor and pastor J. Martin Bailey responded best to what happened at the June General Synod, summarizing the church debate and turmoil Watergate could cause even in religious institutions:

> Delegates at least five times turned aside efforts to bring a statement on the Watergate affair to the 9th General Synod.
>
> Their refusal even to discuss the issue seemed particularly odd at what was essentially an activist Synod meeting, while the President's one-time counsel, John W. Dean 3rd, was testifying before TV cameras.
>
> Although many delegates lost sleep to see the Senate hearings replayed, they scratched the first draft of a statement on "A sense of moral breakdown" that included a passing reference to Watergate. One of the small groups assigned to discuss possible resolutions refused to consider Watergate. The Executive Council ignored an appeal from the president

of the church to bring the issue to the floor. The Synod itself blocked the efforts of the Reverend Lawrence L. Gruman of First Congregational United Church of Christ, Madison, Wisconsin, to raise the subject in plenary debate. Even after 19 delegates from nine conferences prepared "A statement of concern about Watergate," the issue remained dormant.

One member of the Executive Council explained to me that "it is too late for the church to speak out." The press and Senator Ervin have done their work well, he said; "What can we add?"

It is true that bandwagons are for politicians rather than prophets. Third fiddle is hardly the instrument for a Joshua or a Nathan. Yet it is hard to explain the silence of a Synod that dispatched a chartered plane-load of pilgrims to stand with Cesar Chavez for justice and reaffirmed the call of previous Synods for amnesty toward war objectors. In the face of an issue with the magnitude of Watergate, silence must reveal more than apathy. At a time like this, only those who condone Watergate have remained quiet.

Like Richard Nixon, I have something of a sense of history. I regret that future students will search in vain through the records of the 9th General Synod for a word of confession and judgment.[52]

Liberal Christianity criticized conservative pietism for promoting an individualism that contributed to the crisis atop the government. Miriam Wallach, a layperson in the Lutheran Church in America, agreed with Albert P. Stauderman, who had voiced concern about a "spiritual illness of our people" that focused on too much individualism and not enough understanding of community. She asserted, "I have felt for some time now that as stewards of this wonderful earth, we have certainly done wrong. Each has looked to his own gain and not thought of the consequences that might harm his neighbor nor the resources that are ours to use." She clearly laid the guilt on inward looking Americans who failed to account for the greater good, a subtle charge against pietism's focus on the self.[53]

But it was the *Christian Century* that had the sharpest words for conservative theology. James M. Wall made a lengthy comment about it in a May editorial. While he criticized "a new kind of situational ethics: corporate misconduct in the name of a higher cause," he saw the problem in "pietistic conditioning, and for this we can thank those among us who have found it easy to celebrate personal piety while ignoring systemic evil." Wall insisted a focus on individual conversion and its subsequent tendency to self-righteousness fostered an environment where the greater good was subservient to the self. He acknowledged the good in pietism and its discipline and concern with personal behavior, but went on to say, "In its distorted form, pietism celebrates disciplined personal behavior as ultimate. By focusing on specific personal 'sins,' one greatly simplifies ethical decision-making. If the Watergate hearings can be discerned as a landmark in American history, we must record that what they reveal is the result of pietistic conditioning." Wall pointed out situational ethics failed here because it narrowed the questioning to whether anyone was killed, robbed, or hurt, which missed the systemic problem, "for the destruction of a system designed to protect the rights of all is a destructive act that kills, robs and hurts" everyone. But, he continued, "Only men conditioned by a distorted pietism could have tolerated such misconduct." Thus Wall saw in Watergate a chance to take on pietism as too insular and oblivious to the greater good.[54]

An unattributed July editorial continued this reasoning. White House aide Jeb Magruder testified before the Senate Watergate Committee and referenced an alleged lesson he learned from Yale chaplain William Sloane Coffin, who taught Magruder at Williams College in 1958. He claimed Coffin's support for burning draft cards led him to rationalize his own "civil disobedience" in the form of illegal behavior on behalf of the president's reelection. Most likely authored by Wall, the *Century*'s editorial would have none of this argument. Calling Magruder's entire defense "shallow and deceitful," the editorial explained he merely attempted "to make the radical-to-liberal left the real villain in this national tragedy." It stressed even the Senate committee allowed him to portray himself as a "young ideologue led astray by the illegal acts of a respected ethics professor." First, the periodical pointed out that Coffin acted and spoke in public, while Magruder operated in secret. Theologically, it explained "Jesus was involved in civil disobedience when he deliberately pulled an ear of corn on the Sabbath. He knew that the religious law of the day forbade such an action, but he disobeyed that law in full view of the public in order to make his point that man was not made for the Sabbath, but the Sabbath for man." The writer then charged that Magruder therefore flunked his ethics lesson at Williams College

while he "passed marketing by Bob Haldeman's school." Magruder ultimately represented to the *Christian Century* "a religious challenge—the
challenge to hold firm to a belief in an ethical standard rooted in an
authority higher than that of an elective office." Warped conservatism
and individualistic thinking guided those responsible for Watergate and
mandated true Christians expose and denounce them.[55]

In the first year of Watergate, liberal to moderate Protestants viewed
the situation as a serious moral crisis. Unlike their conservative counterparts, they held no affection for Nixon and so easily came to criticize the administration. They spoke of arrogance of power; evil hiding
in the darkness; and the need for open communication, honesty, and
Christian witness to bring about a changed political climate. They also
began to write against pietism and American individualism as the root
causes of the distorted value system giving rise to the scandal. Yet liberal
Christianity also shaped solutions and held out hope for the future. If
Christians took responsibility for their part in failing to speak out, they
could then correct the mistake and reincorporate a socially responsible
Christian ethic into the public realm. In this way, their claims resemble
conservatives who called for a Christian revival to heal the nation. They
diverged in seeing this as an issue for collective action focused on the
greater good and a concern for all of humanity. Comfortable because of
their history of power over American culture as the dominant Christian
voice, mainline Protestants were prompted by Watergate into forceful
political commentary before others joined the fray.

America as a Christian Nation amid Early Watergate Travails

The concept of America as a Christian nation during Watergate evolved
from its more elementary role in the 1972 presidential election. Conservative Christians of the early 1970s contributed to a national resurgence
of patriotism as the Bicentennial neared, and as Americans struggled to
put the Vietnam War, the tumultuous 1960s, and the current political
troubles in the background. Nation reverence as practiced by conservative denominations began to grow as they spoke of America as a
uniquely Christian country and linked US ideology with Christianity.
Most liberal to moderate Christians shunned displays of such religious
patriotism and instead took the opportunity to long for an infusion of a

broader, more universal morality to save an adrift nation. Rather than a form of country worship, religion for them served more as a prophetic warning that did not spare any country. In either form, the understanding of Christianity's influence on America within Protestant circles framed their responses to the political crisis confronting the nation.

The Southern Baptist Convention led the way in bringing a passionate form of patriotism into the Christian community. Despite a history since the Reformation of religious persecution that prompted a heightened fear of state religion, the success of Baptists in the United States and the government staying out of their affairs nurtured an atmosphere of honor and respect for American democracy. In other words, American Baptists no longer feared the US state or felt a tension between praising American liberty and limited government and striving for revivalism and sober public morality. Through resolutions and the holding of "Christian Citizenship Sunday," the SBC became the leader in expressing an explicit Republican Theology.

Amid Watergate and widespread mistrust of the government, *Alabama Baptist* editor Hudson Baggett noted a common belief among Southern Baptists: "We do not have to express a blind loyalty to country in order to be patriotic. We need to insist that government officials and citizens adhere to high moral principles and be honest enough to see our faults. But we cannot afford to get such a one-sided view of things that we become blinded to the many good things about our nation." This statement summarized how many within the SBC justified some of the hyperpatriotism they displayed throughout the Watergate crisis, and nuances those who accused them of conflating nation and God into one entity.[56]

The 1973 SBC "Resolution on Integrity and Morality in the American Political System" embodies the conservative idea of America being a Christian nation. It began with the proclamation, "The Bible teaches that government is ordained by God" and American politics were founded on law, freedom, and justice. The current abuses of power in government called for Christians to speak out by merging a commitment to the "American constitutional principle of government" with the biblical "principle that 'righteousness exalteth a nation but sin is a reproach to any people.'" The resolution's first part, then, sounded similar to other Watergate reactions, but the next part diverged when it resolved, "We do not become a part of any growing pessimism regarding the American political process but persist in the hope that Christian citizens will demand integrity," and it also commended government leaders. Finally, it "further resolved, That we call upon all Christians to involve themselves more actively in the American political process to the end that God may be glorified and that the nation may be strengthened as a guarantor of liberty and justice for all." This last statement linked Christianity to the American government.[57]

The Southern Baptist Convention inaugurated Christian Citizenship Sunday in 1973. Previously, a few regional conventions recognized it, as well as local churches. Bringing it to the national level gave it a higher profile and more advertising dollars. It seems an unlikely coincidence this commemoration came about in a year when most Americans could reasonably feel the onset of decline. Baptists sought to heal the nation and move away from turmoil and questioning of the government with an infusion of their own principles onto the national stage. Winn T. Barr, the chairman of the Christian Life Commission of the Kentucky Baptist Convention, said as much to the *Western Recorder*. He felt "no annual observance came at a more appropriate time than Christian Citizenship Day this year on July 1. Our nation has been shaken by the Watergate affair. Confidence in government is low. We desperately need to be reminded of our Christian responsibility in government and to the civil order in which we live." The national Christian Life Commission's director for Christian citizenship development concurred in his announcement of the day. C. Welton Gaddy wanted Christians to exercise their responsibility as good citizens because "grave immorality in government" demanded "Christian citizenship." Linking this to his faith and job, he asserted, "A time-tested proverb warns that all that is necessary for evil to triumph is for good men to do nothing. This truth is especially relevant today. A person may be a good citizen without being a good Christian but one cannot be a good Christian without being a good citizen!" In this way God and country merged in his mind, necessitating Christian Citizenship Sunday. The SBC organized an honoring of the nation, in its view to obey the command God ordained government, but coming much closer to the church worshipping the nation.[58]

The Southern Baptist Convention did not stand alone in mixing its own faith life with a more general sense of the United States as favored

by God. Many within the Lutheran churches made similar proclamations. Without setting aside a specific day of celebration, for example,
the Lutheran Church—Missouri Synod weighed in with its own understanding. The managing editor of the *Lutheran Witness*, Albert W. Galen,
called on Lutherans to join a national observance of the 197th "year as a
free nation 'under God'" on July 4. He explained the Pennsylvania Sons
of the Revolution would sponsor the tapping of the Liberty Bell by the
descendant of a signer of the Declaration of Independence, followed by
thirteen rings from the tower bell at Independence Hall. Loudspeakers
would relay the celebration from coast to coast. He noted, "Pealing good
news by bells is old tradition. Lutheran bells are invited to help revive
the tradition on Independence Day." While not the same intensity as the
SBC's setting aside of a day for Christian citizenship, it certainly placed
the LCMS in a patriotic camp and asked its congregations to join in a
celebration of the nation.[59]

An organization created to speak on behalf of the Lutheran Church—
Missouri Synod, the Lutheran Church in America, and the American
Lutheran Church also contributed to religious reverence for the nation.
The director of the Lutheran Council in the U.S.A.'s Washington, DC–
based Office of Public Affairs and Government Relations made several
comments in this regard during summer 1973. Robert E. Van Deusen
told the *Lutheran Witness*, "Dismaying though some of the [Watergate]
disclosures have been, it would be tragic if they led to a widespread disillusionment with government as a whole or with democracy." While
all citizens of the United States patriotically participated in the political process, "for Christians the responsibility is even greater, for we
acknowledge the sovereignty of God over the nations of the world, including our own." This meant one must faithfully pray for the nation
and ask God's forgiveness "for its mistakes." Van Deusen articulated
the Lutheran theology of God ordaining government to protect people,
which meant a duty to participate in politics while also uplifting the
nation in a patriotic way. In his office's own periodical, Van Deusen furthered this line of thinking when he asked readers to observe "some of
the elements of genuine love of country" even amid Watergate. These
included a Christian taking part of the blame for government corruption, being true to conscience, and taking one's faith life into account
regarding the government. He finished, "In these and other ways, citi-

zens of the United States hammer out the true meaning of patriotism on the forge of political participation." In a separate article in the same issue, he championed the American system of government because the "built-in checks and balances" affirmed the viability and safety of the government, giving him "faith in the essential fairness of the system." While not as overt as the SBC or even the LCMS's participation in ringing of the bells, Van Deusen contributed a voice of Lutheran patriotism in a time of crisis.[60]

Conservative to moderate denominations articulated these forms of pushing America toward a Christian worship to a greater degree in 1973 than they had during the election year. Also, they acknowledged Watergate now, having shied away from it in 1972. The scandal did nothing to dampen their patriotic spirit as they uplifted the nation and blurred the lines between church and state, Christian faith and nation worship, and patriotism and Christianity. These tenets would hold true for them throughout the crisis, becoming the bedrock on which they constructed hope the country would survive Watergate.

Unsurprisingly, their liberal counterparts viewed the United States much differently. The United Church of Christ held no such observances, nor did its leaders articulate a vision of nation honoring that came close to this kind of worship. Rather, its leaders strove to maintain a distance between patriotism and Christianity, so the UCC could focus on its faith and prophecy without risk of idolatry. A lengthy editorial in *A.D.* made this point in the context of Watergate. This piece prophesied Gerald Ford's words of August 1974 when it declared the American dream had become a nightmare. It linked the political scandal to racism, sexism, the Vietnam War, Cambodia, the abuse of the environment, and other national ills. In an ominous tone, it continued, "Theologically speaking, these events have demonstrated human sinfulness and finitude, just as the rise of Hitler in the 30s did in a more dramatic way." It applauded constitutional checks and balances with the hope this government could overcome the moment, but added, "We will do well to affirm that part of our heritage which has contributed so much to the general welfare of our own people and of the whole world. But it is equally important to look critically at the failures of our system." In a more direct shot at turning the United States into a Christian nation, the editorial concluded: "Christians in every community can help to restate the American dream in terms which avoid chauvinism and false pride but which promise liberty and peace." Others took a similar stance.[61]

Christian Century editor James M. Wall wrote an article that criticized the national tendency to exalt the presidency and blamed part of Watergate on this behavior. After Nixon addressed the nation on April 30 and pled with Americans to allow him to return to "the larger duties of this office" and put the Watergate investigation in other people's hands, Wall determined to write about it. He feared Nixon dismissed "lower-level foolishness" because the president attended to loftier matters. Wall labeled it "a belief by Mr. Nixon and the majority of the American public that the presidency is a sacred office." Or, more bluntly, "We are dealing here with nothing less than nation-worship and with the office of the President as the ultimate deity of that worship." That explained to him why so many wanted to absolve the president of any guilt in Watergate— not because they so admired Nixon but rather because, if the president committed a crime, it would undermine presidential reverence. Wall prophetically warned, "Always in the worship of something less than God there lurks the fear that the idol can be destroyed. It is the nature of man to sense inwardly that misplaced worship never brings full satisfaction; hence the neurotic search for reassurance that the object of misplaced worship is invulnerable." Wall demanded Christians separate their faith from their love of the government.[62]

Christian Century readers sent Wall letters to the editor that agreed with his assessment. William Henry Young argued, "In order to divest ourselves of the immoralities which come from setting up a political office or a social system as being sacred and above question or reproach we need to reject all pretenses of theological certainty and become humble learners" when citizens tried to grapple with humankind's problems and fix them. He feared too many Americans failed at this task and instead made the government a sacred institution, which violated Young's understanding of a Christian calling. Immanuel Nielsen also wrote, "After the events of political scandal, it may be wise to stress integrity as the fundamental requirement of sound government." A Christian should therefore look for such responsible behavior in politicians without assuming any one of them or any office never disobeyed this edict. The readership of the leftist Protestant flagship periodical also distanced themselves from a patriotic celebration of country through faith.[63]

These denunciations of idolatry placed the *Christian Century* and the United Church of Christ firmly in the liberal camp. They feared nation worship threatened the country and allowed for Watergate and the continued controversy because people blindly followed the presidency and nation as institutions to revere. In contrast, moderate to conservative denominations pronounced an even stronger desire to get the churches involved in patriotic celebrations as the year wore on and Watergate became a bigger and bigger story. The lines here blurred between Christian faith and patriotism. According to information about Christian Citizenship Sunday and other ways to honor America, worshipping the Christian God came with a simultaneous veneration of America. As the Watergate scandal intensified in the coming months, so, too, did this debate about America as a Christian nation.

Conclusion

Following Richard Nixon's reelection, Watergate escalated from what at first seemed like a minor political escapade into a serious national scandal, though not everyone agreed about what it meant. Little proof available to the public linked the president directly to the episode, which left the scope of the matter up to interpretation. The Christian community engaged Watergate based on their Protestant heritage of working to influence society, their previous political leanings, and their differing religious philosophies.

Those who had disliked Nixon and his policies since at least his 1968 election were inclined to believe his entire administration was corrupt. They viewed the White House as the center of arrogance of power and called for a collective Christian action to demand higher moral and ethical behavior from their national leaders. This call included a desire to investigate Watergate. In that way, they tended to believe Watergate reached the top of the executive branch and threatened the entire federal government. Conservatives, in contrast, trusted Nixon and called on Americans to believe him until concrete evidence proved otherwise. They condemned the illegal Watergate activities but believed they were not the result of a systemic failure. These Christians leaned theologically toward traditional pietism, insisting a broad-based national revival would bring God's favor on the nation to heal whatever ailed it.

Whether articulating these liberal or conservative political and theological points of view regarding America's faith, Watergate, or the president specifically, Christian America ventured further into discussing
Watergate into summer 1973. Christians' political engagement began to
increase, albeit more slowly for conservatives than liberals. Many hard-
ened their previous points of view, sniped at one another, and held to
their established conviction about how to handle politics. The ongoing investigation into the mushrooming national crisis soon consumed
more attention from all religious leaders, and in doing so intensified
their reactions. It became a bigger step into their continued activities in
politics.

3

A Favorable President or Most Dangerous Man?

Watergate continued to expand in scope from July to October 1973, as investigations implicated more White House officials. Christian political commentary expanded along with it. Just as Americans invested more attention and worry into the matter, so, too, did Protestants, albeit in very different ways. Conservative Protestants, especially among evangelicals, remained reluctant to condemn, singled out only those already convicted or who had confessed, and clung to a belief Nixon played no part in it. Already hostile liberal Protestants intensified their rhetoric against Nixon and his administration. They called for a collective Christian outcry to force change and restore moral integrity to Washington, DC. Other Protestants lived somewhere between these two camps and addressed Watergate in other ways. No matter where they fell on this spectrum, they all ramped up their involvement in the political turmoil as it, too, escalated in intensity.

The Senate Watergate hearings provided Christians with grist for their mills. For example, Senator Sam Ervin, the committee chair, castigated one witness because those in power sought "to nullify the laws of man and the laws of God for temporary political advantage." He then quoted Galatians 6:7: "Be not deceived: God is not mocked: for whatsoever a man soweth, that shall he also reap." Summarizing the episode, the *Christian Century* explained, "These summer hearings are dismal reminders of man's evil. But the hearings are also suggesting that, in ways not always discernible to man, the Word announces itself in the midst of evil." This editorial reflected important aspects of liberal Protestant thinking about Watergate—namely, a disdain for the administration, balanced against a faith the American people could solve the problem together. Brooks Hays, a former Arkansas congressional representative, Southern Baptist Convention president, and special assistant to both President Kennedy and President Johnson, provided a contrasting conservative point of view. His remarks targeted only those found legally culpable, but not the president. While he criticized their "contempt" for rules, Hays minimized the scope of the problem. His solution was therefore simpler than those of liberal Christians: "One must inevitably turn to theology for the needed words" to cure the malaise of Watergate, and "love is such a word." Nothing at this time brought liberals and conservatives together or reconciled their points of view, but these months solidified their conviction to participate in the Watergate conversation.[1]

This chapter begins with the revelation by Alexander Butterfield, a former presidential appointments secretary, during Senate hearings that Nixon operated a recording system in the White House that might provide evidence about conversations. This set in motion a months-long legal battle over release of the tapes to investigators. Underscoring the White House ethical deficit, Vice President Spiro T. Agnew resigned on October 10 for misdeeds as governor of Maryland. The period ended with the Saturday Night Massacre, when Nixon fired the special prosecutor investigating Watergate, Archibald Cox, after the resignation of Attorney General Elliot Richardson and the termination of Deputy Attorney General William D. Ruckelshaus, who refused to do so. Robert Bork, who became acting attorney general, carried out Nixon's orders against Cox. The abolition of the special prosecutor sent shock waves throughout America, escalating the Watergate controversy. These four months witnessed an intensification of the storm that increased speculation about how far the scandal would spread through the US government.

American Protestants confronted these events in ways that reflected their established outlooks. Liberal Christianity had the most to say by far, with harsh criticisms of a sinful president and calls for collective Christian action for the greater good. Conservatives still trusted Richard Nixon, regarded the Watergate capers as the work of isolated individuals, and expounded on a long-held faith that prayers for America and conversions of individuals would lead the nation out of Watergate. They commented on Watergate far less frequently than liberals but more than they had even a couple months earlier. Others found a unique path that combined the liberal critique of the president with pietism. Christians worked to inject theology into the national conversation about the spiritual crisis infecting American politics. They all now participated in regular political discourse because Watergate cried for Christianity to add moral and ethical integrity to the government.

Conservative Perseverance

Conservatives of all stripes paid attention to the national drama as it intensified during the summer and into the fall of 1973. In the infrequent comments they made, they expressed cautious trust in the president and admonished fellow Americans that he and all the accused deserved the constitutional presumption of innocence. They also toed the White House line the crisis was a minor infraction getting too much attention. Moderate denominations also advised leniency for the president and wanted their churches to tread carefully before making final judgments. Conservative Protestants in 1973 were clearly in a holding pattern, even as they ventured further into the fray to counter liberals with their own point of view and determined to remain in the political conversation.

The case of Charles W. Colson as White House insider turned evangelical Christian shaped conservative Christian reaction in these months. Colson came to the White House as a Republican operative known for an acute understanding of the political arena and a willingness to do almost anything to accomplish Republican victories. He first made a name for himself working for Massachusetts senator Leverett Saltonstall, joined the Nixon campaign in 1967, and gained an appointment in 1969 on the White House staff (technically as a liaison to special interest groups such as organized labor and white ethnic voters, but more accurately as a trusted fixer). Nixon particularly liked Colson's ability to get tasks done expediently. Colson helped create the White House enemies list, monitored national security adviser Henry Kissinger's telephone calls, plotted to firebomb the Brookings Institute, and had at least prior knowledge about Watergate. More notoriously, he brought G. Gordon Liddy into Nixon's service. From there he assisted the Watergate cover-up. As the scandal became more public and pressure increased on the White House to act, Colson was forced to resign in March 1973. He was indicted in March 1974, pled guilty in June, and served a seven-month prison sentence. After his March resignation, Colson underwent a conversion experience on August 12, 1973, substituting an addiction to Republican politics as a sort of god he worshipped for a hard-line, evangelical Christianity. During this chapter's period, in which his conversion came at about the halfway point, Colson became a conservative commentator. His blend of evangelical faith and patriotic defense of the president embodied the quintessential Republican Theology as applied to Watergate.[2]

Though Nixon and his staff pressured Colson to resign, he was still treated as an unpaid adviser to the administration in private practice. From the outside, Colson continued to criticize the intense focus on Watergate in Washington, DC. Like many within the White House and conservative Christians at large, he often attempted to paint the break-in as a minor offense Nixon opponents blew out of proportion to gain political advantage. He wrote to one person, "The city is so obsessed with Watergate that almost everyone has lost sight of the much more critical problems that really affect the kind of country we will be living in for the rest of our lives and our children's lives." He complained, "Frankly that has been the most depressing part of this whole thing for me. I have gotten used to most of the brickbats, but I didn't give up three and a half years of my most productive years to see the country go down the drain over a political circus." As with other conservatives, including Christians, Colson concluded Nixon was the victim of a Beltway crucifixion. After invoking the Fifth Amendment before Congress, Colson hoped he would "be in a position soon to speak out again, not only hopefully to establish my own innocence with respect to some of the very unfair and unfounded accusations that have been made, but more importantly to help the Committee get the truth about the President's innocence." He assured another person, "Believe me, your faith in the President is well placed and I hope you will continue to show your faith in him." Colson expressed this faith to the president himself when he wrote: "To resign would clearly surrender the place in history you have justly earned. If, God forbid, you should be impeached, I am convinced that history would record it as a vicious, unprincipled and partisan act on the part of Congress." Because Colson with his insider access to the White House, if not the president himself, felt this way, it stands to reason many other conservatives would follow his lead. These sentiments came around the time of his conversion in August, though public knowledge that Colson considered himself born-again would not come until December. Colson never altered this perception. As late as

1987, he defended the administration and claimed protecting government secrets set Watergate in motion, a minor burglary compared with the threat to national security. Such a conviction coming from an exemplar of the power of transforming conversion served to solidify for conservative Christians their belief in Nixon and their downplaying of much of the Watergate proceedings.[3]

Conservative Protestants minimized Watergate in a number of other ways, too. First, conservative entities failed to discuss Watergate on a regular basis, therefore relegating it to irrelevant or minor importance. Second, when they did mention it, they saw it as an isolated misdeed that was easily cleaned up. Last, they invoked the constitutional principle of innocent until proven guilty, stressing Americans had too little information to judge Nixon. As Floyd M. Stephens wrote in a letter to the editor of the *Alabama Baptist*: "Let us be as fair with President Nixon, whom many of us view with favor and hope, as we have been with other administrations whose ideas were further from our own." This sentiment expressed the desire to allow the process to play out, since conservatives believed the administration's line that a liberal media and the Democratic Party went after it more harshly than any previous presidency. This set the matter more in a political context than a moral and ethical one.[4]

Even the resignation of Vice President Agnew evoked a defense of Nixon from *Christianity Today*. An October 1973 editorial explained the president knew about Agnew's case all along but could have done nothing to prevent the resignation because "he could not have sided with Agnew as though he were innocent without getting involved in a cover-up of the same kind that marked the Watergate tragedy." In this way, the loss of a vice president became a way to praise the president's integrity. The editorial further explained Agnew received fair treatment in being forced from office because "the essence of justice is that he who performs the deed shall eat the fruit of it. Considering the nature of his crime and the positions of trust he held, his punishment is minimal." But the editorial continued with the idea that the vice president's "case differs from those of the Watergate rascals in one important regard: they acted for a cause they professed to believe in; Spiro Agnew acted to line his own pockets with money." Not only did the Agnew incident serve to buttress Nixon in their eyes, but the editors went so far as to make an ethical defense of the Watergate criminals because their crimes served a higher purpose, at least in their own eyes.[5]

Evangelicals were not alone in articulating this conservative point of view, as evidenced by a rift within Lutheranism. The reaction from *Lutheran* readers to commentary from the moderate Lutheran Church in America's main periodical demonstrates this fact well. After editorials against the administration appeared, several readers lashed out in letters to the editor. In declaring her prayers to God to guide the president, Hilda Schoenig felt "Mr. Nixon has efficiently performed his presidential duties and I have complete confidence in his integrity and his administration." Nothing to date caused her to waiver, and thus she took umbrage at her church's periodical. Another reader agreed, writing, "I for one am not disappointed with our President. You write nothing of the great accomplishments our President has done in the few years of his Presidency. Such as the far more important accomplishments of ending the war in Vietnam, bring [*sic*] Russia and China to negotiate Peace and trade agreements." Still another, who asserted her dismay that the *Lutheran* so openly questioned the administration, believed "this entire issue has been blown out of proportion." These more conservative voices from within a moderate church body show many viewed Watergate as inconsequential in comparison to Nixon's accomplishments.[6]

Other Lutheran lay writers restated the administration's defense that Watergate represented nothing more than a meritless political attack. James C. Dickert explained, "I am acquainted with a few sore-head losers from the last election who are less concerned with morality than with rancorous and vindictive recrimination." He presumably included editors at the *Lutheran* in this thinking because his letter reprimanded the magazine for carrying editorials about Watergate, a political matter, in a religious magazine. After also trumpeting the president's foreign policy, entire political career, and attempt to reverse "liberal trends of past administrations which held out false promises," Louis L. Mast blasted not only the Democratic Party and the president's detractors for harping on Watergate, but also his own church periodical. He accused editors, "It is you and your element in the Church which will have to seek amnesty from the public," not the president, for the partisan approach he alleged they took toward Watergate. The bile did not stop with one disgruntled reader: "It's typical of hypocritical moralizers to try to divert attention from evils close to home by pointing an accusing finger at higher ups, such as President Nixon and Watergate." Though J. Hebert failed to itemize these overlooked evils, the closer-to-home reference obviously indicated moral problems he had with the LCA leadership. Sounding much like the administration itself, William Kopf added, "I might also add that many Democrats have engaged in 'shady' practices against members of the 'opposition' as well as against people in their OWN Democratic party. No, I am not saying that 'two wrongs make a right'—I just want to 'clear the air' so to speak." Thus, some Christian defenses of Nixon and his men were quite impassioned in 1973, after a year of hearing and dealing with the Watergate matter.[7]

Expressions such as these naturally flowed to the notion the president was innocent until proven guilty. Kopf wrote a letter before the one just quoted and noted only "concrete evidence" could tie Nixon to a cover-up or anything to do with Watergate, none of which he had seen. He exclaimed, "I have heard more 'hearsay' during the Watergate Hearings than I have in all of the prior years of my life—and—I am now 62 years of age." He also agreed with Nixon's assessment of the media: "It is a known fact that newspapers never did like Richard M. Nixon, so it is impossible for any newspaper to be impartial in their judgment of President Nixon." At least for this reader, Nixon's constant harping about the media for unfair treatment got through, and was used against the *Lutheran*. Another lay Lutheran agreed with the president about the media, pointing his aim directly at the associate editor, Edgar Trexler, who opined against the president for Watergate immorality in July: "Associate Editor Trexler joins the company of a host of journalists who have indicted President Nixon before the evidence is in and he compounds injustice by imputing his indictment to 'all of us.' It is not true by a long shot that 'all of us are profoundly disappointed with our presidential leadership.' Let Mr. Trexler speak for himself; but let him not presume to speak for me." John P. Banta more calmly but forcefully wrote, "You are wrong in having found the President guilty even before the investigating committee has completed taking all testimony and in the face of the President's own words. Right now the only thing obvious in Watergate is that the President and his underlings did make some pretty bad judgments, but that is not immorality." Conservative Lutherans thus let the LCA's *Lutheran* know their position, thereby giving historians a way to gauge the breadth of Nixon's support among them and the potency of White House damage control tactics.[8]

Furthermore, even the most liberal of the denominations faced conservative opposition in 1973. J. Martin Bailey, editor of *A.D.*, and his staff, as well as writers for *Engage/Social Action*, placed anti-Nixon editorials in the periodicals of the United Church of Christ. Supporters of Nixon employed much of the rhetoric previously seen to respond to them. Lay reader Lee D. Rustin explained, "You have violated the basic principle of every person's right to be heard before convicted. You have convicted Richard Nixon before the evidence is in so far as Watergate is concerned. In may be proven that he is guilty, but as of today it has not been." Kelly Janes added the familiar list of Nixon's perceived accomplishments, especially in foreign policy, and asked, "Don't shoot the piano player; he is doing the best he can." A pastor from New Lebanon, New York, more forcefully reprimanded the editors in a complaint that their too liberal bent rankled his parishioners and led to defections from the United Church of Christ. He avowed, "This kind of publishing makes me ashamed. I am not alone in this. Many of the laity are questioning the Christianity of the U.C.C. We will remain behind our elected President and give him our cooperation until January, 1977, and then we will do the same for our next elected President. please don't force the united church into further losses by such printing."[9]

As reported in chapter 2, the UCC General Assembly failed to pass a direct resolution regarding Watergate, which prompted J. Martin Bailey to sharply criticize the delegates for failing in their responsibility to Christian witness. This editorial, too, brought condemnation from conservative readers. And in this case, because the issue occurred at the church's official assembly, the writers framed their argument in a theological context. Ralph P. Ley, who was president of the UCC Wisconsin Conference, held a doctorate in divinity, and apparently knew Bailey personally from the tone of their letters, protested Bailey's take on the convention proceedings. He complained one representative from his own conference spent too much time on Watergate, failing to address "other items confronting General Synod" of greater import. This lack of attention to more pressing religious issues led him to admonish, "I feel the comments in *A.D.* in this regard were very inappropriate." Some of this reasoning went along the lines of Watergate belonging strictly in a political realm, not a religious one. The tone grew sharper when J. W. Steinman, a layperson from Cincinnati, Ohio, objected to Bailey. Interestingly, once again Bailey took criticism from someone who appeared otherwise friendly, and not simply an anonymous reader. Steinman wrote in August 1973 he was "delighted that General Synod had the good sense to remain mute in the face of apparent goading by those who find a congressional inquisition an adequate substitute for a court of law." He further complained about the "church hierarchy" venturing into politics, but guessed "it must be expected when we leave the field of theology and travel uncharted social and political paths." He finished with a stronger statement: "Your last paragraph refers to the lack of a *word of judgment* from the Synod. Perhaps the Synod felt Christ's work did not include playing judge and jury on something as complex and as yet *untried* as the Watergate 'cover up.'" Unlike the Ley letter, Bailey published Steinman's response in the October issue, thus giving readers a true sense of some of the negative comments.[10]

Evidence suggests Bailey, despite a persistent dislike for the president and growing alarm about Watergate, listened to conservative readers. *A.D.* ran a cartoon that depicted Nixon, mocking his fear of the "liberal media" and implying his followers naively believed the president. Victor P. Croftchik lashed out that *A.D.* had no business with such blatant political images and stated, "I guess I'm one of that 'dumb silent majority' that reporters are so far above." In this case, Bailey issued an apology and informed Croftchik, "This cartoon was drawn before the Watergate episode erupted and I frankly wish we had not carried it." Even Bailey appeared to think it went too far afield for a proper religious periodical, and in this case he understood the offense his more conservative readers took at the magazine's actions.[11]

In ways such as these, conservative Protestants ramped up their voice of support for the president heading into fall 1973, invoking his being innocent until proven guilty and insisting the debate had no place in a religious context. They therefore backed the president, whom they saw as successful, and did not want to see their church body attacking him before the evidence clearly linked him to a crime. They increased their Watergate commentary to counter liberal attacks and, in doing so, amplified their participation in politics, a move that grew bolder in the coming months. They were now in the political fray to stay.

Conservative Theology

Throughout this period, conservative Protestants also continued to advocate for a public morality based on evangelical pietism. It is interesting to note that conservative commentators, as opposed to most moderate to liberal Christian entities discussed later, seldom mentioned President Nixon in their reflections because they presumed him innocent. Nonetheless, they recognized the moral problems associated with Watergate had a religious context, and they entered the national debate about the causes of and cures for government corruption.

The conservative theological argument continued along familiar lines. Editorials from various Southern Baptist newspapers reveal this thinking. Floyd A. Craig, the director of public relations for the SBC Christian Life Commission, wrote for the *Western Recorder*, "The Watergate experience has certainly shown us that no government is so big that it cannot be shaken by untruthfulness and deceit." Sin and corruption existed everywhere because of human depravity, which prompted Craig to turn away from solely worrying about the nation's government in order to also remind readers that "no denomination is too big to be shaken by the similar kind of experience." In other words, Watergate represented a typical human problem, and Baptists had better concentrate on their own arena and prevent it there. Printed in the *Arkansas Baptist Newsmagazine*, a sermon by William L. Bennett at the First Baptist Church in Fort Smith, Arkansas, similarly directed Baptists' attention back to themselves, instead of focusing on the national problem. He said, "The enemy is not out yonder. As Pogo said, 'We have found the enemy and the enemy is us.'" He then explained enemies warred against the United States and demanded Christian attention because only repentance could save the country. He added that democracy only worked when infused with a morality the Christian church offered. A lack of reader criticism suggested laypeople agreed with their Baptist leaders. As Max E. Shirk succinctly put it in a letter to the editor of the *California Southern Baptist*, "It seems to me that the Watergate mess is but a symptom of a great illness which pervades this nation." He urged that only the training of young people in "Christian ethics and character" could pull America in the right direction. Thus, conservative theology started with the revivalistic premise that universal human sin caused Watergate, which in the grand scheme amounted to but one example of a general threat facing the country. Even as people went to jail and the Watergate investigation led to major resignations and Senate hearings, this line of reasoning minimized the event itself and turned attention toward the one source of healing: pietist Christianity.[12]

Evangelicals looked to prayer and salvation as the surest weapons against universal sin, and Colson as a shining example of their power. Colson, facing prison and a career in turmoil, proclaimed, "I have found a great deal of comfort in prayer." He continued: "Understanding through prayer that in the long view of things each of us is much less important than we think and that our own desires are less important than that which God has willed, may help you keep balance in this time of trial." This reflection shows Colson drifted at this juncture toward his future calling in evangelical pietism: reform yourself, and the rest will follow. He had a lot of company. The attempt to create an organization called Evangelicals for Social Action prompted Walden Howard, editor of *Faith at Work*, to explain the "administration's behavior . . . highlights the ambiguity which Christian understanding forces us to recognize. Human nature is not altogether trustworthy." While he thought certain safeguards might prevent future activities like Watergate, he emphasized that "the concern of Christians must be to promote that climate of openness within a society which encourages trust, respect, and dignity for every individual." And individual Christian action in this regard would perform that task. As the national mouthpiece for evangelical religion, *Christianity Today* put it most plainly: "The nation needs regenerated people, and this is the business of 'revivalism'; and it needs keepers of the Law of God, which is at the heart of a pietism that emphasizes ethical absolutes."[13]

Indeed, *Christianity Today* took this opportunity to defend itself against critics who questioned the simple notion of piety as a grand solution to all societal ills. Commentaries in August and September 1973 contributed to this Christian theological/cultural war amid Watergate. An unattributed editorial on August 31 stated it wanted to address two concerns about Watergate and religion. First, it forcefully pointed out the admitted Watergate criminals should get lumped into the same category as Daniel Ellsberg in their criminality. In other words, if conservative activists such as John Dean and Jeb Magruder were criticized,

Ellsberg deserved the same condemnation. The immorality must take on a bipartisan tone, or the editors feared it would become a liberal attack on conservative politics and nothing more. The editors' second point emphasized that "none of this can be laid at the door of revivalism and pietism." Though detractors labeled pietism a myopic force too often individualized, leading to a belief that doing anything for the "right side" was justified, *Christianity Today* claimed, "Watergate and Pentagon Papers malefactors may have had plenty of religion; what they lacked was genuine Christianity and obedience to the Ten Commandments. If they had refused to lie, cheat, and steal, there would have been no Pentagon Papers case and no Watergate." In other words, their lack of piety caused the problem, and people turning to a pious frame of mind would fix what ailed the nation. Harold Kuhn furthered this reasoning. Claiming the liberal media assigned responsibility to personal pietism because it stressed individual conversion and behavior that ultimately became "blindness to corporate or systemic evil," Kuhn cried foul. He thought "New Morality" and its defense of the Pentagon Papers release and other antigovernment activities also lacked an ethical basis. He thought it unfair to take the issue of Watergate as a national concern and turn it into an argument unfairly and simplistically blaming all things on evangelicals.[14]

The Baptist Joint Committee on Public Affairs, headquartered in Washington, DC, as a think tank for seven Baptist bodies, contributed to the conservative theological ruminations over Watergate with an October 1973 "Statement of Concern" by its executives and lay leaders. The committee specifically met because of the growing Watergate crisis and published the statement in their *Report from the Capital*. In classic Baptist fashion, it first upheld the importance of the separation of church and state but added, this "does not mean separation of religion from government or politics, nor should it imply the divorce of religion's basic moral and ethical principles from the conduct of public affairs." The statement then reaffirmed a faith in democracy and expressed gratitude that "there is today a widespread reaction against this abuse" of political power. "Indeed," it continued, "we view this reaction as evidence of the intrinsic strength of our American tradition." The statement further emphasized the democratic principles of consent of the governed, the danger of too much concentration of power, the obligation of government to protect civil liberties, and holding public officials accountable for public and private conduct. Its conclusion turned toward the more conservative line of individualism and an implicit pietism: "We express our faith in the ultimate triumph of right and of the truth in a nation whose citizens are dedicated to justice and righteousness in every aspect of life. In this confidence, we urge our people to exemplify and to require character and integrity in both public and private life, and to discharge responsibly their duties as citizens. Moreover, we encourage our Christian young people to seek for themselves a vocation through which they may make their contribution to government and to society in general." Their statement set out no structural reforms and did not address how to deal with tangible problems. Instead, it fell back on one person's duty to engage Christian principles and thereby create a ripple effect into the government to encourage right behavior. In this way, when many conservatives steered away from specifics about Watergate, the Baptist Joint Committee added its conservative theological point of view.[15]

In communicating this action through Baptist Press Release, which sent dispatches to all of the regional Baptist press periodicals as well as to the national media, the Baptist Joint Committee's director elaborated on what compelled them to address Watergate. James E. Wood Jr. explained, "At the moment we are in the dark ages of public affairs in America." Unlike most conservative commentary at the time, Wood's words acknowledged the "prostitution of government power" that included lying and illegal activities to gain an election victory, but he did not bring Nixon directly into his comments. This "dangerous" behavior necessitated a Christian response. As the primary Baptist lobbying entity in Washington, DC, the Baptist Joint Committee could not easily ignore the growing scandal to hide behind general statements about universal sin. Wood and his colleagues therefore addressed the matter in an oblique way, in terms of human sinfulness, the need for Christian ethics in public life, prayer, and revival. Conservative Protestants had firm theological convictions guiding their increased political commentary, a force that became more pronounced as they asserted their will on the political sphere.[16]

Lost Credibility

In August 1973, the *Christian Century* ran a cartoon of a little girl sitting on her grandfather's lap, asking, "Grandpa, did any other presidents besides George Washington ever tell the truth?" The message from editors who chose it seemed clear and, not surprisingly, signaled that liberal Protestants viewed Nixon much differently from their conservative counterparts. For a group that mistrusted the president from at least the beginning of his first administration, if not before, the rapidly cascading revelations about Watergate swept away whatever scant credibility Nixon had left. Liberals used whatever venue they could find to add their voices to the chorus of those challenging the president's hold on the office and to insert themselves into American society to protect the greater good.[17]

Much of this anti-Nixon rhetoric stressed the administration's bold arrogance. UCC pastor William F. Moore of Pilgrim Church in Wheaton, Maryland, stated this is an article for *A.D.*: "The President has met the limits of arrogance, misplaced trust, self-isolation, and continued self-justification." He further wondered why the White House had lost all sense of humility and trust, then took aim at Nixon's hosting of White House prayer services. Instead of seeing them as signs of morality and Christianity in the administration, Moore labeled them "the ultimate symbol of arrogance; where he hosts God, his staff checks prayers, and those who disagree with him are no longer welcome." Fellow UCC editors at the *Washington Report* increasingly mistrusted the White House as a source of any truthful information and cited the alleged robbery of the office of Daniel Ellsberg's psychiatrist by Nixon's men to report "there is fear that he wants to be a monarch." These UCC beliefs found company in the offices of the *Christian Century*.[18]

Again the liberal Christian newsmagazine employed political cartoons to make its point. On the front cover of the September 26 issue, captioned "Disabled Veteran," in a hospital bed surrounded by whirling tragedies labeled as Watergate, moral paralysis, and 'Nam, lies a yawning and bored Uncle Sam. James M. Wall lamented the administration attempted to blame antiwar protests and civil rights demonstrations for the Watergate crimes, because they supposedly created a climate of mistrust and illegal investigations under Democratic administrations the

Republican White House now had no choice but to follow. Wall stated the Watergate hearings were therefore "forced upon us by an administration which refuses to lead the American people, preferring instead the political method of fallacious argument to avoid dealing with the sordid truth." By bringing up the Pentagon Papers, claiming Democratic presidents did the same thing, or insisting all politicians engaged in some sort of dirty activities, Nixon and his associates revealed their conceit. In other words, the arrogance of power created a climate in which the White House blamed others for the problem and avoided addressing Watergate specifically as the result. As before, the limited reader criticism suggests *Christian Century* readers by and large agreed with these editorial claims. Lowell A. Anderson, pastor at Our Savior Lutheran Church in Mesquite, Texas, wrote to Wall, "Nixon has got to be one of the most dangerous men ever hoisted to the top of the political pinnacle in this country." This arrogance of power appalled liberal Protestants.[19]

Quite naturally, the belief in this sheer arrogance led liberal Protestants to witness the ways in which Nixon and his men often saw themselves as above the law. Countless accounts of the Nixon White House and histories of Watergate have already revealed, from the president down to lower-level officials, an attitude of invincibility and being above reproach reigned, paving the way for Watergate and other nefarious activities during Nixon's presidency. Liberal Christians were among the people already pointing this out to Americans in the moment. A former Vietnamese diplomat who taught, lectured, and wrote in the United States made this point in an article pondering how K'ung-Fu-tzu, or Confucius, might react to Watergate. Tran Van Dinh asserted he "would be disappointed if he were to visit Washington in 1973. Surveying the political scene, he would complain that 'in vain I have looked for a single man capable of seeing his own faults and bringing the charge home against himself.'" The article further articulated that in never admitting wrongdoing, the administration accepted Nixon's illegal activities as justified. But Mary Turnbull, an *A.D.* reader who frequently wrote poems or short rhymes and sent them to the UCC periodical, prophetically warned in "Watergate Revelations," "No human reaches such perfection / He no longer needs inspection."[20]

Blind self-importance in the Nixon White House made it inevitable according to liberal Christianity that abuses of power would follow. Albert Vorspan complained to *Christian Century* readers about a current "dark ages of religious social action." It reduced social welfare advocacy, created congregations afraid of public action, shrank budgets for church programs, and generated a troubling silence from religious leaders in view of the "repellent immorality in our government (including the White House)." But he found most dangerous the "assaults on our constitutional liberties and on the programs of social justice which have given some hope to millions of the poor, the weak, the sick, and the elderly." Instead, the executive branch ignored law and order, despite its platform to the contrary, in order to maintain its own hold on power. Some within the United Church of Christ who agreed with this sentiment lobbied for campaign reform bills because the public could no longer trust its politicians to behave ethically: Frederick L. Hofrichter, who worked for the Social Action wing of the UCC in Washington, DC, on lobbying efforts, wrote, "No law can make a dishonest man honest, but legislation such as this can make it more difficult for basically honest men to be drawn into patterns of deceit and abuse of power." The government needed to act, and Christians could add their voice to calls for legislation to curb future Watergates. Liberal Protestants clearly endorsed a collective religious and political action plan to bring about a legislative fix to the problem.[21]

This line of reasoning finally led to some of the first cries for impeachment from the liberal Christian community. Allan R. Brockway, a Methodist pastor but also editor of *Engage/Social Action*, a periodical published jointly by the United Methodist Church and the UCC, began this argument already in July 1973. He wanted the president removed by either resignation or impeachment, and thus by September blasted those who wanted more evidence before proceeding with such a drastic step. He wondered how much more people needed to learn, because "we the people already have the facts on efforts to subvert various Democratic candidates, the deal with the milk industry, the concerted effort to discredit a free press, the corruption and politicizing of the FBI, the SEC, the IRS and other government agencies, the establishment of the 'plumbers' unit, the protection-type solicitation of campaign funds, the judicial persecution of the Berrigans and Ellsberg, the ITT and Vesco, and the revelation of the tapes." He concluded that "we already have more than enough" to bring charges against Nixon and wanted it done immediately. While not many, even among Nixon haters, played the impeachment card just yet, that sentiment existed, and the latest events pushed some toward it.[22]

Even if they shied away from impeachment, leftist Christians found other ways to try to influence American society. As referenced previously, the United Church of Christ led a campaign against the administration's attack on the free press that, by fall 1973, contributed to further delineations of illegal activities and abuses of power. Dennis E. Shoemaker, editor of *Trends* magazine of the United Presbyterian Church, wrote for *A.D.* because it was jointly published by the United Presbyterian Church and the UCC. He defended the religious press from accusations it should print only official denominational policies because readers deserved to hear from Christian leaders about faith's relationship to the public realm. He reported, "Until the Watergate scandal broke, probably not more than 2 percent of the American public was deeply concerned about the assault on the media by the present Administration." Calling it a "war on journalists" that nonetheless demanded attention, Shoemaker declared the "major problem before us is clearly derived from the present Administration's contention the press is not sufficiently 'objective,' which, in part, is double-speak for not sufficiently advocating Administration policy." He explained the public finally awoke to the high stakes of the matter because stripping the media of its rights ultimately endangered "the concept of freedom itself." Or, more bluntly, "A controlled press means a controlled people, a nation of dupes."[23]

Liberal Protestants at this point took the gloves off completely when dealing with the Nixon White House and therefore led Christians into more pronounced political activity. Religious leaders and the laity alike had by and large disliked this administration from early in Nixon's presidency because of his conduct in the Vietnam War and lack of vision regarding social justice. As the years passed and illegal actions by people within the Republican Party and eventually the White House came to light, it simply solidified this already established mistrust. Liberal Protestants' charges became more vehement against Nixon, leading to some of the first calls for impeachment from the Christian community. And, to be sure, these political statements about the administration were undergirded throughout with a carefully articulated theological response to Watergate.

Liberal Theology Sharpens Its Edge

As the Watergate investigation intensified once Alexander Butterfield revealed the existence of the White House tapes, the theological argument from liberal Protestantism became more forceful in adding a faith-driven voice to the national debate. These Protestants were using their theology to drive their message into the public realm.

Like conservative Protestants, liberal theology regarding Watergate began with the notion of sin being embedded in humanity and, in the case of the Nixon administration, leading to the illegal activities. Liberal Protestants voiced this opinion in a variety of ways, including poems. Carolyn Keefe provided one such poetic expression for the *Christian Century*:

> WATERGATE FUNHOUSE
>
> we are in a long hall of doors
> where convergence ends
> at mid-points rather than extremes.
> Pull the knobs and be surprised,
> no skeletons or ghosts,
> just smiles hanging headless
> above the smart blue suits,
> nothing scary here
> where we could find
> our way out.

Her poem indicts the Watergate conspirators but adds allusions to what many would find behind doors throughout the United States, especially since Keefe emphasized the "mid-points rather than extremes." A litany written for the UCC's General Synod in 1973 also played with the idea of human depravity, national sin, and Christian responsibility in the midst of it:

> LEADER: From arrogance, pompousness,
> and thinking ourselves more important than we are,
> PEOPLE: May some saving sense of humor liberate us.

LEADER: From the temptations of self-pity,
the enjoyment of poor health,
and the exploitation of others through our own weakness,
PEOPLE: May we have the grace to cease.

LEADER: From being bearers of despair,
of cynicism, and of ridicule for what is young
and just getting started,
PEOPLE: May we be delivered.

LEADER: From being bearers of new narrowness,
of making fun of what is old or traditional,
yet filled with meaning,
PEOPLE: May we be spared.

LEADER: For permitting our own lack of belief
to tear down the faith and efforts of others,
PEOPLE: May we be forgiven.

LEADER: From making war and calling it peace,
special privilege and calling it justice,
indifference and calling it tolerance,
pollution and calling it progress,
PEOPLE: May we be cured.

LEADER: From telling ourselves and others
That evil is inevitable while good is impossible,
PEOPLE: May we be corrected.

TOGETHER: God of our mixed up,
doubting, aspiring, insurgent lives,
help us to be as good as in our hearts
we have always wanted to be;
help us to hold the vision
of your place and of your people;
give us strength to claim you
in our visions and in our realities;

may we be truly one in the Spirit,
one in the Lord.
Amen.

The litany never mentions Watergate explicitly, but it says enough for an alert worshipper to recognize a disease within the current government. Words such as "arrogance," "exploitation," "cynicism," "special privilege," and "evil" were part of the American Watergate lexicon and unmistakable in their reference. Anyone participating in this prayer would interpret the inclusion of a hope to mean replacing the Nixon administration in part with the help of the prayer of UCC members. Speaking to the sixtieth annual meetings of the National Lutheran Editors and Managers Association in September 1973, *Lutheran* editor Albert P. Stauderman further discussed his difficulty in finding "a label" for Watergate. He stated, "The story isn't Watergate, but it's related to it and bigger than the incident." Immoralities in government were "moral problems which reflect upon the religious life of our land," or perhaps the lack of a vital national faith life. Voices such as those simply informed Americans that human depravity contextualized Watergate. Leftist theological reflections began at the same place as conservatives, acknowledging that sin lay at the heart of the crisis.[24]

But liberals and conservatives diverged thereafter, with conservatives looking inward, while liberals sought to inject Christian social values in rather more public venues and political causes. For example, the United Church of Christ took action regarding a television station's license in Jackson, Mississippi. The controversy involved WLBT-TV, after the station was proved to allow racial discrimination and racist programming. Protection from the Mississippi state government gave cover for the Federal Communications Commission's license renewal for the station. The UCC protested. Its involvement dated to 1964, because of the denomination's posture in advocating for the rights of racial and gendered minorities. This incident wove its way into its thinking about Watergate when the UCC Office of Communication charged that "political leaders in Mississippi who are close associates of Frederick C. LaRue, the Watergate figure, 'improperly exploited' their political affiliations to 'obtain favored treatment from government agencies.'" LaRue was John Mitchell's chief adviser and a major backer of G. Gordon Liddy's role in CREEP.

LaRue had advance notice of the Watergate break-in and cooperated in the cover-up, including distributing hush money before he became the first person in the administration to plead guilty in 1973 to obstruction of justice. Yet he never testified against Nixon or others involved. LaRue's affiliation with the Mississippi officials in this licensing controversy led the UCC into pressing for the Federal Communications Commission to reopen hearings on WLBT and its future. The UCC and fellow opponents insisted LaRue's connections here precluded a careful, fair, and honest renewal process, a symptom of the greater problem of Nixonian corruption.[25]

Christian Century editors ignited a similar discussion about Nixon and morality with an article by Milton Mayer about Quakers and their affiliation with Richard Nixon. Nixon grew up in a Quaker household, with a mother who strictly adhered to the faith, but he gradually drifted farther and farther away from its tenets. For example, Nixon served in World War II, and Quaker pacifism played no role throughout his political career. He generally attended other Protestant churches while in Washington, DC. He was not beyond calling on his Quaker upbringing for political capital in campaigns or in reminding people about his devout mother, but otherwise he left his Quaker faith in the past. Mayer, from the Center for the Study of Democratic Institutions in Santa Barbara, California, roving editor for *Progressive*, and author of *If Men Were Angels*, used this past to call on Nixon's home congregation in Whittier, California, the East Whittier Friends Church, to cast him out of the congregation. Expulsion could be accomplished simply by removing someone from the church rolls for failure to change or alter a certain behavior. Mayer stated that Nixon "evokes a pride and contention" with a "cheerless" demeanor and lack of answering to God. Nixon only sought "public power" and was "a hard man to hold in the light, but held in the light he must be—at least by Quakers." Though Mayer also wanted the Friends to "labor with him tenderly," the fact he "has never kept himself clear of the blood of men by word, or writing, or speaking" demanded the action Mayer requested. Readers debated Mayer's argument. One letter to the editor wondered what disownment would accomplish because "it wouldn't keep Nixon, already in his lame duck years, honest. It wouldn't cause any dramatic change in his ideology or in his use of public piety (or the absence of it) for political purposes." Rather, this writer worried it might make Nixon into a sympathetic religious martyr at the worst possible time. Note that the writer did not disagree with Mayer's ill perception of the president and took Nixon to task for immoral behavior. Other readers more pointedly attacked *Christian Century* editors for publishing this story. David P. Gaines found the introduction of this idea lacking in Christian sensibility and off the mark, while Arnold P. Von der Porten, a fellow Quaker, defended Nixon and declared, "If the Whittier Meeting should disown Friend Richard Nixon, the way I feel right now, I too would probably dissociate myself from the Friends." The final word on the matter, at least within the pages of the *Christian Century*, came from the pastor of East Whittier Friends Church himself. T. Eugene Coffin explained his meetinghouse wanted to keep lines of communication open with the president despite disagreeing with many of his policies. He contextualized it in the biblical notion of allowing for a "wayward" member to repent and come back to God. He further explained, "The Christian fellowship is not an exclusive club seeking to maintain a certain status by its own effort, but rather a caring community which refuses to abandon those in trouble and which seeks to restore rather than destroy, to heal rather than hurt, to reconcile rather than divide, and to accept the risks involved." Mayer certainly induced a controversy by bringing up the matter, and even generally agreeable readers of the liberal newsmagazine disagreed with him. Nonetheless, the controversy demonstrates the way liberal Christians understood Nixon and Watergate. Moral corruption was enveloping the political world of the nation, centered on the president, and necessitated Christian leadership to change it.[26]

As an indication of the growing desire for Christian commentary, more and more moderate to liberal Protestants called for modern-day prophets to step forward. Editorials to this point and reader reactions to them exemplify such pining. Stauderman again used the *Lutheran* to make such statements and ponder the meaning of Watergate. He explained to one reader, who questioned the use of a religious periodical for political commentary, "There is a deep moral question involved which affects the lives of all Christian people. It should be discussed in our churches as well as in the public press. If we have contributed toward such discussion, we have helped fulfill one of our purposes" as a Christian institution. While that reader disagreed, many more Lutheran laypeople voiced their favor. William E. Diehl's letter to the editor defended Edgar Trexler's July article about Watergate and the condemnation of the administration it contained. Diehl asserted that whether Nixon "was responsible or irresponsible, the fact remains that laws were broken and unethical practices permitted. How can any American not be disappointed in such leadership?" Therefore, he continued, "I reject the implication *The Lutheran* should not devote editorial comment to this, the biggest issue of the day. It will be a sad day for all of us when the news media, and in particular church publications, are afraid to raise a voice of protest when evil deeds are being done in high places." In other words, the church had a moral obligation to decry immoral actions in the government in an effort to bring Christian witness to bear.[27]

A similar conversation ensued among United Church of Christ editors and readers of *A.D.* after editor J. Martin Bailey commented on Watergate and the administration in the summer of 1973. Bailey wrote several personal letters to people who complained about what they perceived as inappropriate political commentary in their church periodical. Bailey's defense centered on the biblical notion of prophetic voices raised against tyranny. He thought it crucial to write about a topic that "cuts at the moral and ethical fiber of our nation" and detailed, "The Old Testament prophets, our crucified Lord, and such near contemporaries as Elijah Parish Lovejoy and Dietrich Bonhoeffer are my tutors on the subject of church involvement in political affairs." He told a close friend who questioned him the courts and Congress had a most important role, but "this does not preclude the role of the church as prophet. David had his Nathan, and was a better administrator for it. Jesus went to the cross not for his acts of love and mercy, but because he was at odds with the Jewish and Roman authorities. It is precisely the task of the church and her modern prophets to raise ethical questions and to speak a word of judgment." Thus Bailey laid out a clear theology behind the way liberal Protestants went after the Nixon administration. As with Stauderman, Bailey found more backers than detractors. To the argument the church must wait until civil courts and Congress spoke on the matter, Ralph Douglas Hyslop thought it odd people wanted such a reversal of the prophetic process as often articulated in the Bible. Rather, he wanted his church's leaders to contribute their ideas to the national dialogue. And Anna B. Robertson specified that political beliefs should align with "religious views and experience" through the use of platforms such as *A.D.* so "those who can speak with a prophetic voice" may educate the UCC laity. She continued, "The Old Testament has many instances of this kind of perception and courage on the part of the prophets who were not afraid to speak out in criticism of the kings of old." Clearly, liberal Protestants felt a biblical mandate to enter the Watergate fray and continued to see themselves as a prophetic voice in the national crisis.[28]

Another aspect of the theological conversation swirling around Watergate was the debate over pietism and situational ethics. As usual, the *Christian Century* framed much of this discussion, as evidenced in a piece authored by Duane R. Miller in September 1973. Miller, the director of admissions and financial aid at Boston University's School of Theology, applied Jacque Ellul's philosophy of "Technique." This technique, according to Miller, "concentrates on the immediate solution of immediate problems" without concern for "values such as truth and justice." The problem with this method was that each solution created a new problem, solved by the same methodology, thus creating a never-ending loop. Miller observed Watergate fit this theory exactly, with CREEP focused only on winning, and thus staffing itself with those intent only on that goal, and nothing more valuable. This prompted the enemies list, leaking half-truths, followed by confusion and subterfuge as these activities came to light. It eventually spawned the paying off of criminals and lying under oath to the Senate Committee. Miller stated Ellul articulated how "the technician identifies the means with the end, and equates the best means with the good. He may cite traditional values, but only to divert attention from his real concern of finding the best means." Miller then accused the Watergate participants of being remorseful not because they acted immorally but because they failed to protect the White House. Miller felt Americans must come to question this use of "Technique" and give up their "faith in the office of the President no matter what the facts are." He concluded, "In the light of Ellul's thought, we see Watergate as a crude outcropping from the Technique that has powerfully influenced society. If by its excesses Watergate helps us to understand Technique, it may prove a significant breakthrough in transforming the morality of our nation and restoring such traditional values as truth and justice." Implicit in these conversations by the *Christian Century* was the notion of an individual worrying only about his or her own concerns, not a larger societal or corporate good. Miller understood this lack of pondering truth and justice, which require communal values outside of a small group's goals.[29]

The delegates to the UCC's General Synod more pointedly took aim at pietism. After watching live testimony by John Dean during their proceedings, they discussed "a general raveling away of the nation's moral fabric." Acknowledging church failure in this capacity, including their own, they wanted ecumenical religious cooperation to replace "privatized self-concern" with "outward-oriented concern for others and for corporate expressions of morality." They further entreated their church body to educate constituents on the import of doing and being for others, not just oneself. In short, this outlook blamed American individualism, evangelical pietism, and the current presidential administration for the nation's travails. Delegates therefore demanded a broader approach to dealing with national affairs, with the hope that a collective morality would reduce the too narrow view of many Americans when they considered moral and ethical issues.[30]

But the United Church of Christ did more than simply criticize one form of theology. The Executive Council's decision to release an October statement about Watergate demonstrates how church leaders articulated their own theology regarding the national crisis after the General Synod had failed to issue a statement. The sharp rebuke by J. Martin Bailey in *A.D.* especially spurred them to act. The Executive Council consisted of a little more than forty lay, clerical, and national leaders, all elected at the General Synod meeting, as well as the UCC president, the moderator, and a presidential assistant sitting as ex officio members with voting powers. The body was charged with acting between General Synods on behalf of the church. Recall that UCC president Robert V. Moss presented a resolution on Watergate the night prior to the June 1973 General Synod. The Executive Council declined to act, instead submitting it to a General Synod small group. The small group did not act on the resolution and also struck references to Watergate from any of its official actions, a move Moss could not explain afterward, though he assumed "their decision was made in good faith." A motion by some delegates to suspend rules in order to introduce a Watergate resolution on the floor also failed. Therefore, Moss and others shortened, polished, and otherwise revised the original June resolution and brought it before the Administrative Committee, which met in September. The Administrative Committee was essentially a select subgroup of the Executive Council. Its members discussed the revised resolution, agreed on the appropriateness of the church making a statement, and decided to recommend the Executive Council take up the matter again at its October meeting. They forwarded the statement, after more revision, for the Executive Council's scrutiny. Thus one can see how UCC polity met the challenges of the era's political crisis in a regular, democratic process guided by prophetic leadership.[31]

The statement itself sheds much light on UCC theology as it relates to Watergate. Because God judged nations as well as people and ordained government for the good of humanity, the church and individual Christians needed to concern themselves with it. Therefore, it continued, "In the light of Christian conscience each of us must judge what is right and what is wrong in the functioning of government, and must act upon that judgment." In other words, not only should the church take responsibility for the moral and ethical well-being of the nation, but it was imperative according to this faith life they do so. The statement next criticized these same Christians for failing to engage all aspects of society in a Christian manner. Corporate Christian values necessitated a believer not look the other way or accept such things as "the spreading of false values," or tolerate "national self-righteousness and idolatry" and "contempt for the law," or contribute "to the corruption of power" through an acquiescence to "public mismanagement" and "scorn for politicians." Having thus established the theological justification for the Executive Council's statement, it presented a method for Christians to use to turn the tide against this problem. The UCC statement urged individuals to act as part of a greater network of people, as part of the larger society. UCC leaders asked Christians to "impress upon the nation that moral responsibility is an essential foundation for the exercise of political authority," to insist on the "imperatives of freedom of religion," and uphold the constitutional principles "that can prevent any branch of government from imposing its will on the nation." The statement further tasked Christians with protecting the right of individuals and holding even the highest offices in the land accountable for their actions. It concluded with the call for Christians to "insist that the maintenance of law and order is a responsibility to all of the people, and that persons in positions of power and privilege are never exempt from this responsibility." In this way, the UCC articulated a theology of action. Like Christians of all theological stripes, it laid part of the blame for Watergate at the feet of Christian laziness. But it then diverged into a liberal viewpoint with the idea the individual should not withdraw or retreat from the defense of the common good. One's personal conversion or beliefs meant little without action including a just and moral government.[32]

In a special issue published in late September, *Christian Century* editor James M. Wall determined by August 1973 Watergate had grown to the point of demanding a broad theological response from a number of prominent theologians. In a form letter sent to professors, pastors, and church leaders, Wall spelled out, "For the moment we feel that a survey of religious leaders like yourself is needed to provide focus for the evaluations that are already beginning to develop." He further explained, "Public discussion of Watergate needs the theological dimension you can provide." Along with the United Church of Christ, Wall wanted Christians to work toward an ethical solution. The people to whom Wall reached out responded favorably. Methodist theologian Earl Brewer's agreement included an entreaty to Wall that "your Foundation needs to make news as well as report it and reflect upon it. Because of your own interests, this is a ready-made issue for an intervention from the perspective of the Christian faith." Vocally taking a stance became a vital component of this liberal periodical's existence if it intended to live out a Christian calling. Joseph Fletcher, from the University of Virginia School of Medicine in the Program in Human Biology and Society, informed Wall about the demand for such conversations, saying he was "swamped" with requests for Watergate comment, lectures, and statements. He viewed it not only as a Christian responsibility to speak out, but also a response to a national cry for such moral additions to the dialogue. Wall concurred in a follow-up letter to those who agreed to participate: "We feel it [the Watergate issue] will be an important contribution to a nation that badly needs to see its way out of the Watergate morass."[33]

While impossible to determine the exact influence this particular issue of the *Christian Century* had regarding Watergate events or on opinions about it, indications reveal a widespread consensus among liberals. Wall explained to readers he designed this issue "to examine the moral dimension of Watergate." Each respondent was asked, "What precisely is the central religious or theological issue posed by Watergate, and how will we as a people find resources to deal with this issue?" It then left it open for their reflections. Various theologians often reiterated the arguments made in the UCC statement in terms of explaining why they commented on this political topic. Dana W. Wilbanks, an assistant professor of Christian ethics at the Iliff School of Theology, justified Christian participation because "the church is called on to live in sharp tension with government ideology and practices, serving as one vital source of the transformation of political ethics in the United States." Theressa Hoover of the Board of Global Ministries for the United Methodist Church also explained, "When loyal Christians plead ignorance of facts as a way to avoid responsibility, blindly accept as gospel the words of elected leaders, and question the loyalty of those who are critical, they actually put the ideas of Caesar above the principles of God. Such has been the situation which has made possible Watergate." Ronald J. Sider of Messiah College relied on the notion of prophetic voices speaking against evil when he stated, "Watergate has strengthened my belief that God is still alive and well, doing precisely what the prophets said Yahweh always does: acting in history to destroy evil men and institutions."[34]

Naturally, most of the commentators focused on the theological origins of Watergate. Robert McAfee Brown, a professor of religious studies at Stanford University, took aim at American egoism and pietism when he wrote the issue "is also the allied one of *idolatry*—the worship of false gods, in this case the false gods of the self and of the self's extension, the tiny in-group." This led to dangerous thinking that whatever protected the president, no matter how unethical or illegal, was justified. Brown linked this problem to a consistent moral failure in the administration, such as "the President's willingness to bomb Cambodia for six months without a shred of legal, military or moral authority to do so." Cynthia Wedel, a former president of the National Council of the Churches of Christ in the USA, more directly took aim at pietism. Such outward virtues contrasted with "inner corruption" throughout American society. Watergate represented but the most significant manifestation of these issues. She hoped the church "could regain its soul" by questioning this behavior in favor of an approach that denounced the ends justifying the means and advocated for the greater good, not individual glory.

Liberal condemnation of pietism and its relationship to Watergate had no harsher critic than Eugene Carson Blake, the former general secretary of the World Council of Churches, who wrote: "Watergate has exposed for all to see that the secular reaction to the dominant rigid Protestant morality of the first century and a half of our nation's history has now produced a culture which at all levels rationalizes our national human greed for material good and for selfish, self-serving power." Similar reasoning came from United Methodist Church bishop James Armstrong, who decried Americans' reactions to Watergate even more than the crimes themselves. He agonized over citizens who worried more about their own well-being than about sin in Washington, thus pondering, "Perhaps the sin is ours. We have embraced false gods and unworthy loyalties. We have confused means and ends. In a power-conscious, public-relations-oriented age, the motives and objectives implicit in Watergate strike close to home." Thus liberal theologians, much like their conservative counterparts who took aim at Watergate's exposure of sin, saw it as a symptom of an illness. Yet for liberals, the mind-set and theological approach of conservatives was the nursery of the disease. Armstrong ended with a hope for salvation in the fact Americans saw "much of ourselves mirrored in the Watergate hearings, and we don't like what we see." Collective Christian action to change this culture, not revivalism, gave the best hope for renewal.

Alan Geyer, the Dag Hammarskjold Professor of Peace Studies at Colgate University, took this a step farther and invoked an even sharper tone in doing so. He pinpointed hypocrisy as the central sin of the Watergate affair, reminding readers, "The prophetic tradition, pre-eminently in Jesus Christ, interpreted hypocrisy as a religious issue of the most ultimate kind." He then criticized pietism because "Watergate is not the first, but perhaps the most blatant, revelation that those in our republic who have made the most conspicuous display of their own piety and righteousness have generated deeply and profane wicked ways." He pointed out Nixon and his administration harped on law and order while conspiring to hold on to their power illegally. They also howled about abuses of government, all the while using the government to harass and undermine those with whom they disagreed. In addition, they promised peace while persisting with the "unjust war" in Vietnam. In conclusion, Geyer stated, "None of us can pretend to know how the

Almighty will judge this willful evil in our nation's leadership. It may be remembered, however, that Dante reserved the lowest circle of hell for hypocrites."

The Boston College theologian Mary Daly contributed a feminist perspective to liberal religious responses. She directed her ire at patriarchal structures in which the world "is characterized by social and psychic models of dominance and submission. Subservience to the prevailing hierarchies involves the whole syndrome painfully visible in the Watergate affair: blind obedience to 'authority,' 'loyalty,' violence, erasure and/ or reversal of threatening facts, false innocence, victimization of 'the Other.'" She also articulated God in the United States had become the American Male, and the president His Chosen One. Despite the deeply entrenched and problematic system, Daly still believed change could occur. She explained, "As the ultimate outsiders, as deviants in the Man's world, women have the psychic potential to break the vicious circle" of corruption and discrimination, and so vanquish the patriarchal structures allowing for Watergate in the first place.

In similar ways, other theologians expressed the notion, darkness not withstanding, that Christian light could remedy the current malaise. David R. Hunter, deputy general secretary for the National Council of Churches, referred to Watergate as "demonic" but continued that this subsequent danger challenged Americans "with forces deep within our being where God can have a way with us. The need for deception must be removed and the capacity for trust restored" with Christian understanding and openness. Thus the *Christian Century* confronted the issue of Watergate as a national problem demanding harsh rebukes of those involved, and the sins at the heart of American society: rampant individualism and a passive pietism. These Christian leaders called for all Christians to assert a greater moral authority over politics via a radical redefinition of its conservative values.

Liberal to moderate Protestants during this era conveyed a sharp condemnatory tone about Watergate as they delved further into the theological issues causing it. While histories of the Religious Right focus on its move into politics, scholars seldom show that liberal Protestants were already operating there. Protestants couched their response in terms of Christian corporate responsibility, and the need for religious voices to imbue the nation with a revelatory new set of values in the manner of the prophets, if not Christ himself. Liberal Protestantism's persistent prophecies added to the growing cries for change and no doubt contributed to the eventual downfall of the thirty-seventh president by revealing him to be not David but Pharaoh.

African Methodist Episcopal Reactions

As Watergate investigations proceeded, the religious responses also became more nuanced and complicated. It also becomes more difficult to classify the various reactions because not all Christian entities marched in lockstep behind a single leader or set of principles. No organization shows this reality more than the African Methodist Episcopal Church. In some ways, it belongs with a liberal point of view because of its antipathy toward Richard Nixon's administration and its civil rights advocacy. Yet in other ways it took a cautious theological approach to Watergate, and its proposed theological solutions more closely parallel those of evangelicals. In other words, by the second half of 1973, the AME set out to blaze its own trail regarding Watergate.

Much like mainline white liberal churches, the AME had a low regard for Nixon. While the denomination could broadly agree with his anticommunist foreign policy, the AME criticized his poor record on race. Despite Nixon's attempts to address economic disparity, they recognized his pandering to white racist southerners with attempts to roll back integration initiatives and his reluctance to follow through on the civil rights movement. The AME also denounced the Vietnam War because it disproportionately affected African American young men.[35] It therefore evolved naturally that AME conferences and individuals condemned the administration's deepening culpability in Watergate. The Chicago Annual Conference, meeting in September 1973, included a Committee on Special Resolutions which deplored racism and poor economic and housing conditions. The committee's report began with "as the United States enters into four more years of the Nixon Administration, the problems of racism, hunger, unemployment and housing, to name a few, remain matters of central concern in these United States. The immorality of 'Watergate' has manifested itself in every aspect of American life." To these delegates, Watergate represented just another problem on a long list of grievances with the president. After recounting why Americans held the president to high moral and ethical standards, *Christian Recorder* editor A. Lewis Williams stated, "Mr. Nixon can no longer be trusted with the grave responsibilities of this government. He should find some legal way to resign for the good of the country." Though he noted he spoke for himself and not on behalf of the AME, Williams fell in line with early calls from the liberal Christian community for the president's ouster. AME youth also added their voice to anti-Nixon statements when their section of the *Christian Recorder* published a cynical telegram that California state senator Marvyn M. Dymally sent Nixon. He lamented that Nixon's enemies list lacked enough African American representation, and thus demanded the addition of his name. In all, the AME found much to dislike in the Nixon presidency.[36]

Yet other conference statements denouncing Nixon presented a conservative point of view. The August gathering of the Michigan Annual Conference provides a case in point. A statement by the Special Resolutions Committee lumped government corruption with legalized abortion and attempts to legalize drugs. After listing such conservative causes, however, the statement reviled Nixon by asserting that "our Country lost" with his election because of his economic and social policies. It concluded with a call for stronger moral leadership throughout the government. In this way, the Michigan Annual Conference of the AME occupied a middle ground. Similar moderation came from the Illinois Annual Conference in September 1973. After outlining American distrust of the administration because of Watergate, a report from the Committee on the State of the Country noted some hope that at least Nixon's addressing of the matter with the media indicated he, too, was angry about Watergate. Yet it also portrayed Watergate as pitting "President Nixon directly against the Watergate investigators." The report optimistically declared the scandal prompted Americans to demand higher moral standards in government, which would improve the state of the nation. Amid the continuing scandal and heightened hopes for accountability, the committee concluded, "The state of the country is a very perplexing one, indeed."[37]

Nonetheless, like both their conservative and liberal Christian colleagues, members and leaders of the AME determined the church must step into the political arena. In some ways, the denomination sounded a typical conservative lament about failed ethical and moral failure. For example, Sidney Simon, an AME member and a circuit court judge of Cook County, Illinois, "lashed out at the Watergate scandal, corruptions in governmental areas, both in churches and other facets of society which has brought about mistrust on all hands." *Christian Recorder* editor B. J. Nolen asserted, "Our moral climate smells to high heaven. Both Church and State must be put back on the track and let the peoples' train get moving again." These commentators blamed church, government, and society for the crisis in America. But such conservative outlooks competed with others in the AME on the subject of what the church could offer.[38]

The Indiana Annual Conference of the AME demonstrates this more moderate tone with reports from two committees. The Special Committee on Resolutions Dealing with the Issues of Today requested the church "speak out against dishonesty in government" and "the low level to which our national government has descended." But it next added a list of liberal, moderate, and conservative concerns Nixon failed to address: "poverty, Watergate, busing, education, drug addiction, prison reform, racism, and abortion." It swung back to a more conservative theology with the conclusion "The church set its house in order that it bring sinners to repentance, bring labors from the corner of the streets and place them in the vineyard of labor." In other words, renewal and focus on Christianity provided the best solutions for fixing the problem. The Report on the State of the Church regretted secular activity moved to the center of people's attention, not the church, and lamented Christians no longer cared about this lost influence. They linked this to a too strong belief in the "political arena," which waned with the Watergate mess. This brought about "demonic fears and inquisitional ethics."[39]

Nothing sums up more succinctly the AME general reaction to Watergate than a poem by William R. Wilkes, an AME bishop. He sides with those investigating the scandal and denounces the political ethics leading to Watergate, while concluding that the conservative call for repentance and coming to Christianity was the best solution:

THE SCANDAL OF "WATERGATE"

It is generally known in every
  State,

About the scandal of "Watergate"
It appears that some political
    "rouse"
Has connected the scandal to our
    "Whitehouse."

Shouldn't this nation be thankful
    to the Washington Post,
For exposing this scandal from
    coast to coast?
These probers will be remembered
    across the years.
By many more people than just
    their peers.

This scandal should bring them
    to their senses,
As they sit down to the table of
    consequences,
As I make this remark, I hurry
    to say
It will happen to us in the "self
    same way."

The moral universe is so structured,
    some wise men say,
That if one gets by with crime,
    he can't get away.
This principle is riveted in the
    order of things,
No matter how much sorrow and
    suffering it brings.

This scandal has corroded our
    global relations,
Because it exposes the sickness of
    a part of this nation,

It far exceeds "The Tea Pot
　Dome"
And could erupt in every home.

It is more than the "Chickens
　coming home to roost,"
It is political corruption, well on
　the loose,
The partisan "plumbers" waited
　to [sic] late
To plug these holes in "Watergate."

But, before we get stuck in the
　mud of despair,
Let's call this nation to action
　and prayer,
With a firm belief that a
　righteous God
Will protect and preserve the
　pure in heart.

The scandal of "watergate" is
　not the end,
It only exposes the depths of sin,
This nation, under God, can get
　the power
To keep on going in its darkest
　hour.[40]

    As liberals and conservatives squared off regarding Watergate, the African Methodist Episcopal Church held true to its hybrid political and theological tenets. It traditionally held to a more conservative theology espousing an evangelical call for coming to the church for salvation and close adherence to biblical teachings. However, as with many black churches, the AME possessed a long history of social activism because of its founding on the issue of segregation in the church and because its members confronted racial inequality every day of their lives. This activism increased more and more throughout the civil rights era as the issues intensified on a national stage.[41] Because Nixon failed in many people's opinions regarding race in America, he lost these denominations, including the AME. Watergate simply added another reason for this denomination to mistrust the president. Unlike its white liberal counterparts, its reactions approached a more rightist tactic of wanting a revived Christianity as the solution. Yet as the Watergate crisis escalated in the coming months, the AME revised its views.

Favored by God or Idolatry?

What shift there was in discussions about America being a Christian nation paralleled differing views between liberal and conservative Protestants writ large. Conservatives held back to see how events unfolded and continued to trust the president and country, while liberal and moderate Christians grew more angry and questioned such nation worship. Conservatives had less to say than liberals, perhaps because liberal to moderate Christians began to more seriously worry about the fate of the federal government. Silence could also signal conservative doubt about Republican Theology tying them too closely to White House wrongdoing.

Yet Protestants of all theological and political stripes shared a common belief that the US government, despite Watergate, was essentially sound. They trusted the system to correct the problem and asked people to keep faith with the positive aspects of government as outlined in the Constitution. Contributing editor J. Elliott Corbett of the United Church of Christ's *Engage/Social Action* wrote, "The Constitutional provision for a separation of powers has served this nation well—even in the crisis. For at a time when the Congress has been weak and the executive branch has failed us, the judiciary system has worked well." To be sure, he regretted that up to now too little had happened to put Watergate to rest, and in other arenas this periodical regularly criticized the Nixon administration. Nonetheless, the liberal Christian entity voiced a continuing faith in the government's ability to work through the crisis. A reader of the *Christian Century* added, "There is, as always, a possible comeback, a revival of nobility and honesty and public service as an honor and trust." In addition to the Constitution working, this person recalled that for most of America's history a sense of service to others prevailed and would reemerge. The Michigan Annual Conference of the African Methodist Episcopal Church declared, "The United States Constitution, the oldest and most successfully written constitution in history, has served the nation with remarkably little formal alteration during its various periods of rapid social changes." In this way, American Christian bodies shared a faith in their nation, but without specifically labeling it as Christian.[42]

This arena still exposed more nuanced theological arguments. Conservative Protestant patriotism emphatically proclaimed a faith in the nation that stemmed from a belief God ordained all government, and specifically blessed American democracy. Though Watergate revealed humans succumbed to temptation, including those holding high office, *Christianity Today* editors felt the "services of watchdog journalists" assisted the country "even if some did so out of ulterior motives." They thanked the mainstream media for exposing Watergate and safeguarding the democratic process, while distancing themselves from journalists' perceived liberalism. They used this maneuver by invoking divine providence. Returning to the sinful nature of humankind, the piece stated all elements of society worked together because "man cannot be thoroughly moral on his own. The more we can build this consideration into our culture, the more justice, peace, and order we will have." The same sentiment came from *Home Missions* of the Southern Baptist Convention, which directly called for the United States to operate as a Christian nation because "the Old Testament reminds us: 'Blessed is the nation whose God is the Lord.' Jesus taught us to pray: 'Thy will be done in earth, as it is in heaven.'" While these comments came in the rationale for the SBC's creation of Christian Citizenship Sunday, Arthur B. Rutledge prefaced the remarks with a lament about Watergate and the need for Baptists to participate in healing the nation, as God expected.[43]

Because conservative Protestants placed a higher degree of importance on God's ordaining of government, they also expected Christian participation in mending the nation's ills, a strong sentiment in the Southern Baptist Convention. The Christian Life Commission sent a letter to all members of the House of Representatives and Senate calling for "a recovery of integrity in the life of our nation" because of the "shocking disregard for morality on the part of those involved" in Watergate. It asked for new legislation to correct political abuses and encourage higher ethical standards and requested the Senate Select Committee continue to investigate Watergate. Assuming a sense of Christian morality existed from the founding of the nation, it ended by encouraging "you as a national leader to exercise to the fullest extent your influence in helping to bring about a recommitment to those basic moral principles on which this nation has traditionally stood."[44]

Though subtle in distinction because they prayed for the nation as did conservatives, moderates to liberals offered prayers that nonetheless demonstrated a different sense that avoided any direct links to God's providential role in the US government. Rather, they implored God to influence the people involved in their decision-making. A UCC prayer for all peoples and rulers of the world printed in *A.D.* noted God governed all the world without favoring the United States. It entreated God to instill in public servants the notion that diverting their power for private ends betrayed the country and to "Breathe a new spirit into all our nation." But even in seeking to enlist in leaders a "holy warfare for the rights of the people," nothing suggested any special favor from heaven upon the United States. Even the more moderate Lutheran version shied away from assertions God particularly favored America. Lutherans, too, sought divine guidance among leaders, but also prayed for citizen engagement that demanded ethical and moral behavior. The LCA hymnal implored God guide the president and those with authority so they "may be high in purpose" without any implication America was a chosen Christian nation. The prayer hoped for American leadership to live Christian ideals without making the supposition they were God's anointed servants. Lambert F. Brose of the LCUSA staff attempted to amend the prayer further, to implore God to turn the American public from all notions of nation worship. The key difference between these moderate and liberal prayers and those of conservatives rested in whether the person praying thought God used America as a special vessel.[45]

In a similar way in the *Lutheran*, the layman Philip C. Becker wrote, "Let us pray that Watergate will lead to a restoration of confidence in government," less polarization in society, and a "repatriation" of men who fled to Canada to avoid the draft. This more liberal call also charged readers to understand dissent did not mean disloyalty to the nation, and love for country should compel everyone to seek true justice. However, true justice did not mean the government itself represented God's will.

The UCC's *Washington Report* quoted John Cotton from approximately 1640, reminding his Puritan faithful that "all power that is on earth be limited" because of human sin. In other words, sinful humans operated governments and therefore necessitated constant Christian vigilance to root out ungodly actions.[46]

A draft prior to the October passage of the UCC Executive Council Statement on Corruption in Government more carefully distanced the UCC from merging Christianity and American democracy. It first stated churches concerned themselves with governments because "God judges nations" and because throughout history "churches have reminded secular authorities of their responsibilities to God and to humankind." The United States was not different from all history and countries, and so was not exceptional. While the statement applied the common refrain for Christian ethics to operate in the political arena and applauded the separation of powers in the three branches of government, it also sought for individual Christians and denominations to work for change through actions, and not wait for God to act.[47]

As often happened because of its different platform and constituency, the *Christian Century* expressed its views more forcefully. Unafraid of a conservative backlash, the editors and writers took aim at the idea of a special status for the United States and instead blamed that for what transpired within the executive branch. In October, editor James M. Wall addressed this issue in his comments about Spiro Agnew's resignation. Agnew, although a moderate Republican for most of his career, swung sharply to the right as vice president. Even more than the president, his increasingly racist and elitist attitudes drew rebuke. Agnew proved his detractors right when his career "came to a crashing halt" after he was forced to resign on October 10, 1973. Evidence materialized that Agnew demanded kickbacks from contractors starting first when he served as a county executive in Maryland, continuing while he was the governor and into his time as vice president. In order to avoid a lengthy trial and possible prison sentence, he pled guilty to tax evasion and agreed to resign. In responding to this latest administrative scandal, Wall noted the Constitution "sustained us as our leaders have failed us" because the founders based it on laws, not "the wiles and manipulations of individuals." He saw "theological wisdom" in how the Constitution protected citizens by diminishing the importance of one person and the whims of sin that go with it. However, unlike conservative calls for trusting the government and God to fix the problem, Wall explained, "Christian realism assures us that all persons who occupy positions of civil power are susceptible to the temptation to misuse that power. Because only God is to be finally trusted, we know to deal with all human assertions" cautiously.[48]

Ralph L. Moellering, a Lutheran pastor for special ministries in colleges and universities in the San Francisco Bay Area, authored "Civil Religion, the Nixon Theology and the Watergate Scandal." He outlined how Nixon still proclaimed his innocence and thought those guilty of any crimes merely became "overzealous" in their attempts to assure his re-election. Moellering explained how this stemmed from the ill-conceived idea their "intentions" were pure and meant to protect the nation with "the defeat of a candidate who consorted with dangerous radicals and the triumph of a man who represents what is best for the people." This hubris was found in too many in the administration. These ideas, which became more and more a failure of how Nixon defended himself in the coming months and coming years, placed the president and his associates on a pedestal above everyone else, as special defenders of the United States and therefore above the law. A nation worshipping its presidency promoted this disease, which manifested itself in Watergate. Moellering identified this as close to a Nixon worship: "The tragedy of this President is that his 'theology' has become either self-delusion or a camouflage for the moral authority which he exerts in his office for ends that are amoral if not immoral." Moellering felt these ideas led the nation down a dangerous path of worshipping false gods.[49]

Whether America represented a nation more favored by God remained a side conversation when Christians discussed Watergate. For conservatives, who remained relatively cautious on Watergate during this period, that stemmed in part from the fact they saw no relationship between the two. Their articulation of Christianity's importance to and even link within the US government promised to protect them and save the nation from God's wrath. It therefore had little bearing on why Watergate occurred, though it could positively move the nation toward fixing the problem. In contrast, moderate to liberal Christians more and more disassociated themselves by separating God's will from institutions governed by humans. Instead of God especially favoring America, liberals saw God as one judging this nation the same as all other nations throughout history.

Conclusion

Between mid-July and October 1973, Watergate heated up as Americans learned that the full dimensions of the matter had not yet been fully realized. The Christian community continued to react and address the controversy in order to imbue society with its value system. Subtle changes occurred within Protestantism that moved these Christians toward a greater recognition of the depth of the problem. Among conservatives, trust in limited government and high public moralism still held sway. They condemned the people already implicated in Watergate, but trusted Nixon's words he was not involved and, like them, wanted to get to the heart of the issue. Enough transpired in these months to force conservatives to admit a serious problem existed, but not enough to alter their trust in the president and their faith in the creative power of personal conversion and prayer. In contrast, liberal Christians came out forcefully as their previous mistrust of Nixon and belief that Watergate threatened the nation intensified. Some of them went so far as to call for impeachment, and as a whole they felt the country needed to move away from individualism and revivalism toward securing the common good by direct action. Liberals also saw a dangerous nation worship, even as their conservative colleagues clung to the hope God's special favor would see the United States through the storm. Still other Christians, such as members of the African Methodist Episcopal Church, registered disapproval of Nixon and his administration, combined with a pietist call for prayer and conversion.

Protestant differences persisted, and they would throughout the crisis. But the fall of 1973 brought enough evidence of wrongdoing by someone at the highest levels of government that no one could safely ignore the ethical calamity of Watergate. Christians debated the degree to which they thought the president himself was involved and criticized each other's theology as applied to Watergate. Without a dramatic point of change or specific date of transformation, all Christians arrived in late 1973 at a place where they discussed politics and attempted to influence the government. Their previous, more cautious approach had given way to more assertive action. Coming events only escalated this national crisis, and with it the Christian response of inserting itself in politics.

4

The Church as Prophet versus Praying for Those in Authority

After establishing a broad Christian participation in Watergate politics by October 1973, the Protestant community solidified recognizable positions, and its responses grew more urgent from November 1973 to April 1974. Those already opposed to the president ramped up their attacks and were joined by the previously more cautious. Even conservative Christians, who long supported Nixon, began to question the value of his leadership. They persisted with their support of him but more circumspectly, describing his sins as no greater or lesser than those of the average American. But too much unethical and illegal activity had come to light for them to ignore it altogether, and so conservatives altered their views more significantly than other Protestants. In doing so, their political activity became more pronounced and matched that of their liberal counterparts.

The common liberal reaction by now assumed presidential guilt and only debated how far the punishment should go. Finding vindication against Nixon, not just the prospect of impeachment, Robert Jewett, professor of religious studies at Morningside College in Sioux City, Iowa, asserted, "A principle deriving ultimately from our religious heritage has been affirmed—namely, that the law is no respecter of persons," not even the president of the United States. He continued, "If the law comes from the king, he is by definition above it. But if, as in the biblical perspective, it derives from God, the chief executive is subject to it." The investigation into Nixon and his associates rose to biblical standards, a prophetic pronouncement of justice in God's name for a prince's weakness.[1]

Conservatives, even as they more deliberately moved against the president, held to their tradition of seeking spiritual revival by invoking divine action and healing. Many now admitted a serious problem existed, though some still held out hope Nixon was not directly involved. But in addressing this new (for them) reality, J. Everett Sneed, the editor of the *Arkansas Baptist Magazine*, best summarized their approach: "One of the greatest needs of the hour is to pray for our nation, our government, and our president. Unquestionably, this stands as one of the most turbulent times in our country's history." He especially pled the president "needs our prayers!"[2]

No single public revelation or official move during these months mortally wounded the Nixon administration. However, events made it clearer even to conservatives that prayer alone would not protect the president or the nation. Nixon proclaimed his innocence with the infamous "I am not a crook" declaration on November 17, 1973, though a month later the White House struggled to explain how an eighteen-minute erasure appeared in the subpoenaed tapes. The fighting over airing the White House tapes continued into April 1974, as the White House prepared to at least release the transcripts. Leon Jaworski was named the new Watergate special prosecutor, so the criminal investigation continued, and the momentum in Congress toward impeachment gathered steam. Most of what drove toward Nixon's resignation during these months happened outside of public view. Still, almost no liberal, moderate, or conservative Protestant failed to address Watergate during these months. All American Christians asserted their voices as depravity in high places further compromised American democracy.

The President Reviled

Liberal to moderate Protestants continued their condemnation of the president, though marked changes appeared by November 1973. The rhetoric against Nixon became harsher and more pointed as these Christian commentators lost patience with his refusal to address Watergate in an open and honest way. The topic of impeachment went from occasional to general, but anti-Nixon Protestants disagreed about the necessity of it and what it might do to the nation. Nonetheless, a serious discussion of impeachment was a watershed moment, and its intensity increased moving forward. Importantly, some conservative Christians joined the Nixon opposition, a sign that increased evidence against his administration had begun to take its toll even among Nixon loyalists. It is clear these Protestants were a significant part of the intellectual fight to end the Nixon presidency.

The critique of the president often continued the familiar mantras about his abuse of power as they had from the beginning, albeit in a more adamant way. The *Christian Century*'s delineation of how Nixon illegally and unethically took advantage of his position is a prime example. John Collins, from the New York Conference of the United Methodist Church, took exception to a *Wall Street Journal* editorial calling for liberal Christian leaders to back off their attacks on the president in order to allow the judicial system to handle the matter. Collins continued, "If we were dealing with people of common morality and respect for our institutions, this might be sound advice. But here is a man whose hallmark in dealing with the American people has been a consistent and bald-faced disregard for truth ever since 1948. He discovered what other tyrants have known: that many people will believe any lie—if it is what they *want* to hear." Nixon therefore become a tyrant at this stage, rather than just a corrupt politician. Collins demanded "relentless confrontation of lies with truth, of distortion with clarity, of amorality with conscience." The same issue found Pastor Larry E. Dixon labeling Nixon's crimes as "an abomination before the Lord" that necessitated swift justice. Charging farther down the path of accusing the president of being an authoritarian, editor James M. Wall asserted, "An inflexible leader is dangerous because he creates fear in his enemies and exploits prejudices among his followers." The accusations had indeed sharpened.[3]

Others joined the chorus of those claiming the president had become unhinged. In the United Church of Christ's *Engage/Social Action*, the director of the National Committee for an Effective Congress and a campaigner for fair elections, Susan B. King, criticized the Nixon White House's abuse of power and advocated campaign finance reform as a remedy. She joined other Christians who outlined the wrongs of the administration and then translated this information into practical action the church could take. Calling Watergate the "darkest side of our political process," King pointed out that moneyed interests influenced elections and tried to hide corruption by buying people off, practices the president, among others, carried to an extreme. Huber F. Klemme, a UCC pastor and the editor of the publication, similarly described the Nixon presidency as "contemptible" and "contemptuous" in so many ways it defied description. The Nixon tapes came into play because of the president's refusal to release them, on top of previous actions, such as the break-in at Daniel Ellsberg's psychiatrist's office, the mass appeal to popular prejudices, the undermining of the special prosecutor investigating Watergate, and the use of the government to attack those opposed to Nixon's policies. These actions reflected the "deliberate tactics of small-minded, power-hungry men. They were not only violations of law or ethics or both: they were so palpably petty as to call in question the fitness of those employing them to exercise any governmental power whatsoever." While Klemme trusted the nation would survive the scandal, he lamented the country would "be a long time paying the price for letting third-rate men run" it.[4]

The persistence of the compromised Nixon presidency enlivened conversations about whether or not the Christian community should back impeachment. However, even the most ardent opponents of the president in the liberal Christian group failed to agree on the matter at this juncture; but this six-month period saw those who pushed for impeachment gradually persuading their liberal colleagues about its inevitability. The debate in the churches mirrored the national debate. It has been noted the prospect of "impeachment proceedings moved steadily forward from October 1973 to their ultimate resolution ten months later," following the Saturday Night Massacre. Liberal to moderate Americans, and even some conservatives, followed this pattern as they gravitated toward impeachment. Liberal Protestants led this charge within the religious community.[5]

Not surprisingly, the *Christian Century* adopted a staunch editorial position in favor of impeachment. Editors opined the Senate trial, which would follow impeachment by the House, "would provide a national 'autopsy' to determine what has brought us to this low moral point." Though it would be an unpleasant process, they insisted the ultimate good of arriving at the truth outweighed any hurt to the nation. They called on Nixon to avoid this entire ordeal by changing his behavior and revealing the truth himself, though they doubted he would do it. By April 1974, the voice of mainline Protestants became louder. An unsigned editorial agreed not only that impeachment should occur, but that all proceedings should be televised because "in a court case, the aggrieved is permitted to attend the trial. In this case, the aggrieved is the American people." These Protestants no longer pondered an avoidance of impeachment but moved to how it should play out in public. A majority of letters to the editor agreed with this position. John A. Cappon of Madison, Wisconsin, wrote the president "has shown that the presidency of the United States is much too big a job for him, and that his qualifications for realistic functioning in foreign affairs are negligible." No one put it more succinctly than W. F. Roberts in an April letter to the editor: "And the man in the White House is even more clearly and presently dangerous" than nuclear stockpiles.[6]

Yet well into spring 1974, *Christian Century* editors held back in calling for a widespread *Christian* call for impeachment. Though they asserted impeachment was inevitable and supported it, James M. Wall also stated, "It doesn't serve us well for church agencies to carry their coals to Newcastle by issuing strong calls for impeachment." Rather, he wanted it left to Congress and due process, presumably to avoid embroiling the church in this nightmare of a political situation. Then, in January, editors contemplated not enough evidence existed to impeach the president, despite their hope it would bring clarity to the situation. Editors could not bring themselves to unambiguously endorse impeachment, instead struggling with the prospect in their deliberations.[7]

Colleagues in the United Church of Christ's *Engage/Social Action* also took up the impeachment issue with gusto. Editor Allan R. Brockway simply stated in December 1973, "The House should quickly pass a bill of impeachment of Richard M. Nixon, President of the United States of America. Such a bill requires a simple majority." An editorial in March 1974 more specifically detailed the reasoning for this stance. Watergate would not disappear "if only we would pretend it isn't here," this writer continued; rather, it "will not go away and the President's efforts to hurry it out the back door are part of the reason." The continued refusal by the administration "to produce requested information and otherwise hamper the pursuit of justice through the Congress and the courts" necessitated the profound action of impeachment.[8]

Other more moderate bodies joined this early cry for impeachment in October 1973. The Board of Church and Society of the United Methodist Church expressed "dismay, shock, and outrage" at the president's abuse of power in response to his Saturday Night Massacre. It marked a sign the administration viewed itself as above the law in their eyes. Such "flagrant obstruction of justice" demanded all citizens react and "not tolerate" it. Because of these actions, the board urged "the US House of Representatives to initiate immediate impeachment proceedings against the President and we pledge our support of such action." The 225-member Board for Homeland Ministries of the United Church of Christ concurred a few months later. The board passed a resolution asserting the nation "reached a breaking point" because of "arrogance of power without conscience" and "abuses of authority." Speaking in what it called a "tradition of love, but also in a tradition of prophecy," the board called for Congress to impeach the president. In these two cases neither group assumed impeachment automatically meant removal of the president. The inability to get at the truth led them to these statements, so Congress could gain the power to discover it and put the nation back on track. No doubt many felt a trial would lead to Nixon's ouster, but they wanted the official process to take place first.[9]

Dr. Howard Schomer, chair of the United Church Board for World Ministries, wrote a letter to Peter W. Rodino Jr., chair of the Committee on the Judiciary of the House of Representatives, urging him to take action on impeachment. Schomer outlined a host of abuses by the president, including lies about the Vietnam War, misused funds, income tax avoidance, and obstruction of justice. This behavior made it impossible for the American people to trust his leadership, and Schomer feared three more years of it might destroy the country. He further noted, "Unless the Judiciary Committee findings not only exonerate President Richard M. Nixon of literal law-breaking but of this moral untrustworthiness which has brought the highest office of our government to the lowest esteem it has suffered in our two-century history, I believe that Congress will have no choice but to vote for impeachment." By writing directly to Rodino, Christians were doing more than just discussing Watergate. They were now lending a different kind of moral weight to the issue of impeachment.[10]

As with the indecisive editorial position of the *Christian Century,* other anti-Nixon liberal Christians did not want to take the drastic step of impeachment just yet. A reader of *Engage/Social Action* disagreed with the editors' vehement advocacy of impeachment. Explaining he disliked the president, Kenneth A. Coates continued, "But I question seriously whether the church should so easily denounce *any* individual (even with quotes around his name) as *the* evil." The writer of a *Christian Century* guest editorial worried international enemies might take advantage of the political turmoil in Washington. Rabbi Dov Peretz Elkins of Congregation Beth El in Rochester, New York, therefore argued against impeachment, even in the case of a president whom he described as "reputed to be duplicitous and paranoid." He also ironically observed people seemed shocked that a president with a history of ruthless politicking brought dirty dealings to the White House: "Recognizing his overwhelming potential for evil, I did not vote for Richard Nixon. Yet now I find myself opposing his impeachment." He feared a vacuum of power might embolden US enemies to act, a reality "beyond the point of worthwhile risk."[11]

This period in the Watergate saga witnessed the first exodus of conservatives from the president's camp. Some of the new conservative opposition to Nixon came from a small segment of the evangelical community that never supported him wholeheartedly because of his domestic policies. Evangelicals for Social Action adhered to a typically conservative theology but diverged from other evangelicals in advocating for strong social programs to assist the marginalized and poor. Organized in November 1973 at a conference in which participants wrote and signed the Chicago Declaration of Evangelical Social Concern, they did not create a national membership organization until 1978. Nonetheless, from its inception in 1973 with the Chicago Declaration, the leaders advocated among evangelicals action on injustice, racism, women's equality, and a generally more left-leaning domestic policy. They therefore often aligned with liberal Protestantism on such issues as the civil rights movement and Lyndon B. Johnson's Great Society.[12]

Evangelicals for Social Action accused the presidency of having lost "in some history page the concept of Servanthood." The organization abhorred the notion the government operated in a system of the ends justifying the means and from "a theology of national security which has left the realm of reality and has entered that of the absurd." This action proposal asserted, "We deplore the sin of the lust and abuse of power by President Nixon and some political leaders," and called on them to therefore "exercise just leadership by publicly confessing their sins." The statement listed Watergate and Vice President Agnew's transgressions specifically as reason for this stance. The declaration also deplored the administration's attempt to stifle publication of the Pentagon Papers and criticized the secret White House taping system, as well as a litany of other "harassments" of innocent people through tax investigations and clandestine burglaries. While nothing particularly new or revealing came from this statement, the defection of evangelicals was a turning point in how many Christians spoke against Nixon.[13]

Other even more conservative Christians joined ranks with the defectors, as this period from November 1973 to April 1974 saw the splintering of conservative Christianity. Several Southern Baptists began to question the president publicly. While not a majority within the SBC, their willingness to speak out in a denomination otherwise firmly aligned with the president signaled changes to come. Foy Valentine, the executive secretary of the Christian Life Commission, often adopted more moderate stances than many of his clergy and lay colleagues, including a staunch opposition to the Vietnam War and advocacy for the civil rights movement. In November 1973, he therefore wanted "the church to shed its timidity and speak boldly concerning the current moral crisis in government." He specifically asked Christians to back the special investigations so they could determine the truth and thereby correct the problems infiltrating so many parts of the government. The executive secretary of the Texas Baptist Christian Life Commission also warned Jesus was "Lord of our politics" and therefore accused the White House of committing "spiritual offenses, not just legal and ethical blunders." These "offenses against the spirit of the nation" meant religious leaders should weigh in on the Watergate crisis. And these SBC leaders had certain backers among the laity. One anonymous writer to the *Arkansas Baptist Newsmagazine* wanted fellow Baptists to "pray for our President to tell the truth or resign." The writer felt this was the only way to restore faith in the nation and called into question Nixon's "sense of values." While a minority voice, such sentiment put more pressure on the legal and political system as the anti-Nixonian rhetoric moved from a continued liberal attack to a broader Christian one.[14]

While this Baptist call for prayer matched the typical nonpolitical response of conservatives, liberal Protestants created more overt forms of direct action. Fred L. Hofrichter and Tilford E. Dudley, the associate on legislation and the director of the UCC Washington Office for the Center for Social Action, respectively, provided a very specific way for UCC leaders to act. They sent an open letter to a variety of people in April 1974, asking them to appeal to their senators to vote for campaign finance reform. Campaign finance reform came out of the Watergate crisis, because extralegal activities were funded prior to a new law that disclosed donor names and how campaign donations were spent. Previously, that rule applied only after a person became a nominee. The earlier law allowed for slush funds for covert purposes; for example, CREEP had almost $2 million in cash on hand before the new law took effect. And the letter clearly requested that UCC clergy further contribute their religious authority not merely to influence an internal Christian dialogue but to mobilize the laity to force change. A letter to the editor of *A.D.* similarly asked for Christian participation. Charles F. Gregg thought "stimulation of Christian churches" forced altered policies around the globe, including the ending of US participation in the Vietnam War and de-escalation of tensions in the Middle East, among others. Contributing to the push for change in the federal government would keep average citizens from total despair and support a movement toward better integrity and ethics in government.[15]

As the nation as a whole came to more and more uncertainty regarding their president by April 1974, so, too, did more and more Christians. Led by the liberal Protestants who had struggled against Nixonian policies and behaviors for some time, the rhetoric against him became sharper and more pointed, including the opening discussion about impeachment. The addition of more moderate to conservative Christians in this conversation seemed to spell doom for the president as his leverage and support continued to slip away. To put it mildly, they had immersed themselves wholeheartedly in the political process. And while much of this generic conversation appeared without mention of which specific faith tenets persuaded the various people to this point of view, to be sure a theology undergirded their stance.

A Theology of Change

As articulated by the *Christian Century* and the United Church of Christ, the liberal Protestant denunciations of the Nixon administration and calls for church bodies to engage in the public Watergate process were rooted in liberal theology. They grounded their opposition in the viewpoint the Christian community served as a moral watchdog over society and was therefore obligated to work toward whatever necessary changes might resolve the problem. This notion accompanied a firm biblical foundation that reminded everyone of Christian hope: with God's love and fervent Christian action, better times could emerge for the United States. Their faith called them into political action.

The United Church of Christ and its publications most consistently voiced how the church must not abdicate its safeguarding of public morality to secular institutions. William Nelson, a retired pastor and past president of the UCC Board for World Ministries, applauded the Pentagon Papers and Watergate disclosures. He explained that "no position of prestige is sacrosanct" but pointed out the media, not the church, brought this to America's attention. He therefore wanted the church to serve "between despair and hope," going forward so it could become part of a national solution. Similarly, an editorial in the same issue of *A.D.* complained "we, the people, share the responsibility" for Watergate by overlooking the importance of morality in politics. As a church, this meant the need to "confess our own sins" before moving into the realm of placing blame or guilt on other people.[16]

But once Christians acknowledged their own failings, UCC leaders wanted them to act to bring change. A contributing editor of *Engage/ Social Action*, who also advocated for impeachment, explained succinctly, "Whatever the legal implementation required, it appears that the churches have a moral duty to express their concern over the question of integrity in government." *Keeping You Posted*, published by the Washington, DC–based Center for Social Action of the UCC, often justified its existence to readers, and Watergate provided the perfect example. It explained it functioned to keep members of the church body informed about key issues in government, and in turn to help shape a Christian response to various concerns.[17] J. Martin Bailey, *A.D.* editor, most poignantly explained this point of view in a letter after a church member wrote of her frustration with the denomination's journal taking political stances regarding Watergate:

> Your note indicates that you believe we are concerned more with politics than with Christ. If I am concerned with politics at all, it is because I believe that the gospel of our Lord impels me to a concern for my fellow human beings and for active participation in the life of our great country. This is what I believe the meaning of the Incarnation is all about. God is

at work in the world, in and through persons, in and through governments. It is the task of all Christians to play a responsible role and it is
especially the task, I believe, of the church journal to hold a standard of
ethical participation before the members of our church. If the church
journal cannot stand for integrity and honesty and the unity of God's
people, who can?

No one better articulated how Christians navigated the dangers of
churches being drawn into partisan politics while upholding the obligation of religion to guide and shape societal ethics and morality. Bailey's
sentiment stretched across liberal Christianity and led to more pointed
calls for the church to reestablish the political arena on firm moral
grounds.[18]

UCC periodicals therefore delved into the matter of churches, and
thereby Christians, contributing a moral grounding in the political
arena. A letter to the editor of *Engage/Social Action* simply stated, "The
church has long been silent on issues on which it should speak" and
therefore encouraged the editors to continue placing the church at the
center of ending the national crisis. Explaining that sin spread from
those at the highest level of government to every Christian, Sydney J.
Neal, a lay member and treasurer of the UCC Metropolitan Boston Association, insisted in *A.D.* that Americans also owned the "break-in
and breakdown" of Watergate. In order to cure the ills, he explained the
power each person possessed "to break the habits of secrecy and manip-
ulation and to turn back—as individuals, communities, and nation—to
a respect for the law that stands above us and all the people who stand
beside us." Interestingly, such a pronouncement mirrored conservative
longings for a revival to cure the nation. The difference theologically
rested in the subsequent action of liberal declarations because it suggested turning to the church merely began the process of infusing the
political system with morality.[19]

Moreover, these entreaties for the church to act rested on a self-
consciously biblical foundation. Larold K. Schulz, executive director of
the UCC Council for Christian Social Action, utilized the Old Testament
confrontation of Ahab and Micaiah, a biblical story about "the arrogance
of power." Like Ahab ignoring and banishing the prophet Micaiah, so
Schulz felt the current administration had treated the media and other

detractors, because they mimicked Micaiah when they refused to speak only what the king desired to hear. Comparing the biblical tale to the current crisis, especially Nixon's firing of Special Prosecutor Archibald Cox in the role of prophet, Schulz wrote it provided "a sense of *déjà vu*." Attorney General Elliot Richardson appointed Cox, a Democrat, in May 1973 as a special prosecutor in charge of the Watergate investigation. The investigation by the former US solicitor general and then Harvard Law School professor became instrumental in publicizing the White House taping system and litigating to release the transcripts. In October 1973, during the infamous Saturday Night Massacre, Nixon purged the top ranks of the Justice Department until Robert Bork agreed to fire Cox, because the president feared the direction and success of the investigation. Schultz's comparison to Ahab and Micaiah gave an appropriate biblical analogy to current affairs. But while the sin of arrogance rested on the president, Schulz further articulated how individuals, including those in the Christian community, too often allowed such wrongdoing to persist: "God's judgment requires more faithfulness from us if we are to fulfill the requirements the Gospel places upon us." He explained God expected the church to play the role of Micaiah and to state what "God wants said rather than what the world wants to hear." He curved the sermon-like article back to a lesson of hope and action when he concluded, "It is not too late. We are forgiven for the past; it is the future that counts. . . . If Watergate is to have any positive impact, it requires our action. There is yet time to be faithful."[20]

The *Christian Century* joined its liberal colleague in grounding its anti-Nixon and reformist advocacy in a biblical context. Editor James M. Wall complained a desacralized mind-set too easily removed individuals from the greater political world. He contextualized this concept by using Paul's reference to paganism in Ephesians 4:18–19 that stemmed from being ignorant and thereby alienated from God. He explained too many people dismissed Watergate or even defended the administration's actions because "only inhabitants of a desacralized world could approach the horror of Watergate with cool logic and rational explanations that evoke the admiration of corporate executives." Writing at Advent, Wall turned it into a more hopeful message by explaining Christians still could change the situation and add their voice positively to reform: "The gift of Advent overcomes defeat without promising a victory that is seen. If nothing—including death, life, angels and principalities—can separate us from the love of God, then victory and defeat, gain and loss cease to have ultimate significance. This is Christian hope in a Watergate world." A letter to the editor saw a New Testament lesson in Watergate as well. This reader described Jesus as a teacher and servant of the people, in contrast to the Roman government "lording" power over the people. He sought to have the "custodians of public trust" seek such a servant/ teacher role instead of "being lords and masters with the consequent arrogance and misuse of power." This Christian model for American leadership, much like Wall's Advent message, would turn the nation toward a brighter future.[21]

Numerous liberal Christians rang out these hopeful messages as they fought for a moral and ethical US government, including UCC leaders. *Washington Report* continued the theme of the church as prophet amid Watergate, explaining, "The manner in which we answer as Christians will determine whether they are Prophets of doom or Prophets of Hope." Larold K. Schulz, executive director of the Council for Christian Social Action, detailed this theological belief as it related to Watergate with the following message of optimism:

> But through it all, there is hope. Hope that we will be able to overcome even this national tragedy and move toward fulfillment of the promises contained in the documents of our national life—the Bible, the Declaration of Independence, and the Constitution. Hope is based on the indications that the democratic system works, even when severely tested by arrogant persons with selfish and evil motives. Hope is based on the outpouring of opinion from citizens who care about truth and justice. And hope is based on the gospel of Jesus Christ, which indicates that, through it all, God comes into history and overcomes evil with justice, mercy, and love.

Reverend Barbara W. McCall restated this sentiment even more forcefully for *A.D.* when she wrote, "There is an increasing conviction that, despite inflation and accompanying budget cuts, despite war and rumors of war, despite dishonesty in high places, it *is* time to rejoice. To quote one who spoke eloquently on this subject at a recent meeting, 'It is time to rejoice because, in our confused world, we have salvation!'" For a church body as negative about the current climate as the UCC, it bears mentioning it also proclaimed a message of Christian hope to overcome the corruption of Washington.[22]

Liberal Protestantism thereby placed its criticism of the Nixon White House and government within its theological beliefs. This exegesis and faith life explained why liberal Protestants so vehemently entered the debate regarding Watergate and wanted a voice in the fate of the current administration. By outlining Christian responsibility to engage in such matters, and articulating the role of modern prophet, they justified discussing politics within liberal denominations and religious periodicals. They retained a unique position for efforts toward pushing the nation toward a more moral and ethical behavior in government. Finally, by transforming what otherwise seemed dark, depressing, and dangerous into a message of Christian hope, liberal Christianity attempted to craft a positive faith message out of the bleak national picture.

African Methodist Episcopalians Take the Gloves Off

The African Methodist Episcopal Church, which previously held a middle ground between conservative and liberal Christians, by the second quarter of 1974 aligned itself with those vocally opposed to the Nixon administration. The new AME response owes something to Christian theology articulated by the leftist church bodies, but the AME added a more conspicuous racial element. A church body that came to accept discussions of race in America during the civil rights movement continued to do so well into the Nixon administration, a result of the denomination growing disenchanted with the president's record on race relations. This antagonism between the president and the AME over race in America framed much of the church's criticism of the White House, whether or not it involved Watergate. And evidence from the Nixon archives indicates the president and his staff returned the antipathy.

Sometimes this AME stance regarding Watergate came with the simple notion the nation must follow through with the investigation to the bitter end once it started. Carroll R. Chambliss, a chaplain in the US Navy, delivered an address to the Naval Station Chapel in Mayport, Florida, on February 10, 1974, with this point. He noted the president himself declared in his State of the Union address "one year of Watergate is enough." Chambliss agreed but hoped "he did not mean you can suddenly stop in the midst of legal and moral judgment and bury the hatchet and forget it ever happened." Rather, he explained, "once the genie is out of the box it must be dealt with, followed around until the full course is run" and the truth exposed. He wanted whatever findings materialized from the Watergate affair to "be binding," whatever the consequences. While the chaplain's remarks are more neutral compared with those of most liberals, they demonstrated the AME wanted the truth revealed. His comments at least indicate this church body would not accept further cover-ups.[23]

The theology buttressing this AME outlook in many respects mirrored that of other anti-Nixon Protestants. It began with the assertion Christian bodies were obligated to play a prophetic role in society, and even rebuked other denominations that failed to act in this way. Noting "the A.M.E. Church is on record many times as deploring 'Watergate' and all it implies against the spiritual, moral and fraternal lives of Americans," one *Christian Recorder* article applauded the National Council of Churches for a statement about Watergate, but wanted other church bodies to join the chorus. Nannie Julia Wilkes, the supervisor of missions in the Thirteenth Episcopal District of the AME, spoke of a woman's role in society and insisted women must raise a host of problems before the nation and demand solutions to poverty, discrimination, and civil liberties. This gendered notion of women protecting the moral integrity of the nation continued, asserting such "feminine" attributes more forcefully would "contribute to the prevention of a possible future Watergate conspiracy and/or moral breakdown" in government.[24]

Adding to these ideas of prophets and Christian women becoming part of the solution, the Eighty-Seventh Session of the Michigan Annual Conference passed a special resolution about various national problems, including Watergate. Because "the credibility of our government has now tied its lowest ebb in history" due to leaders feeling the ends justify the means, the statement regretted how this thinking was "winning a battle but losing a war." The president and his men triumphed in the 1972 presidential election but then spiraled the country into chaos with a poor economy, lost prestige in international relations, and an erosion in popular confidence in the government. The assembly therefore included in this resolution: "Whereas, Watergate is declared by this body as an immoral act may it be highly resolved that corruption in Government is too steep a price to pay to be tolerated in any form and greater moral leadership highly advocated." In other words, the AME abandoned the current administration and challenged the nation to bring about a positive change for the future.[25]

Naturally, the African Methodist Episcopal Church grounded its Watergate pronouncements specifically in biblical exegesis. The denomination had moved to a more activist political stance since the civil rights movement largely because of the Christian mandate to help fellow humans. Citing Nehemiah 8:13, one article for the *A.M.E. Church Review* explained the story of admitting sin at Jerusalem's Water Gate, paralleling it to the United States' own Watergate sin. In the biblical story, the people gather to hear Ezra read the law to them, weeping at their transgressions and wanting to repent of these sins. The writer explained, "Then as now, the participants were high government officials. But in that incident, the confessions were voluntary!" Thus the current nation needed the church to assert the lesson and demand change in order to move the country toward a biblical response to the crisis. Such comparisons between the Bible and modern America served the denomination well in expressing why the AME felt compelled to speak about this detrimental political issue.[26]

As with many Americans in general and Christians specifically, the national government's travails prompted introspection for individuals and entities of all kinds. The AME wanted Watergate to remind them of their imperfections and help them avoid scandal within the church body. In an editorial for *A.M.E. Church Review* of one-sentence thoughts or random ideas, Opal Dargan made this point. The columnist mused, "Bets are being wagered that if certain people would talk, the A.M.E. Church could have its own Watergate affair; misplaced trust and mismanaged funds." The editorial planted the seed for wondering about scandal within the denomination and hope for repentance in the AME. *Christian Recorder* writers pondered the same thing. E. William Judge wondered if a Watergate could occur in the AME. He asserted, "All of us know that it can happen." He offered concrete solutions for avoiding such a calamity, specifically noting leaders must obtain honest and forthright feedback from a number of sources, and act on things needing to be fixed. Much like others who identified Nixon's propensity to isolate himself, Judge wanted his denominational leadership to hear from the entire church in order to better serve it. He explained, "When any leader gets to the point where he does not want to get intelligence from the people he is on his way to 'Watergate.'" The biblical proclamation "Ye shall know the truth and the truth shall set you free" applied in this instance, according to Judge. In this way, the AME engaged Watergate on an introspective plane, and not as a government problem, myopically focusing on the White House.[27]

When the AME glanced inward, it often saw race in a way no other denomination studied here could. The AME First Episcopal District passed a resolution in November 1973 offering a glimpse into Watergate and race. Calling him an "unknown, patriotic, loyal, faithful employee," the resolution addressed the lack of acknowledgment given to Frank Wills, the security guard who discovered the taped door at the Watergate building, which ultimately led to the discovery of burglars at the Democratic National Headquarters. His act led to the American public's "shock" and the subsequent events known as Watergate. The resolution called for Wills to therefore receive "some recognition by the government for the performance of his duty" and commitment to law and order. Absent such a federal response, the district demanded the AME host "Frank Wills Day" and thereby assist him economically. In addition to uplifting Wills, the tone of the resolution and discussion around it surmised his race contributed to ignoring his role in Watergate. Whereas white investigators, lawmakers, lawyers, and other officials came into prominent public attention, Wills fell into obscurity, an indication of the continued racism haunting America.[28]

Broader racial concerns also contextualized Watergate for the AME. *Christian Recorder* writer and pastor Lonnie C. Wormley, who chaired the Social Action Committee of the Forty-Ninth Session of the Southern California Annual Conference, asserted simply that Nixon's record on a number of things prior to Watergate made it almost inevitable such a scandal would materialize. He pointed out the president had done nothing "to mitigate the racial and urban crisis" in America, instead shunning the issue of race at every turn. Wormley asserted "the 'cover up' of Watergate is analogous to the President's failure in domestic programs." As a call to arms, Wormley wanted the church to lead African Americans toward political action to solve the problem: "Nixon and company is an anathema to the progress of black folks. The time is far spent and the hour has now come for us to assert the political clout—the ballot box." Watergate had pushed the AME from denouncing Nixon to denomination-wide action against him.[29]

Evidence demonstrates the AME's disdain for Nixon was mutual. As was common for him, Nixon dismissed the denomination and its concerns because it failed to support him. The correspondence over a requested meeting reveals this fact. Michael Thompson, who worked for Thompson and Associates in Annandale, Virginia, attempted to gather AME bishops to meet with the president because he knew them through his "various activities in the Washington D.C. area." He wrote Patrick Buchanan to request a gathering in order to "assist" the president during "these trying times." He also wanted them included in a prayer service, much like Nixon held with other religious leaders who visited the White House. Thompson specifically wanted the meeting to focus on issues of poverty and welfare.[30] A White House staffer took the initiative to investigate the matter and to report on how to respond to Thompson's letter. The report first quoted Stan Scott, an African American special assistant to the president, who said "most of the Bishops of the AME Church were not supporting of the President last year. Several, in fact, made statements against the Administration." Scott therefore recommended against Thompson's request. A couple of people inside the White House continued to push for the meeting, but only as a worship service because the White House could use it for publicity in order to make Nixon look better on race relations. Because of the varying advice, and especially because AME bishops failed to back the president, the report concluded, "We just acknowledge the letter and thank Thompson and say we will keep it in mind." The curt reply to Thompson obeyed this directive: "We very much appreciate your interest and thoughtfulness in this instance. While a time is not foreseen now when the President could have the Bishops come in due to his extremely heavy schedule, your suggestion is being carried on the forward calendar." Of course, nothing ever came of it because Nixon only met with those who supported him, and even they had increasing difficulty gaining a presidential audience the deeper the administration submerged into Watergate.[31]

This mutual animosity cleared the way for the AME to join the growing chorus of religious entities seeking an ouster of the president on moral and ethical grounds. A denomination associated with a more conservative, evangelical theology had moved leftward in the political realm over the last thirty to forty years because of the civil rights movement and its demand for an end to discrimination. The early 1970s saw progress in this area but a long way to go toward completing it, and a president and his staff seemingly trying to reverse the trend. A devout theology that adhered strongly to biblical principles therefore merged with a social ethic to create hostility toward the White House from AME leaders and writers, as well as laity who attended the various conventions.

Coming to Terms with Reality

While liberal Christians solidified their opposition to the president and grew in their ranks, conservative Protestants who had long supported the president entered a difficult period. Many of them still backed the president and hoped for a resolution maintaining Republicans in office while ridding themselves of the Watergate problem. They placed their continued hope for Nixon in a theological context and warned against Christians too quickly casting stones at others. Still, the mounting evidence against the administration strained credibility to the point even these stalwarts altered their tone and ventured further into politics.

Southern Baptist supporters accepted a reality in which the president made mistakes but on religious grounds cautioned against a crusade against him. E. M. Cullen, a lay editor at the *Western Recorder*, opined, "You know we are all human beings and I am sure everyone [*sic*] of us have made some mistakes in 1973, so let's not be too hasty to criticize President Nixon, for he is, too, just a human being subject to mistakes." He thought even George Washington erred and thus concluded "what would help President Nixon now, most of all, would be to pray for him, everyday [*sic*], and for all our national leaders." In this way some conservatives inched toward accepting Nixon's sin, if not a punishable crime, but sought a sort of Christian forgiveness or prayerful assistance to mend his ways and thus continue in office. The executive secretary of the Kentucky Baptist Convention voiced similar sentiments in March 1974, acknowledging Watergate weakened public trust and induced a "negative" mind-set. Noting no one liked "to be duped" or "misled by charlatans," Franklin Owen nonetheless advised against falling into "negativism, suspicion, distrust" because it "can kill the spirit of leaders." Instead, he implored Baptists to pray and maintain positive thinking, even when it came to the president. In these ways, conservatives admitted they could no longer view Nixon blamelessly, but neither would they abandon him.[32]

Baptists turned to the Bible as did other Protestants. Herschel H. Hobbs, pastor emeritus of First Baptist Church in Oklahoma City, delivered a radio broadcast on *The Baptist Hour* contextualizing his response to Watergate and the president with 2 Kings 19:15–19 and Isaiah 37:15–20. Hezekiah, the king of Judah, wavered in his faith as an Assyrian king prepared to march against Jerusalem after sending a messenger to demand surrender. The prophet Isaiah counseled Hezekiah to trust the Lord would deliver Jerusalem. Indeed, the Lord sent an angel to the Assyrian camp, killing a multitude of its soldiers overnight, and thereby forcing their retreat. Hobbs noted these texts because he personally felt 1973 was the most tumultuous year in his life. Acknowledging the corruption of the body politic and the need for reform, Hobbs nonetheless applauded Nixon for having "done an unprecedented thing in revealing to public gaze his political and private business matters. One shudders to think what a Pandora's box would be opened should all public servants be required to do the same." In putting the matter in these terms, Hobbs criticized government corruption but continued to defend and trust the president. Returning to Hezekiah's story, Hobbs warned his readership: "Do not point an accusing finger at the White House, Congress, the Governor's office, or City Hall. Put your finger on the real cause of the trouble—sin and rebellion in your own heart. For it is there that God looks to find the seat of sin or righteousness in our nation." Hobbs came to terms with Watergate as a national sin but minimized worries about Nixon in part by believing the president revealed the worst of it, and by demanding each person address his or her own sin before condemning the president.[33]

Christianity Today published an article by Pastor John A. Huffman Jr. to address Watergate. Huffman, the pastor at First Presbyterian Church in Pittsburgh and a former pastor at a Presbyterian church in Key Biscayne, Florida, added his personal experiences with Nixon to the conversation. Nixon frequently visited Key Biscayne with his close friend

Charles "Bebe" Rebozo and found it a calming and relaxing respite from his duties as president. He often vacationed there prior to becoming president and after the 1968 election bought two homes there as a presidential compound. During the six years they interacted at Key Biscayne, Huffman came to "greatly appreciate" his friendship with Nixon and his family. He refused to condemn the man or declare absolute innocence: "For me to make fallible human judgments on incomplete data would be foolish." He thus instructed readers to address their own sins and "then be free from the possibility of your own Watergate" before going after the president. He explained, "Watergate puts a mirror in front of me, alerting me to the cover-ups in my own life." Pietism once again extended the solution, as did biblical stories. Huffman explained integrity and personal honor would make people happier than political gain at the expense of high ethical standards. To prove his point, he noted Joseph went to prison for refusing the advances of Potiphar's wife, but "now he stands in the pages of history as an eternal winner, a man of character who would not adapt to the expedient." Huffman explained Joseph's story revealed Christians will "lose at many points in this world" though Christ promised "he who loses himself shall find himself." This commentary on Watergate added *Christianity Today* to the chorus of conservatives who came to denounce Watergate without yet suspecting Nixon of direct involvement. When it came too close to accusing the president, evangelicals turned to the refrain of sin in each person to avoid commentary against the man they thought represented their point of view.[34]

This approach by conservative Protestants therefore brought a much different response regarding the possibility of Nixon's impeachment from the debate in liberal circles. While most right-leaning Christians still avoided the topic of resignation or impeachment, *Christianity Today* provided an interesting view on the matter in a November editorial. First, the editorial declared, "We are opposed to his resignation," despite the serious charges against him. They worried this course of action may "leave us in doubt" about his guilt and "would also enable his accusers to evade the heavy responsibility that must fall upon them if the charges are false." In a much different take on impeachment than that of liberal Christians, the editors sought impeachment rather than resignation or other solutions. Unlike others who assumed impeachment would lead to Nixon's ouster from office, this evangelical position expressed a hope the president could thereby be exonerated.[35]

Complicating the study of Protestant reactions to Watergate are members of liberal denominations who disagreed with the general antagonism toward Nixon. An excellent example comes from writers to *Engage/Social Action*, a joint publication of the United Church of Christ and the United Methodist Church, which often took the harshest line against Nixon and his administration. December 1973 letters to the editor allowed readers to respond to an attack on the White House from the July 1973 issue. R. W. Wicker complained, "A Christian is willing to wait until all the facts are known and to understand the situation before condemning and sentencing without a fair trial, yet you whose views are completely prejudiced have already made up your minds as to the guilt of the President and the administration. Your article is not only unchristian and slanderous but extremely unfair and not representative of our church." C. L. Leighton mustered even more indignation, proclaiming the editor of the July piece "should be fired, impeached, or otherwise thrown out for his own lack of Christian principles." Again returning to the notion of a fair trial before a public condemnation, he warned, "Woe be unto you when the Almighty asks you if you condemned the President without fair trial or established guilt, and your honest answer sends you to the burning pits of hell." Even as various investigations heated up heading into spring 1974, many American Protestants steadfastly backed the president, called for a fair trial, and censured their liberal colleagues for prejudging him.[36]

Whether from conservative, moderate, or liberal Christians, Nixon received so many letters from people proclaiming their support and assuring him they prayed for him regularly the White House prepared a standard reply. It assured the recipient of the encouragement such expressions of support gave Nixon and wanted the person "to know how much I [Nixon] appreciate not only your thoughtful telephone messages but the prayers which you have offered in my behalf." He promised to continue working for the shared "great goals" for the United States. The same sentiments went to people who attended White House prayer meetings or the National Prayer Breakfasts. A form letter in the Nixon archives states Nixon did "believe America's rich spiritual tradition is a source of enduring strength to our Nation" and reminded him "of the unfailing trust we must continue to place in God's will for the future of our country." Whether Nixon ever actually read these form letters remains unknown, nor is it possible to determine the depth of his actual belief in the spiritual convictions they relayed. Regardless, they demonstrate well into 1974 conservative religious believers persisted with their faith in the president, to the point of writing to him as much. In turn, as the number of Nixon's backers dwindled, the administration embraced these believers and relied on their continued goodwill.[37]

As noted in chapter 3, by 1974 evangelicals gained what they viewed as inside knowledge about the White House through Charles Colson, a 1973 Christian convert and former White House insider. Colson's conversion is hard to assess given his reluctance to embrace or even acknowledge his own criminality. Even after his March 1974 indictment and later prison sentence, Colson insisted, "I can't think back on anything that really troubles my conscience or of any time in the three and a half years I was in the White House that I felt I was even bordering on criminal activity. That fact makes the indictments very hard to take." Given the known activities in which Colson participated, it makes his claims of repentance a bit suspect when he still failed to admit fault despite his conversion and guilt according to the criminal justice system. Even in his autobiography and later writings in which he regretted his callous behavior and many of his White House deeds, he danced around the depth of his own culpability, instead regarding himself as a fall guy or scapegoat. As late as 1987 he continued to argue that a genuine need for secrecy because of the Vietnam War and the Cold War explained and exonerated the climate of fear and investigation in the White House that spawned Watergate. This attitude at the time encouraged conservative backers of the president. In fact, Colson asserted "people will realize the magnificent things this President accomplished" and see those who served him as only wanting to help the country. He concluded, "Those who have conspired to bring about his downfall will be exposed for what they are." Conservative Christians believed Colson's authenticity as one of their own and clung to his insistence on the administration's innocence.[38]

Nonetheless, investigations by Congress, the judicial branch, and the media steadily uncovered information that gave even some stalwart conservative Protestants pause. Though less common than conservative Christian support for the president, some conservatives questioned their commitment to Nixon. It required a certain courage in conservative circles to join moderate to liberal Protestants, so it stands to reason it took the strong evangelical credentials of *Christianity Today* to pioneer the trail. The Saturday Night Massacre in fall 1973 started the periodical's questioning of the White House. Editors applauded "the way they (Richardson and Ruckelshaus) responded to the challenge of conscience" and refused a presidential order they saw as immoral. While admitting the president had the legal right to fire them, it begged the editors to wonder if Cox in particular was "fired simply because he refused to obey a presidential directive, or was it because he was getting close to the heart of the Watergate tragedy? Was he readying or coming close to discovering some evidence that would damage the President irreparably?" The Christian journal, a newsmagazine co-founded by Billy Graham, shrank from impeachment; however, it called for the president to fully disclose the truth. The weight of evidence and the legal dodging by the White House through early 1974 intensified the evangelical periodical's unease, a sure sign Nixon's cover-up had unraveled more and more.[39]

Another conservative church body, the Lutheran Church—Missouri Synod, similarly grappled with the new realities it faced because of Watergate and the general state of politics in America. While continuing a somewhat Lutheran tradition of shying away from direct political commentary about Nixon, LCMS leaders wondered about the current national climate. An editorial about the upcoming American Bicentennial provided a case in point for the *Lutheran Witness*, which commented on patriotism and its theological outlook on the matter. A brief editorial noted the "continuing post-Watergate fallout" had shifted the overall religious press from triumphal celebrations of the nation to something more subdued. This article explained that "more recent church voices on bicentennial proposals carry more prophetic—even eschatological—tones." The church's main periodical backed a more subtle ecclesiastical observation reflecting biblical prophecy over celebrating American spiritual exceptionalism. Interestingly, no other Christian periodical or denomination specifically referenced the Bicentennial during this period. Perhaps Protestants across the spectrum felt unable to muster much patriotic fervor in the current climate. Yet the LCMS in this regard indicates the country longing to celebrate but doing so in decidedly muted terms. The LCMS found itself searching for answers and balancing its traditional quietism with patriotism amid a political world falling apart.[40]

Conservative Christians under Nixon gained access to the president in new and important ways, a sign of their increasing move into politics and the sway they would come to have over the Republican Party. This newfound respect in larger political circles must have made it difficult to accept the guilt of the president as it pertained to Watergate. Their brand of Republican Theology agreed with his notion of limited government but needed him to maintain public moralism. In undermining Nixon's moral and ethical authority, Watergate could damage their own integrity if associated with him. This factor, at least in part, explains why conservative Christians continued to hold to his innocence and trusted his words. The very foundation of their American religious/political ideology depended on it. This stance related to the fact they belonged to a large cohort of Americans who continued to believe the president. Amid the Cold War and throughout the post-1945 period, such faith in the commander in chief remained common, even after the tragedy of Vietnam. Nixon's own words of faith and the assurances by conservatives such as Charles Colson solidified this point of view. It would take more than right-leaning Protestants had heard to date to push them off this position. Gradually, and to their dismay, Nixon's behavior accomplished just that. As foreshadowed by *Christianity Today*, if the president told the truth, he had nothing to hide. Unfortunately for them, he was hiding a lot.

Revival and Prayer

Conservative Protestantism's public support for the president should not be misunderstood as ignoring the moral and ethical crisis consuming the United States. In many ways, it seemed all too predicable to them because they long lamented a perceived drifting of America away from traditional values and religious belief, toward secularization and rebellion. If anything, conservative Protestants added this political crisis to the litany of concerns they had coming out of the 1960s, about youthful anarchy, the "God is dead" philosophy, women's rights activists, drugs, lawlessness, homosexuality, and a realm of other such conservative concerns. Conservatives called time and again on the one sure force to combat the creeping immorality that threatened the nation: revival and prayer. Though seemingly redundant in its refrain, this bedrock of conservative theology did more than simply parrot the same message over and over; it adapted itself to the circumstances and traumas of the time to give comfort and vision to the conservative message about Watergate and all the other "evils" America faced, and it morphed into a stronger political imperative moving forward.

Conservative Protestants still framed the problem first and foremost in the context of human sin. Without accepting this vital theological framework, no matter how seemingly redundant, none of the rest of their exegesis or moral ruminations made sense. The *Ohio Baptist Messenger* reminded readers about the "darkness of moral blackout in the government" creating a crisis of mistrust and cynicism, a darkness no doubt rooted in human depravity. In a letter to the editor of the *Christian Century* responding to the prominent theologians who commented on Watergate, Gould Wickey felt they ignored "the sinfulness of man," which only one writer "dared to mention." The *California Southern Baptist* summarized this position most clearly: "As long as American people do not seek to know and do the will of God, they will be buffeted from one crisis to another. They will be caught by great promises and whirled up to heights of expectations only to be dropped then to the depths of disappointment by the failure of persons and procedures." Nothing more than human sin caused Watergate, one of many maladies confronting the United States.[41]

Naturally, evangelicals rested heavily on biblical support. Sometimes this exegesis came in simple pronouncements to an audience that was already versed in evangelical theology and, presumably, needed no detailed explanation. *Christianity Today*'s November 1973 editorial explained, "American society, if it is looking for guidance as to what is right, not merely 'constitutional,' must turn back to an authority it has largely abandoned: to the Bible, the only perfect rule of faith *and practice*." The short statement contains hallmarks of conservative religion and Watergate: it avoided mention of President Nixon in favor of a more ambiguous reference to societal problems, mistrusted purely secular solutions, called for a revival of traditional Christian practice, and declared only such a conversion would heal the nation. *Alabama Baptist* editor

Hudson Baggett explained the Bible taught times of crisis assisted the Christian in turning toward God for solutions better than periods of prosperity. He suggested this return to Christianity would uplift the nation because "God's primary purpose for man is that we be like God and represent him in the world. Such ill will, suspicion, hatred and lack of trust force us to look for a way of hope. Current events remind us in a plainer way than ever before that our hope lies in the direction of God's purpose." Thus grounded in the evangelical view of the Bible, leaders once again pled for the American people to pray.[42]

Indeed, the common idea that the power of prayer would save the nation was a constant in conservative theology during Watergate. Baggett, in his Watergate ruminations in February 1973, implored readers to put their country ahead of individual or small-group needs and to avoid partisan considerations, noting, "Above all, there is a need to pray that God's purpose for our nation will be carried out." He further warned the United States was not "exempt from the judgment of God" and prayer would prevent repeating past mistakes by countries ultimately facing God's wrath. In short, Christian prayer could save America not just from Watergate but also from ultimate destruction. Ohio Baptists echoed this sentiment at their 1973 state convention held in Columbus. They resolved for Baptists to pray for national leaders during the "moral and physical crises" faced by the nation as a way to turn away from criticizing leaders and instead to pray for them "as admonished to do in the New Testament." This statement likewise avoided mentioning Nixon specifically and directed attention toward the broader need for Christian prayer as the solution. When the US Senate proposed a National Day of Prayer for April 30, 1974, *Ohio Baptist Messenger* editor L. H. Moore joined this chorus when he asked "every individual Baptist, and every church make this day" one of prayer, "indeed."[43]

Other gatherings of evangelicals made similar appeals for prayer, such as the fall 1973 meetings of Evangelicals for Social Action. With a more socially liberal outlook than their evangelical peers, this organization blasted racism, militarism, sexism, materialism, and turning away from the poor, especially pointing out evangelicals shared much blame for these problems. The statement the group released in November 1973 thus took aim at a number of issues and avoided direct reference to Watergate. Nonetheless, it alluded to the political crisis and insisted prayer must play a vital role in correcting what ailed the country. With an evangelical lament that Americans too often turned away from God, it called for repentance and for "our nation's leaders and people to that righteousness which exalts a nation."[44]

Though a majority of conservative entities in this study espoused an evangelical point of view, other conservatives who did not share it joined in calling for prayer to save the nation. The Lutheran Church—Missouri Synod, after its late-1960s swing to the right, joined the chorus of those worried about the country and wanting prayer to heal it. One correspondent to President J. A. O. Preus liked the concept of a National Day of Prayer and asked her denomination's president to add the LCMS to this cause. She asked, "Wouldn't it be wonderful if all Lutherans would unite with other Christians in our nation to humble ourselves and pray and seek the face of God, and turn from our wicked ways so God can forgive our sins and heal our land?" Such holy pleas might defeat "the rulers of this present darkness" and prove to God the nation's loyalty to God, thus gaining God's favor.[45]

In addition to these widespread cries for prayer, perceptions about the executive branch also played a role in the conservative theological outlook regarding Watergate. *Christianity Today* wondered if "we created, in the modern presidency, an office that so combines awful responsibility, vast power, and messianic pretension that no mortal can occupy it without suffering personal disaster." Perhaps, editors asserted, "Christians should examine their consciences, inquiring whether they have followed the biblical injunction to pray for those in authority—or have left them as easy prey to spiritual wickedness." The sin of humankind, and particularly of Americans, caused Nixon's illegal activity, not necessarily the man himself, by abandoning him to a difficult office without support of heavenly entreaties. The message ended with the predictable hope for the future: "To that extent that we have not prayed, we can begin now, too late to undo past disasters but in time to forestall new ones." Editor L. H. Moore of the *Ohio Baptist Messenger* concurred, writing, "One of the most meaningful resolutions passed in many state conventions of Baptists this fall was one which urged Christians to pray for the President, for those in government." He explained simply asking God to help the president "to do right" could do much to restore sound government.[46]

Less so than their liberal counterparts, but important nonetheless, conservative Protestants thought prayer needed further action from their ranks to ensure a better future. The Southern Baptist Convention participated in a fellowship breakfast for Baptist congressional representatives in fall 1973, where religious leaders articulated how Baptists could employ their beliefs to assist the nation during the Watergate scandal. They did not want the church body to mandate political action and especially wanted to keep the government out of their religious affairs. Still, they insisted individual Christians held a responsibility to remember their faith life when voting and governing. As SBC president Owen C. Cooper charged the assembly, because "Southern Baptists are deeply concerned with Biblical morality," they wanted this faithfulness to manifest itself in American leaders. He further articulated Christians disliked those who used government for personal gain and sought to "deceive voters or violate basic personal rights and liberties given to us by almighty God and guaranteed for us by the Constitution." He outlined the way SBC members could use their godly platform to seek change amid chaos in government. C. Welton Gaddy, part of the Baptist staff at the Capitol who put the breakfast together, prayed "leaders in this room may be among those in this 93rd Congress who by moral leadership secure once again the shaking foundation of this democracy." Baptist leaders concluded the gathering with a hope all Christians would more meaningfully engage the political process in order to heal the government, a perfect example of their adherence to Republican Theology.[47]

The Baptist Joint Committee on Public Affairs issued a statement on October 3, 1973, echoing these points. The Joint Committee consisted of eight national Baptist bodies, including the SBC, that lobbied on behalf of Baptist causes and communicated with Baptists across the nation about news affecting Baptist denominations. In a public letter to Senator Sam Ervin, James E. Wood Jr. explained the statement allowed churches to study "the moral and ethical principles in public life and the abuse of political power in American life." He continued "Baptists believe in the fundamental principles of democracy and we are alarmed when we become aware of the misuse of power and the erosion of public morality in government." The statement itself well established the Baptist theology at play here and bears quoting:

Believing that separation of church and state does not mean separation of religion from government or politics, nor should it imply the divorce of religion's basic moral and ethical principles from the conduct of public affairs, we voice our concern over some recent developments in public life and reaffirm our commitment to the fundamental principles of democracy.

At a time when there is widespread distrust of the government resulting from the abuse of political power, we need to be reminded of the premises upon which our government was constituted. We are gratified that there is today a widespread reaction against this abuse. Indeed, we view this reaction as evidence of the intrinsic strength of our American tradition.

The times call for an affirmation of trust in the basic principles of the American system of democracy. These include: (1) government's powers are derived from the consent of the governed; (2) the harmful potential in any concentration of governmental power makes necessary the distribution of powers among those who make, execute, and interpret law; (3) government is to protect the rights and liberties, and to promote the well-being of all people; and (4) all public officials must be subject to law in both public and private conduct.

In affirming these principles, we express faith in the ultimate triumph of the right and of the truth in a nation whose citizens are dedicated to justice and righteousness in every aspect of life. In this confidence, we urge our people to exemplify and to require character and integrity in both public and private life, and to discharge responsibly their duties as citizens. Moreover, we encourage our Christian young people to seek for themselves a vocation through which they may make their contribution to government and to society in general.[48]

Statements from state and regional conventions and newspapers affirming the sentiments of the national leadership trickled further down the line within SBC polity. The Colorado Baptist Convention resolved Christians must give "moral examples in communities in which they live by eradicating the harsh, destructive, hypocritical statements so commonly directed toward all authority." Moreover, Baptists should respect the government while also looking to change aspects of it that failed to match their Christian convictions. Bob Terry, acting editor for the

Western Recorder, reminded readers in November 1973, "With elections Tuesday, we can begin by helping elect officials with the moral courage and the faith in God to stand for what is right." C. R. Daley echoed this point, stating rules and regulations could not instill morality and ethical conduct in politics, business, or religion, but only "persons of honor and integrity" could do so. He furthered this thinking with the statement "It is better to change personnel than to keep tightening up the rules in an effort to force ethical conduct from an unethical person." The leaders and people issuing them, as well as the Baptist faithful receiving them, could well understand the relationship of these ideas to Watergate: they could confidently play a role in correcting the problems in government. Far from shrinking in fear and hiding behind the separation of church and state, they sought to exert their moral will on the situation through pietist action.[49]

Dr. Herschel H. Hobbs, pastor emeritus of the First Baptist Church in Oklahoma City, delivered several sermons on *The Baptist Hour* that delved further into the Baptist theology as it applied to Watergate in winter 1974. Hobbs had a prestigious history, in terms of his SBC leadership and national renown, having authored numerous books, pastored the First Baptist Church from 1949 to 1972, served two terms as SBC president from 1961 to 1963, and served as vice president of the Baptist World Alliance from 1965 to 1970. This acclaim included a national radio broadcast of his sermons. In three sermons from January 1973 and one from March, Hobbs brought out three themes shaping his understanding of Watergate and the general decay of good government: the role of ancient prophets and warnings to Israel, the sin of the United States, and the urgency of repentance.

Hobbs rooted his sermons in Old Testament prophets admonishing the kings and people of Israel for sin and for ignoring the prophets' warnings. God's wrath fell upon them as a consequence. One sermon outlined the life of Amos, which began at a secure time for Israel, perhaps at the height of its power, but preceded its fall to the Assyrians forty years later because "she was wallowing in sin, luxury, and false security." Amos spoke against the oppression of the poor, the corruption of justice, sexual immorality, and drunkenness. He represented for Hobbs the righteousness of the prophets as they battled the depravity of Israel to no avail. The prophets sometimes met with success, as demonstrated by the story of Isaiah urging Hezekiah, the king of Judah, to pray for the protection of Jerusalem from the Assyrians. The angel of the Lord passed over the Assyrian camp to kill the soldiers, which prompted their retreat and the safety of Jerusalem. Here, then, Hobbs juxtaposed the tragedy of ignoring the prophets and the triumph secured by invoking God's power.[50]

Moving toward the contemporary situation, Hobbs began one sermon with, "It is my judgment that the greatest need today in preaching is to echo the message of the ancient prophets." He explained the United States paralleled the privilege of Israel and, "like Israel, we have failed to use these things as opportunities to witness for God to a lost pagan world." More damning, he charged that "our nation is more flagrant in its sin than ever before in its history. No ancient pagan nation exceeded ours in this category." Hobbs prophesied against the nation for what he saw as its many sins because otherwise it would "bring upon us divine retribution." He stated, "We have sunk to unprecedented depths of sin. As a whole, while pretending to be religious, we have by our evil and corruption even dared God to do anything about it." The list of America's sins was long and included "breakdown in morals; corruption and confusion in economics," international relations, pollution, poverty, sexuality, and turning from God, much like Israel of old. And within this litany of sins, Hobbs often cited the problems facing the national government: "The Watergate affair has set off a chain reaction of investigations which reveal judicial injustice and abuse of governmental power—in bribes, kickbacks, and purchase of legal advantages—from local to national levels." He particularly bewailed that too many justified these problems with the excuse "everyone is doing it" and worried "the compounded tragedy is that only the top third of the iceberg is visible. Who knows what lies underneath the water level?" Hobbs warned, "No nation in history has so defied the moral standards of the Ten Commandments and survived. God is patient. But there is an end to even His waiting before judgment falls." He quoted Billy Graham's declaration, "If God does not punish America, he should apologize to Sodom and Gomorrah." Or, in Hobbs's own words, "America is like a giant animal seeking to devour itself. At the time when our nation should be giving moral and spiritual leadership to the world, we are held up in shame for all to see."

This horrendous situation prompted Hobbs to outline what his listeners could do in order to protect America and avoid the tragedy of Israel when it ignored Amos. Not surprisingly, he called for repentance and revival. Noting, "Uncle Sam's trouble is not in his stomach but in his heart," Hobbs called for the nation to "purify its heart" through "repentance and a turning to God." As always, Hobbs avoided blaming only those in government, instead stating people from "the White House to the lowest hovel in the land" must participate in the revival in order to save the country. In this regard, individuals confronting their personal sin could then pray for the nation and bring God's will upon themselves and the masses; everyone held responsibility for both the deep sin and bringing about the possible solution. In fact, Hobbs blasted those who sat in "glass houses" and criticized public officials in order to "make political hay out of the moral sickness that has seized upon our political and social order. Far better would it be if each of us would search his own heart and cry out to God for forgiveness!" He further delineated, "A nation cannot repent and pray in response to governmental decree. It must come from each individual heart." Again he articulated an intense pietism when he asked followers to "put your finger on the real cause of the trouble—sin and rebellion in your own heart. For it is there that God looks to find the seat of sin or righteousness in our nation." He finished one sermon with, "Will we heed? We had better do it. For if history and the Bible tell us anything, it is either that or death as a nation." As with prophets, Hobbs took no joy in condemning the nation or for portending God's wrath but felt compelled by his "commission from God" to speak these "truths." No one better articulated the conservative evangelical theology in the period. Hobbs took up the prophetic mantel and charged the nation with willful sin that spawned the United States' travails, including Watergate. And, instead of endorsing specific solutions or targeting specific problems, he preached individual conversion to save the nation to the exclusion of all else.

Perhaps nothing exemplified the truth of how this theology might change the nation better than Charles Colson's conversion. While Colson explained his conversion publicly in a variety of ways, his personal correspondence to people illustrates the deep-seated nature of his beliefs and thrilled those looking for an example of how conversion might save the country. Though doing so was painful, Colson explained he examined his previous life and found it wanting: "I never like to look back, but I suppose if I had slowed down before to really take stock of myself, that I might have found that all of my values were not quite what I would like them now to be." On the one hand, such statements demonstrated how he came to see the need for personal redemption, to be freed from the addiction to politics by the consuming power of Christ. On the other hand, they reveal a very careful Colson, unwilling to reflect too deeply on his previous actions or assume full accountability for what he had done. However, he admitted to others something about the work of a presidential assistant "brings out the worst in people's personal charac-teristics. In my case, I would like to think it was the pressures and not the arrogance of power. But whatever the past, I have found a new set of values in my life which are much more meaningful and enduring." Thus Colson saw himself as saved from sinning in the White House to living his life for God. Colson often blamed the errors of his previous existence on a rudderless life and rejoiced he found redemption once brought to Christ.[51]

Several standard answers he sent to the many admirers who wrote to him further elucidate his perception of himself at this juncture. He hum-bly insisted, "I haven't had the impact, I have merely been His instru-ment" in terms of the larger significance of his conversion in the lives of others. He frequently asserted he was "apprehensive over the publicity about my own experience," but the accolades and support from sister and brother Christians "have made it more than worthwhile." Colson embraced this new outlook, to the point he wrote one person about his son's bewildered reaction to his father: "Wendell doesn't quite under-stand what a 'Jesus Freak' is and I think it came as a shock for him to think that his father might be one. But then I have been shocking my son for years, so he's probably getting used to it." Colson further vowed to turn away from politics once the "Watergate anguish is past," instead wanting to take his new faith and craft a "more meaningful" career. He wanted everyone to join him in prayer to bring more and more people to Christ in order to protect society.[52]

Even so, he continued to struggle with his role in previous crimes. He frequently questioned whether anyone "in times like these" could receive "fairness in the judicial system" but trusted the "truth" would prevail and "whatever happens, I know that God uses us in ways that we cannot understand." He even claimed to accept the twisted notion he would be found guilty despite his protestation of innocence because, "no matter how unjust some of the charges seem at times, I know what ultimate justice is and that gives me a great deal of inner peace." This framework for his situation brilliantly allowed him to feel righteous in his newly converted life. He adeptly exonerated his old ways without saying he did anything criminal, foresaw the writing on the wall indicating he would be convicted, anyway, but vowed therefore to use it to further Christ's message. He maintained this stance when declining an initial plea bargain because "I couldn't as a Christian . . . in conscience accept it because it meant pleading guilty to a charge of which I am innocent and it also carried with it the implied suggestion that I would give testimony that in conscience I couldn't give." Colson had moved seamlessly into this evangelical and conservative realm of thinking. His pietism protected him as he moved forward in life and assured God had a plan for him regardless of what happened.[53]

National publicity about Colson's conversion demonstrated its far-reaching importance to the evangelical community. No less than *Christianity Today* featured a story about his experience. It detailed how Tom Phillips, an old Colson friend, guided Colson to Christ in August 1973, but Colson remained quiet about it for some time, "fearing it would appear self-serving." Colson insisted his spiritual quest began before Watergate, but his constant prayer ultimately led him to a point where "Christ gave him joy and freedom from fear in the middle of all his troubles." Privately, the *Christianity Today* editor and author of the story on Colson assured him, "Your courage in speaking up will, I'm sure, be a source of inspiration to others." And, indeed, it was for thousands of evangelicals who claimed it as proof positive for pietist theology. This one single conversion, in their minds, changed the course of the nation and might lead others to God's word at a time when they thought the nation desperately needed it.[54]

This theological framework, while seemingly simplistic at times and certainly redundant throughout the Watergate affair, informed how evangelicals, and many of their conservative Protestant colleagues, understood the current political climate. Republican Theology relied on public moralism by individuals in order to function. Conservatives prayed for revival and conversion to save the country before Armageddon, a mantra that picked up steam because of Watergate and fueled the Religious Right's fervent political ambitions moving forward.

Lutherans in the Middle

Like the African Methodist Episcopal Church, the Lutheran Church in America stood apart during this period of the Watergate affair, not easily labeled as liberal despite often aligning with liberal Protestants, but neither did it lean conservative. In a rather characteristic American Lutheran fashion, the moderate Protestant denomination found itself studying the issue and only slowly attempting to shape a response to the national problems. As LCA president Robert J. Marshall explained to a layman who wrote to question why the church failed to speak about President Nixon's possible impeachment, "It is my opinion that at this stage not enough has been proven about the president's behavior to allow the church to speak officially." Still, a careful reading demonstrates the LCA's cautious approach to the matter did not mean the church and its followers remained silent.[55]

Not that other Christians failed to understand this obvious point, but much of the LCA's struggle with Watergate stemmed from how complicated it viewed the matter. Albert P. Stauderman, editor of the denomination's official periodical, the *Lutheran*, explained this very fact in editorials he wrote during the winter of 1973–74. While most Americans focused attention on the national level, Stauderman pointed out that Spiro Agnew's resignation from the vice presidency "began in his case at the local level." Corruption, therefore, materialized at the international, national, and local levels, leading Stauderman to remind readers to examine all the complexities of the political climate, not just one person or party. He also cautioned against a cynical viewpoint because "proper perspective" demanded Christians see, "with few exceptions, those whose duty it is to enforce the law or to make our laws are conscientious, reasonable and above reproach. Cops or politicians who take graft are a tiny minority." He also applauded the system for "ferret[ing] out wrongdoers, right up into the highest offices in the land," a sure sign of the "health and strength" of America. Still, he acknowledged Watergate caused "an erosion of confidence in government and in people. Prominent political figures have stooped to deception, which is nothing new."

And he understood some of this attitude resulted from the situations being "so complex that no one can grasp the whole picture." In short, Stauderman articulated the LCA viewpoint that Watergate exposed a mess in America, from top to bottom, with no easy political or theological fix. In a sign of what other Lutherans would similarly argue, he urged readers "to rededicate ourselves to faith that God is present and active in our world and in our lives. Then we can live triumphantly, no matter what comes."[56]

Other LCA voices sought to reflect carefully on the nation's political problem and add the church's voice in a deliberate way. In January 1974, the LCA's Division for Mission in North America issued a report from its Department for Church and Society listing many problems facing the church and nation, titled "The Moral Crisis." While only a first draft designed to generate discussion, it framed well how the LCA was approaching Watergate. The report contextualized that Watergate fit with a number of other recent and immediate problems facing the country, including the continued struggle for civil rights and racial equality, the division over the Vietnam War, local political scandals, and business participation in the election process. In this regard, Lutherans seldom isolated Watergate as a unique or special problem. This litany of anxieties prompted a national "mood of 'malaise'—at the very least genuine concern, often anxiety and even despair." And this very complexity spoke to why the LCA took such care in framing a response. To alleviate some worry, however, authors stressed it was "not a bad thing for Christians to question their basic societal values; on the contrary it is a good thing and all too rare!" In other words, the silver lining of the turmoil rested with it prompting the Christian community to reevaluate its role in society and then act. Though seldom with very specific instructions as to what exactly Lutherans should do, these LCA leaders inched toward possible solutions. For one, the report called for Christians to act as "reconcilers. But that does not mean standing in the middle between conflicting claims, trying to find the lowest common denominator or a median compromise. Rather, it means reconciling people with each other and with ourselves." Instead of continuing to fight or exacerbate the situation, this concept asked LCA members to assist in healing all of the national wounds. Indeed, the current climate provided them "a tremendous opportunity to test the spirits and ourselves, to challenge deceit, dishonesty, and selfishness in public and private places in the land and internationally and to bring to bear our best witness, courage and insight on all the problems that the human family faces."[57]

Other LCA voices articulated a similar message, suggesting a widespread agreement with the "Moral Crisis" statement. Paul C. Empie, a prominent Lutheran leader, president of Lutheran World Relief, and former general secretary for the USA National Committee of the Lutheran World Federation, articulated almost the exact same approach to Watergate. Explaining "disclosures about the illegal actions of certain government officials" represented "only symptoms, not the disease," Empie wrote, "A probing of our national life will be productive only if it is deep." He blasted conservative piety as "superficial" or so blindly patriotic as to verge on idolatry and stated, "Christian integrity would seem to require that we examine ourselves on at least the following points." This scrutiny included focusing on justice and peace, building toward support of "corrective government action" based on Christian conscience, and loving enemies. It was a classic Lutheran response, with a plodding analysis yet strong desire for Lutherans to be present in their world in order to heal what ailed it, leaning both toward the right and the left at the same time.[58]

Despite the slower approach the LCA took to reaching strong opinions or issuing clear statements, moderate Lutheranism wanted to speak relevantly about Watergate. These Lutherans lived with a tension between careful examination and a history of avoiding controversial topics, while also striving for a Lutheran presence in the public sphere. One option came from local congregations voicing their concern, which eliminated the complicated task of national unity even though it perhaps reduced the influence because it came from a smaller group. The church council of Holy Communion Lutheran Church in Racine, Wisconsin, wrote to LCA president Robert J. Marshall with its ideas about how Lutherans could contribute to Watergate discussions. Citing the "moral decay" in the United States as "exemplified by the Watergate scandal," the council lamented Lutherans said too little on the subject. Its members felt it wrong for the leadership of the church to remain silent and requested the church act more as the "Old Testament prophets as they were inspired by God to speak out against the wickedness and corruption of their day." This letter represented classic Lutheran ecclesiastical practice, where a congregation articulated a concern and then used its elected denominational president to generate a moral Lutheran presence.[59]

Paul Simon, at that time a professor of public affairs at Sangamon State University and later a senator from Illinois, offered a model for individual Lutherans to also act in his keynote speech at the Lutheran Forum on Social Concern in Cleveland: he attacked politicians for governing according to opinion polls and blamed the church, in part, because it often failed to ask or demand that national political leaders also reveal bad news. He wanted a more "compassionate" government *and* church that dealt with reality in a warm and caring way but without ignoring the ethical and moral crisis facing the country. He further told this gathering of Lutheran leaders, "Your combination of faith and insight into the needs of society gives you a marvelous position to lead both our church and our government."[60]

Robert E. Van Deusen, director of the LCUSA Office of Public Affairs in Washington, DC, and editor of *Focus on Pubic Affairs*, also discussed Watergate and its meaning for Lutherans in America, in his case both as an individual Lutheran and as a national leader. He blamed Watergate not on the specific abuse of power but "the tolerance of that abuse" by American citizens, including Lutherans. The resulting "cynicism and disillusionment" became a bigger problem when the unchecked elite seek any means necessary to keep themselves in power, which only worsened the conditions. Van Deusen went on to suggest a unique remedy. He recommended Lutherans simply pay more attention, in their voting habits and in the expectations they place on their civil leaders. Rather than become consumed in the wave of apathy and despair, they should rise up and use the ethical and moral teachings of their denomination to change the current political climate for the better.[61]

LCA president Robert J. Marshall urged moral leadership in private letters to local and national leaders, including Gerald R. Ford in December 1973 on his elevation to vice president of the United States. He acknowledged Ford came "to office in a difficult time. You have borne lengthy and probing investigation. You have responded with forthrightness and comprehension. This is what I would have expected from you as the result of your contribution to the breakfast meetings with churchmen during the past year" they attended together. While a kind and congratulatory letter, it also served to remind the future president America's religious leaders expected a great deal of him going forward, thus allowing Marshall to use his position to establish a Lutheran presence at the highest levels. Marshall also appealed to his church body, as with an article in the *Lutheran* in which he explained how Lutherans could assist the country. He reminded readers, "A Christian must be a moral person even in a time of decline in public morality. A Christian is required not to accept the generalization that 'everybody is doing it.' He dare not become cynical and say, 'You can never expect anything good to come out of politics.' To be cynical is to reject the implication of Christian hope." In order to live out their theology, then, Lutherans must bring to public life their moral underpinnings.[62]

In many respects, the Lutheran Church in America played its historic role of a moderate Protestant voice during this period of the Watergate crisis. Certainly LCA extremes on the right and left existed. A laywoman declared the president was not "a crook" and warned her denomination's periodical against editorializing against Nixon because "it is the freaked out misfits" and the media "who are trying to destroy" the nation. A lay attorney argued the opposite, wanting the LCA to press further in denouncing the president. But for the most part, these Lutheran representatives grappled with Watergate carefully, yet this approach did not mean passivity as they simultaneously worked to exert their influence on public opinion and to influence policymakers.

Conclusion

The period from November 1973 to April 1974 witnessed investigations in Congress, by the media, and by the newly appointed special prosecutor that gathered evidence but failed to produce a smoking gun. The White House maintained presidential innocence, labeling Watergate as insignificant and accusing the press and Nixon's detractors of manufacturing a false crisis. Nevertheless, the Christian community ramped up its involvement. The Saturday Night Massacre in October and the trickling out of other information propelled Protestants to sharpen their messages and raise their voices.

Differences still divided the responses. Liberals' hostility toward the administration intensified, and they became the first to debate impeachment. While not yet unified about backing that measure, they dialogued about it and came together in believing the president deserved some form of sanction. Theologically, they called for prophetic action to force a nation gone astray to bring morality back to the public sphere. They were now joined by the African Methodist Episcopal Church, whose enmity of Nixon focused on his poor record regarding race and poverty. The Lutheran Church in America stood apart, proceeding more cautiously into public debates and preferring to study thoroughly before proclaiming a position. The LCA leaned against Nixon, but only select leaders made that stance public. This period saw the most change from conservative Protestants. Too much proof came to light for them to continue to hope for innocence from the administration and even the president. But their acknowledgment of this fact came with the condition the president was a sinner, like everyone else. Most hoped he could exonerate himself and used Charles Colson as proof born-again politicians could stay God's judgment on a sinful nation and government. Republican Theology depended on public morality, which became harder and harder for them to find within the executive branch.

All told, the Christian community became more vocal, political, and partisan. While Christians hardly agreed on what theology to apply to the situation, they all attempted to direct it. The United States needed an infusion of Christian leadership, that only churches, Protestant leaders, and religious periodicals could provide. This contribution became all the more crucial by the middle of 1974, when Watergate escalated into a full-blown constitutional crisis forcing the first resignation of a president in American history. Christians contributed their voices to the dark political moment and decided to remain thereafter as a guiding light.

5

The Bleep Heard round the World

No period during the Watergate scandal moved as dramatically and quickly as mid-1974. In May, judicial action forced Nixon to release damaging transcripts of private taped White House conversations. By July, the US Supreme Court ruled unanimously that, in addition to the transcripts, Nixon must release the actual recordings, which was followed by the House Judiciary Committee passing the first three articles of impeachment with the charge of obstruction of justice. Nixon complied with the tapes release in early August. The content proved the smoking gun to many because of conversations the president had within a week of the initial Watergate break-in, exposing how early he knew about it. Even Republicans on the Judiciary Committee who opposed impeachment at the end of July changed their vote as a result. Faced with imminent impeachment and almost certain conviction in the Senate, Nixon resigned on August 8, 1974.

American opinion therefore went from contention about what really transpired to a general consensus that criminality consumed the entire presidency. Christians followed these events closely and reflected this almost universal agreement about Nixon's wrongdoing. Liberal Protestants felt vindicated in that proof validated what they had argued all along about the administration's immoral and unethical behavior. They therefore intensified attacks and calls for impeachment. Moderates joined the liberals. Yet the clearest change came from conservatives. The tone and conduct of the president as revealed in the transcripts of White House conversations shocked them into opposition. Evangelicals and their conservative compatriots could no longer even hope Nixon was innocent and instead searched for ways to end the national nightmare. It would include a more persistent and permanent move into politics, to match their liberal and moderate colleagues.

These last months of the Nixon administration left Christian Americans from across the spectrum distraught, angry, or both. The *Christian*

Century reached the limits of disgust. It vilified "the man who early in his political career smeared Helen Gahagan Douglas as the 'pink lady'" and never stopped the unethical quest for victory at any cost. Watergate was not a misjudgment Nixon "felt at the time were 'in the best interest of the nation.'" Editor James M. Wall continued, describing Nixon's final address as "so far removed from the reality of what he had done in office that it stunned national leaders and television commentators into respectful praise, leading some to mutter that it was his 'finest hour.' It was not a fine hour." Rather, Wall claimed, it plunged the presidency to a new low and crafted a call for liberal Protestant intervention to save America's political process. In the *Ohio Baptist Messenger*, editor L. H. Moore echoed, "Few, if any, of the crises our nation has faced have revealed the nation in such moral weakness" as Watergate. Moore gave voice to the particular hurt of conservatives: "It is a pitiable thing to watch Ichabod being inscribed on the brows of those we trusted and whom some of us defended. It is a dismaying experience to see the leader of a nation fall because of inner weakness." He asked Christians to weep for themselves, for the country, and for its leadership. But, like Wall, he proffered a means to reverse this downward trend. He stated, "It is time for prayer that the God who watched over the birth of this nation and nourished it will preserve us in this trial." His brand of Republican Theology invoked God's previous favor, hoping, "If this crisis could bring spiritual renewal that would revive the nation to morality and ethics consistent with Christian teaching gain would come from our loss. Christians should pray to that end." Amid the shared lamentations about the country, the two sides still fought over how to respond theologically as democracy equipped them with the ability to add their voices to the conversations.[1]

Liberals Sensing Blood in the Water

At first glance, little changed in the general reporting about Watergate from liberal to moderate Protestant entities. Yet their persistent scrutiny of Watergate laid important groundwork for the shifts in their theological outlook discussed in the next section. Still, their all-purpose coverage and their religious reflections grew even sharper in tone during the most tumultuous period of the Watergate scandal. But criticism of Nixon and his inevitable resignation segued to articulating a Christian vision for how to recover from the crisis, action requiring Protestant immersion in politics.

A May editorial in the *Christian Century* by Martin E. Marty commented on the release of the White House taping transcripts and in many ways summarized the bitterness and sarcasm of many liberal Protestants. Marty noted many thought the "conversations would permanently taint Nixon's image as evangelical, square America's Moral Man," but revealed him "as a man who doth frequently sin against the commandment not to take the name of the Lord in vain. He is a profane and dirty conversationalist." Marty then mocked those surprised by Nixon's language and fantasized this interaction: Marty pleads "Say it ain't so, Mr. Nixon," to which the president responds, "*Bleep! Bleep!*" Marty found it ridiculous too many people focused on Nixon's foul language, not his illegal activities. In fact, in this commentary, Marty came the closest to siding with Nixon because he demanded readers understand all presidents, including Nixon, were human. To him, Nixon fell in the eyes of his followers for cussing on the tapes, a rather mundane fact of human life.[2]

The commentary was more direct and pointed from other sources. An unsigned *Christian Century* editorial in the next issue, most likely by editor James M. Wall, more methodically outlined the current news and problems, having nothing to do with Nixon's language. Instead, Wall asserted Nixon sought "not to admit error, but to cover mistakes. 'National security,' used on other occasions to harass political enemies, was now proposed as a solution to his own personal dilemma." He continued to point out the president and his associates fought for two years to hide the truth and "have thrown overboard data and victims when it became necessary." He continued, still to that day, the president remained "deceitful" and told lies regularly to the public. On behalf of the United Church of Christ's *Engage/Social Action*, Douglas G. Ebert succinctly stated "the nation is sick of political corruption, and Watergate in an abomination to us all."[3]

A June editorial by Wall probed the significance of American journalists who kept the Watergate story alive by searching for sources and seeking answers to questions the White House desperately tried to avoid. *Washington Post* reporters Carl Bernstein and Robert Woodward led the journalistic charge in probing into the matter; their dogged pursuit of important revelations to the American public became a crucial cog in the machine exposing the Nixon White House, along with Congressional activism and judicial investigations. Wall thus applauded the two, stating "the amazing part of their saga is not all the work they did to uncover the secrets, but that they did it all with so little help from fellow journalists." He regretted the public dismissed Watergate as irrelevant for so long because too many in "the media" sought to reassure the public to protect their profits. While appreciating that a free press depended upon readers and viewers for revenue, Wall also emphasized the press must possess a "zeal" for seeking "the truth" because "in its finest moments the press brings light into darkness." He turned toward the religious nature of his commentary in concluding "man is by nature geared toward corruption; but he is also plagued by an instinct for the higher calling of truth. In some circles this is called conscience." Since June, Wall moved past the release of the transcripts and Nixon's language. None of that surprised him or altered the trajectory of his opinions against the Nixon administration. He continued to teach *Christian Century* readers about the lessons from Watergate and what was needed going forward to secure the nation, both legally and morally.[4]

A majority of Christians within the liberal community by this period had decided for impeaching the president. From the tepid reception of it in April 1974, impeachment discussion took center stage in their deliberations by late spring and grew in intensity until Nixon's resignation. Tilford E. Dudley, the Director of the Washington, D.C. office of the United Church of Christ Center for Social Action, wrote to members of the House Judiciary Committee in May, beseeching them to pursue the best evidence on which to seek impeachment. He felt the "sanitized transcript substitute" of the White House tapes only made matters worse, and the actual recordings themselves should be reviewed. Absent this openness, Dudley thought impeachment inevitable. An *Engage/Social Action* contributing editor advocated impeachment and enjoyed the irony that the administration, well known for its many wiretappings, "should find itself the victim of wiretapping it conducted absentmindedly on itself." The UCC therefore consistently called for Congress to impeach as an act of justice. A letter to the editor of the *Christian Century* took a cue from John Dean's cancer metaphor to colorfully write, "If surgery to remove a gangrenous limb is delayed, can we expect to become stronger in our fight against the deadly infection already circulating in our system?" Marge Roberts demanded removal of the diseased limb in the form of impeachment.[5]

An overview of Watergate coverage in *A.D.*, the UCC's official periodical, demonstrates a sense of hope for the future, even as it insisted no one must escape judgment. Editor J. Martin Bailey commented frequently on Watergate. Despite the president's "repulsive" character as revealed by the Watergate tapes and the "petty and illicit acts" of his administration, Bailey explained Nixon's resignation "was widely acknowledged as proof that the American system is both capable of cleansing itself and inherently healthy." Led by Christian convictions, he hoped Americans would "challenge our leaders to greater moral stature by expecting more of them." He also stated, "Watergate trials and the distasteful impeachment processes at least indicate that the American system is resilient and free enough to purify itself. The fact that the news media's reputation improved shows that the role TV and the daily press played in uncovering crime has been appreciated." Left unmentioned and difficult to calculate is the extent to which he and other liberals assisted this media effort by keeping the matter in front of Christian readers with a theological context. And their commentary about Watergate in these final days of the Nixon administration emphasized the vital role the churches and Christians in general played in American society and politics.[6]

The Church's Voice in America

Liberal Protestant views of Watergate were so dire, they led them to articulate a theological call to arms. These Protestants believed in the necessity of a more churchly presence in the public realm, self-reflection on the problems the nation faced, and a deliberate effort to infuse their ethics into American life. As the executive vice president of the UCC's Board for Homeland Ministries, Howard E. Spragg, explained in *A.D.*, "The church should help lead the United States 'out of the morass that is Watergate.'" He continued, "Bitter and divisive days are ahead as the nation is tested in the crucible of impeachment proceedings. Let us hope that justice may reign, but that we emerge reconciled." Such reconciliation demanded the church's action.[7]

James M. Wall used the *Christian Century*'s respected platform to delineate the theology behind this call for Christian action. A May 1974 editorial echoed a more general, nonpartisan Christian theology of setting the problem in a greater American context, not just a "cancer" on the White House. He explained the "real horror" was not Watergate, "but that what happened reflects so accurately the value system the nation has come to accept as Standard Operating Procedure." He turned this reflection toward the left when he blamed that attitude on America's focus on winning, whether in sports, business, or politics, and whether by an individual, group, or the greater majority of Americans. The Watergate tapes and actions in Washington, DC, differ "only in degree from nationally accepted norms. Once we placed the highest priority on winning, then 'at any cost' means what it says." He pointed out too many people found life's meaning in "winning." Christianity, on the other hand, labeled this "a losing proposition." Furthermore, he stated, "Faithless people prefer to celebrate heroes who smash all opposition with total abandon" and thereby prove "total victory brings ultimate satisfaction." In contrast, Wall felt Christianity understood life was God's gift, "not something to be won." Wall's statements imply a rebuke of pietism, which Wall believed concerned itself with perhaps winning one's soul at the expense of indifference to the social fabric. Christianity could therefore alleviate the suffering as exposed in Watergate by repudiating this winning culture and teaching that sacrifice for the sake of many mattered more.[8]

Robert E. Van Deusen added a Lutheran hue to this theology. The Lutheran Council U.S.A. director of the Office of Public Affairs wrote about the upcoming impeachment proceedings in July and detailed how Lutherans must operate in this situation. He felt they "will need to participate responsibly in the healing of wounds and the reconciling of differences both in their congregations and in the wider community." Like Wall, reconciliation for Van Deusen fell upon Christians, as a theological duty after previous years of strife. Van Deusen also wanted readers to remember all Americans held responsibility for the crisis because, "if moral standards in public life have eroded, the absence of the church as a vital opinion-shaping, standard-setting force may be partly to blame." It was crucial to revitalize politics by reclaiming an ethical and Christian message: "As our nation enters the third century of its experiment in democratic government, we will need a creative rebuilding of the structure of public life on tested foundations. The church should be part of that process." Watergate exposed a flawed America needing a renewed Christian spirit in order to lead it back to a moral grounding.[9]

The United Church of Christ, too, accused American society of being part of the problem. J. Martin Bailey, editor of *A.D.*, worried about integrity in government but warned against "the temptation to be satisfied with a scapegoat. We must search our own hearts and exorcise the forces in ourselves that have contributed to the decline of our economic, political, and spiritual institutions." In *Engage/Social Action*, a joint publication with the United Methodist Church, editor Allan R. Brockway explained it this way:

> Watergate is the name for an incredible maze of crimes, indiscretions, immoralities, and just plain stupidities that have their common focus in Richard Nixon and the national administration he headed and heads. But Watergate is also the name for a rude awakening on the part of citizens all across these United States. The awakening is so rude, in fact, that it may not be inaccurate to understand it as the dying of a myth.

He continued:

> Whatever the version [of the myth], the same elements are there: personal integrity pays both for the individual and for the public; avarice and greed (whether for money or power) destroy both the individual and the body politic. This myth is dying in our midst and the name of the dying is Watergate. The myth is not yet dead—in fact, it could be said to have quite a vital spark remaining—but it is growing weaker. Should it finally die, the nation and its citizens would be considerably impoverished.

For Brockway, the church—institutionally and as individuals—must demand both a changed behavior in the public realm and accountability for those who so failed the nation. In short, he stated, Christians had a theological duty to "actively support the impeachment of Richard Nixon" not only to solve the specific problem but also for the better moral grounding for the country. Or, as applied to President Nixon, he explained, "Mr. Nixon as an individual will survive through the atonement of Christ. The nation will survive through the judgment of God as expressed by the Congress of the United States."[10]

The debate that liberal Protestantism engaged with conservatives over situational ethics also crept into their theological stances in Watergate's final acts. Increasingly after World War II, but especially heading into the 1960s and 1970s, liberal Christians began a more strident advocacy for contextually based ethical approaches, as opposed to rule-based laws that failed to value unique circumstances. Conservative moralists decried this intensified reliance on "situational ethics" as hypocritical and indulgent, while liberals viewed it as more humane and authentic. UCC pastor Huber F. Klemme found it self-serving that certain testimonies by Watergate participants framed their defense in situational terms. They claimed the greater national good of Nixon's reelection legitimized their unethical and illegal actions. While conservative Christians used this example in an attempt to discredit situational ethics and promote their more rigid moral codes, liberal Protestants saw this as a gross distortion of situational assessment of the crimes. Civil disobedience, for example, to protest the immoral Vietnam War, differed drastically from illegal actions to secure an election. When *Christianity Today* made the argument Nixon employed situational ethics to justify the cover-up, Martin E. Marty blasted, "I do humbly issue the following rejoinder: M*A*N*U*R*E." He continued, while situational ethics "intends to be situational, it also intends to be ethical. Mr. Nixon's admissions, stripped of euphemism, may be translated thus: 'I lied, I conspired, I obstructed justice to save my neck and my regime.' That is situational but has nothing to do with the ethical." The actions surrounding Watergate represented unethical, immoral activities liberal Protestants denounced and were hardly analogous to their ethical stance on certain protests or understandings of difficult events. The liberal argument was consistent from the beginning of Watergate: a nation adrift must revitalize itself with a Christian message of high ethical standards that worried about the whole community. They were determined to influence the political realm.[11]

The LCA Abandons Caution

Historians often pigeonhole American Lutherans under "quietism," sometimes justifiably because Lutherans avoided controversial topics in order to maintain internal tranquility, and at other times prematurely, primarily because too little scholarship explores Lutheran history. Regarding the Lutheran Church in America and Watergate, both of these observations held true. Until summer 1974, the LCA was not as self-consciously active in that political crisis as other Protestants, especially when compared with its moderate to liberal colleagues. While its leadership condemned the administration, it refrained from overt public action and from issuing strong official statements. However, the LCA jumped into the fray by late spring 1974. The 1974 LCA Convention articulated a Lutheran theology for the public realm, which led to an outline of what Christians should do to help the nation through the moral and ethical emergency of Watergate. It even found itself embroiled in a Watergate-type scandal, mirroring the mistrust and turmoil swirling throughout the United States. By August, as the prospect of impending impeachment impelled Nixon's resignation, the LCA had cast aside historic Lutheran quietism.

LCA theology began with the notion of original sin and, like Christians throughout the nation, pointed out that everyone sinned, not just those in power. As Robert Van Deusen stated in the *Lutheran* and other periodicals, the absence of the church from public debate and politics allowed for the collapse of national moral standards. Without excusing the Watergate perpetrators, he asserted Christians, out of their benign neglect or their sin of omission when it came to the government, enabled them. Another Lutheran explained an outlook similar to that of LCA president Robert J. Marshall, that the excessive scrutiny by scholars, the media, and American society in general led to a "delight" in the "flagellating of superiors in government, in church, in business and finance" without concurrent attention to mass guilt or collective individual sin. *Lutheran* editor Carl T. Uehling acknowledged how this led Americans to a state of demoralization, "without a sense of purpose or destiny." Although everyone shared blame in the matter because of sin, all were not without redemption because "we were died-for long before our nation was founded. We could find in Christ who is 'alive and let loose in the world' that we have new hope for this world, too." Lutheran concepts of sin and redemption lay at the heart of the LCA Watergate response.[12]

Other Lutherans also employed a Lutheran theology of Christian help for the secular realm in Watergate's last summer, thereby refuting quietism and illustrating the LCA's affinities with other liberals. Van Deusen's article in the *Lutheran*, just mentioned, first outlined how Watergate was enabled by excessive executive branch authority and sinful society, but then observed, "The churches have a unique opportunity to help their people deal with the emotional strains that will be involved" as impeachment began. Christian reconciliation would heal political divisions and hopefully restore values "by effective involvement in the democratic process." The nation needed to "rebuild" the "structure of public life on tested foundations" with the church as part of the process. Lutheran hope and values, in other words, must play a vital role in fixing the political crisis. Byron L. Schmid, editor of *Lutheran Social Concern*, furthered this notion. Amid the "normal reaction" of "civil impotence, frustration, 'the hell with it'" attitudes, "it is just in such a time as this that Christians are called upon, *in the name of Jesus*, to engage in political struggle and to transform the Nation's bitterness and disillusionment into opportunities and future hope." Schmid therefore urged "each of you to join one of the political parties, if you are not already involved, and work for policies and for candidates of integrity and compassion. Now! November is a bit late."[13]

The official periodical of the Lutheran Church in America echoed this idea in its editorials and articles. *Lutheran* editor Albert P. Stauderman wanted strong moral candidates for president in 1976, explaining only Christians in the election process could bring "unimpeachable honesty" to a world that also demanded "political savvy and aggressiveness to campaign for the presidency." Because America in the 1970s desperately needed "political leaders whose first impulse is to do what is right in the sight of God," Lutherans had to vote and lead. Edgar R. Trexler similarly stated, "The church has a prophetic role to speak to its members and to society, regardless of the criticisms" it may face. *Lutheran* editors also printed an article written for Interchurch Features, a nine-denomination magazine consortium, by a lay Roman Catholic. Despite coming from a different denomination and written for a larger Christian audience, its presence in the LCA's official periodical expressed a Lutheran agreement. Specifically, Michael Novak wrote Christian vigilance in scrutinizing the public realm had been necessary since the founding of the nation and would continue as long as the United States existed. According to him, Christians should deliberately engage the public sphere in order to police its ethical and moral behavior. While the article was vague in exactly what it meant for Lutherans to vote their conscience and assist moral leaders, and certainly the periodical sidestepped any endorsement of a candidate or political party, these ideas encouraged Christian citizenship beyond merely voting.[14]

Privately, President Robert J. Marshall often articulated a left-leaning Christian stance toward war and government social policy, though he was more moderate and careful in public. By summer 1974, however, his statements regarding Watergate were more bold, and he at least wanted Lutherans to understand their vital part in solving the nation's woes. Marshall's report to the Seventh Biennial Convention stated, "In practicing pastoral care for people, the church will need to be concerned for the effect institutions are having on human life as well as for the ideas and attitudes that influence behavior." Christians therefore participated, for example, in the civil rights movement and paid attention to politics, regardless of political affiliation. To Marshall, Lutheran views of the world meant the church must "continue to define the relationship between the heavenly vision and earthly servanthood"; the church, not government, infused morality in society toward everything from interpersonal relations to the environment, from consumerism to "spiritual malnutrition," from the "age of affluence" to the government. In bold, he commanded his denomination, **"It is time for vision to be matched with action. The vision of the Lord, known in crucifixion and resurrection, includes a vision of his body, the church, threatened but still serving."** Retreating into two kingdoms theology (that divorced the secular realm from the spiritual one) violated Lutheran tenets, as Marshall charged his people with the responsibility of carrying their Christian conviction from one kingdom into the other. When Marshall forwarded to Richard Nixon a resolution from the 1974 LCA Convention, he told the press, "All of us must remain morally committed to the welfare of our country and to what is right as is consistent with Christian faith and good citizenship." In a letter to all LCA pastors, Marshall called for the spiritual leaders in his denomination to further carry this message to the laity. He felt combating political cynicism resulting from Watergate "gives us the chance to reclaim public responsibility and leader accountability" from a Christian perspective. The two realms were bound together in Lutheran theology, not forever separated by it.[15]

While less assertive and more careful than other, more liberal Protestant bodies, the 1974 LCA Convention heard Marshall's message and acted in its ratified resolutions. One committee, charged with responding to President Marshall's report, exhorted delegates who wanted to avoid politics that "undeniable theological and ethical considerations" were involved in the use of power by the government and therefore necessitated that Lutherans "erect a steeple" at this crossroads between the ecclesiastical and earthly realms. The committee pointedly demanded it was "incumbent upon the church to address those issues while society is considering them and not to withdraw from that challenge because of fear that the church will be criticized from without and within. The United States particularly cries out for moral leadership. Can our church serve God and remain silent?" They doubted it. Furthermore, the Committee on Ecumenical Relations reported the National Council of Churches, to which the LCA belonged, "urged Congress to act 'expeditiously in the matter of impeachment.'" This message to Congress, however, paled in comparison to a resolution that was amended and passed at the July convention by the entire assembly. Hardly demonstrating a Lutheran quietism, the LCA Convention not only instructed LCA president Marshall to send the resolution to President Nixon but also released it to the public:

> Whereas, during the next biennium, we will be made vividly aware of the heritage of our nation; and
>
> Whereas, the Consulting Committee on the Bicentenary of the United States, in its statement of intent, said: "We hope for the recovery of a true understanding of 'this nation under God' in terms of the continuing purification of Divine Judgment that calls us away from our past sins and into a future of fuller justice and community"; therefore, be it
>
> Resolved, That the Lutheran Church in America express its love for America and its concern over the deterioration of integrity at all levels of government which contributes to the erosion of moral standards, and
>
> Be it further resolved, That the President of the Church communicate this concern to the President of the United States.

The Lutheran Church in America, through its democratic process, demanded action to fix the ethical crisis in government. While it remained a careful resolution, it came from a denomination that shied away from politics, signaling how Lutherans stepped out of the shadows to add their moral voice. Indeed, the Bicentennial Committee mentioned earlier began to plan for the LCA's contribution to this national celebration.[16]

Sydney E. Ahlstrom, Yale historian of American religion and a member of the LCA, chaired the Consulting Committee on the Bicentenary of the United States. As opposed to the more patriotic celebrations of the Southern Baptists or Lutheran Church—Missouri Synod, having for a chair an expert in American religious history led this LCA committee to recommend an intellectual and nuanced commemoration. In this regard, the LCA approached the Bicentennial in a manner similar to that of the academic and minority communities in the United States, as an occasion to celebrate while continuing to fight the ongoing revolution for more equality and an even better nation.[17] Ahlstrom wasted little time in communicating this vision to LCA members. Updating the national convention in July 1974 about the Bicentennial committee, he advocated the two hundredth anniversary of independence should prompt individuals and the church to reflect on the past "and then apply this knowledge to our present predicament." Though, on the one hand, Ahlstrom felt no individual, committee, or even church body alone could "bring about a change in the moral climate of the United States," he also asserted, "As Americans we appeal to a law that is higher than the laws of nations." This combined with a civil religion granting "a solemn commitment to equality, liberty, happiness, tranquility, and justice for all of humankind." He hoped "we all will do what we can to penetrate the moral fog that is encompassing us, and which will get thicker in the ensuing months and years and perhaps reach the darkness of a total eclipse in 1976. We must try to be the leaven in the loaf." Ahlstrom concluded the Bicentennial for the LCA "could become a time of rededication in which an enlarging circle of thoughtful people, by reflecting on our past, and facing our present with candor and penitence might yield a vision of the future that is worthy of our revolutionary tradition."[18]

Ahlstrom communicated these themes in a pamphlet he sent to the newly appointed committee members in November 1974. Although he acknowledged the positive notes to score, he also maintained the current political crisis demanded something more from churches when they assessed American history. While suspicious about why Congress added "under God" to the Pledge of Allegiance in 1954, "for reasons that were at best dubious and mixed," Ahlstrom observed it did "invoke the principle that this nation stands under judgment, under a higher law. And it can safely be said that if our efforts to restore the nation's moral health proceed under that standard, then the Bicentennial as an occasion for moral renewal will succeed." Though, for obvious reasons, the real impact of this approach would take until 1976 to manifest itself nationally, Ahlstrom and the committee reveal the movement of the Lutheran Church in America toward a more pronounced public stance in solving the nation's spiritual problem.[19]

Not unexpectedly, the new LCA impulse to identify and address the evil in Watergate met with a small but loud backlash from conservative clergy and laypeople who either defended the president or simply disliked any political statements. Edna S. Nielsen reminded fellow Lutherans about Nixon's détente initiatives and ending of the Vietnam War, adding "Blessed are the Peace Makers." She felt "heartsick as I cannot understand the attitude of church members and clergy who feel justified in the crucifixion of Mr. Nixon" and instead wanted the church to pray for the man "overwhelmingly elected after serving his first four years." Her attitude obviously demonstrates an enduring conservatism in the LCA throughout Watergate. Others felt individuals and church bodies had too little information and should therefore leave impeachment to Congress. Erling P. Redal explained, "If the founding fathers wanted the tenure in office to be based on the number of letters received or the popularity polls, they would have said so." Reverend Kenneth L. Nerenz compared Nixon to the crucified Lord, stating, "Christ was condemned and executed because of public clamor, not incriminating evidence. We Christians should be the first to oppose any recurrence of this injustice. If public opinion is to decide the President's guilt or innocence, we can ship [sic] the whole impeachment process and let Congress get back to work. Maybe we could all vote by postcard." With near messianic reverence for their president, these LCA members decried the church's involvement in the final stage of the political crisis.[20]

Just as the Bicentennial offered the LCA a positive means of trying to influence the nation and its diseased political system, the national climate of suspicion worked itself out in an LCA scandal of its own. It began in a seemingly innocuous way, with the announcement by the Reverend Dr. Wallace E. Fisher that he intended to campaign against Robert J. Marshall for president of the Lutheran Church in America at its July 1974 Convention. At the time, Fisher, whose doctorates were both honorary, had served as pastor of the Lutheran Church of the Holy Trinity in Lancaster, Pennsylvania, for twenty-two years and authored seven books. In spring 1974, he informed Marshall he would send information to delegates, pastors, and other bodies of the LCA to announce his run for office. He wrote to Marshall in April that he "decided to announce my candidacy for the office of the presidency of the Lutheran Church in America at its biennial convention." Before this moment, no person ever actively campaigned for the office in the LCA, instead relying on a tradition of standing for office if nominated or drafted by peers. At the expense of his home congregation, Fisher sent an "Invitation to Dialogue and Decision" pamphlet to a large LCA audience before the convention and distributed another pamphlet, titled "To the Clerical and Lay Delegates," at the convention. These documents, the debate over them, and the language both sides used link the LCA to the larger Watergate scandal.[21]

Fisher minced few words in the material he distributed at the convention. And it takes little imagination to see how the spirit of Watergate could infiltrate all levels of society, though in this case it seems more that Fisher exploited the national turmoil for his own gain. He wrote, "In this era of increasing distrust of institutions and suspicion of professionals, depersonalization, and national fragmentation, there is a deadening decline in the morale of both clergy and laity in the Christian Church in North America." While he sidestepped any direct accusations against Marshall, he insinuated as much when he continued, "In these times, the president of the LCA must be, above all, a pastor, teacher, and prophet in the biblical sense. Solid executive ability is required, but the pastor-priest-prophet-enabler role must at all times be primary; it dare not be subordinated to the interests of institutional efficiency or institutional security." Readers would certainly understand Fisher judged Marshall a failure in these areas. He promised, if elected, to "seek to develop authentic communication through personal presence, reasoned correspondence, open consultations, collegial decisions, and public proclamation." It is important in a Watergate context to note his use of words such as "open" and "public" because they imply Marshall operated in secrecy, as had President Nixon. Fisher regretted too many mistrusted their national church, and stated, "One cause certainly is the hidden political maneuvering in the church itself, the lack of openness, the dearth of serious discussion," as if Marshall were isolated and making decisions with cronies at the national headquarters. More pointedly in regard to Watergate, Fisher invoked the political crisis to further justify his candidacy. He wanted the church more actively involved in bringing a stronger moral voice to US politics, again stating he would add such morality where Marshall had failed: "How the church and the state in America handle the current storm over politics and Christian piety will determine partially the course of human events—and the human situation—in the closing quarter of this century." Fisher's document contained sixteen pages that described how the current LCA failed its members and the country with its secrecy and isolation and its bureaucratic blindness to reality. Whether Fisher's campaign was a personal vendetta or a theological conflict is something for others to determine. What is noteworthy here is that he freely manipulated the darkest shades of Watergate to advance his candidacy.[22]

Fisher found support among a vocal LCA minority. Kenneth L. Nerenz, the pastor at Emmanuel Lutheran Church in Racine, Wisconsin, exemplified those who backed Fisher. He, too, painted the situation in the church body in Watergate colors. Nerenz explained, "The 'Watergate Affair' and subsequent investigations of the personal finances and questionable campaign practices of other public officials suggests [sic] that the American people are no longer willing to accept the ethical and moral levels of leaders," prompting him to "feel strongly that the greatest crisis facing our country today is a crisis of moral leadership not only in government but also in the church, in business, in labor, in the media, yes even in athletics and education." He gave specific examples for disliking Marshall, such as his support for the LCA's participation in the National Council of Churches in Christ. It infuriated Nerenz that the NCC called for Nixon's impeachment. This statement seemed to align Nerenz with conservative, pro-Nixon Lutherans when at the same time their standard-bearer's material against Marshall otherwise likened Marshall to Nixon. He more pointedly stated the LCA leadership's "irresponsible shooting from the hip at anything that moves does little to bolster confidence in our church leadership. I am not alone in finding it increasingly difficult to trust church leaders to make judgments in keeping with scriptural principles and Lutheran teachings. If the blind are to be led, the leaders must see clearly." Nerenz and Fisher supporters felt Marshall failed in this regard, while Fisher would bring a more open and trustworthy administration to the church body.[23]

Despite the criticism against Marshall, Fisher's campaign garnered minimal support within the LCA. A vast majority of letters to Marshall, to other church leaders, and to the *Lutheran*, as well as other source materials, indicate LCA clergy and delegates alike appreciated Marshall's leadership and supported him. As the Reverend J. W. "Jack" Berry wrote to Marshall from his pastorate at Salem Evangelical Lutheran Church in Fremont, Nebraska, "Knowing you and your concerns as well as your style, it seems to me to be unfortunate that he [Fisher] would suggest that you are operating like some cold-blooded, mechanized corporate executive. Hopefully, the people throughout the LCA view you differently than Fisher seems to present you." Indeed, the results of the convention fulfilled Berry's hope. In the first ballot, 635 votes were cast, with 477 needed for election. Marshall earned 339 to Fisher's 168. Each candidate with at least 5 percent of the vote addressed delegates before the second ballot, on which Marshall was elected to a new four-year term by a vote of 534 to 107. The minutes of the Seventh Biennial Convention note, "The announcement was greeted with vigorous applause."[24]

For his part, Marshall handled the accusations and affair with a dignity befitting his position. While taken aback by the accusations and personally offended, he maintained a high decorum in his correspondence by defending the Lutheran Church in America without personally attacking Fisher and his backers. However, he did not cow to their demands. He detailed the errors he felt their argument contained and stood for reelection in the face of this adversity. After Fisher notified him by letter of his intention to run for the office, Marshall thanked him for the information and blandly added, "In doing so, you are breaking new ground." Marshall then defended himself: "I have not sought any office in the church other than the office of ordained ministry. As in former instances, so now, I will not seek election, but will accept it only if it occurs by the will of others, registered by vote at the convention." Privately, Marshall voiced larger concerns. He particularly worried about "seeing the church move in the direction of copying the style of election for government officials. If we are to have campaigning, we can expect campaign promises that will have to be broken, especially by those who know little about the office for which they are campaigning." As for the Watergate parallels in the matter, Marshall, too, had concerns: campaigning for office "takes money and I would think that Watergate has shown us the extent to which the attempt to outdo another candidate can lead to bad practices. I am in favor of openness. The question is, how is that attained without the injustices?"[25]

Marshall's acceptance speech to the convention capped his principled victory over Fisher. He noted the need for a "place for differences of opinion in the church" and committed himself to working for everyone in the LCA, whether or not he agreed with them in everything. He accepted the office in the "spirit" of belief "we are all committed to having God change our lives." For his part, Fisher, too, demonstrated a graciousness in defeat, claiming "fresh procedures for openness have been established." Fisher also wrote a somewhat qualified letter of congratulations to Marshall: "Many find satisfaction in the fact that my candidacy placed crucial issues before the church. Fresh procedures for openness have been established that will not easily be set aside." This outcome hardly paralleled the drama at the national level. However, it nonetheless demonstrates how already in 1974 Americans began to see Watergate scandals at every turn and couched debates in these terms. It portended a future in which any political dissent, disagreement, or issue, within the government, corporations, or even churches, became an opportunity to blast the opposition as conspiring against the masses and operating in secrecy.[26]

After a long period of only cautious commentary, the Lutheran Church in America made public criticism of Nixon and Watergate by the midpoint of 1974. The LCA chose to move into the political arena out of a traditional Lutheran understanding of the need for moral and ethical guidance from the church. Two kingdoms theology may separate the godly from the earthly realms, but LCA Lutherans lived in both simultaneously, and so worked in several important ways to minister to American politics and morals. It continued this action after Watergate ended and well into the 1980s, when it merged with other Lutheran denominations to form the Evangelical Lutheran Church in America.

The African Methodist Episcopal Church

As noted in the previous chapter, the African Methodist Episcopal Church established its own way of examining the Watergate affair. It combined its evangelical and right-leaning theology and a more leftist political agenda. Their more vocal mistrust and general dislike of Nixon from spring 1974 continued into summer. Yet this church body hardly dwelled on him or even the federal government exclusively, as it also took the opportunity to use the growing scandal as a chance to reflect on human sinfulness. Some within the AME issued renewed calls for Nixon and his administration to divulge the truth of what happened.

When it came to theological reflections about Watergate, the AME sounded like other conservative Christians in emphasizing human sin in everyone. One *A.M.E. Church Review* article explained the Bible predicted corruption and world problems throughout human history, and thus the current 1970s problems were nothing unique or new. It observed salvation came only from faith in God, and protection from evils only from people turning to Christianity. Acknowledging "evidences of moral decline in private and public" realms led some to become "a pessimist," AME theology called people to Christ for a solution. Even with a lost "confidence in the integrity of leaders in local, state and federal government," trust in God would overcome all calamities. *Christian Recorder* editor A. Lewis Williams concurred: "In these Watergate days . . . there is a great temptation for us who preach to black folk to take our text from the headlines of the morning papers. This temptation, we must fight down and repress [because] we cannot afford now to stop preaching the gospel of the Lord Jesus to fool around with some temporary situations that came up in the night and will disappear in the night." A district newspaper echoed this sentiment, glad African Americans experienced gains in equality since the Emancipation Proclamation, yet reminding readers of "an unavoidable and indiscreet awareness that man in all of his vastness of knowledge is still failing in the ultimacy of his social relationships one with the other." As for evangelicals, Watergate revealed the sin inherit in humanity to them. Individual salvation, not finger-pointing at those in politics or the federal government, was what was needed.[27]

Yet the African Methodist Episcopal Church hardly allowed this conservative theology to align the denomination with other Christian conservatives in the political realm. By May 1974, six ministers at the 102nd Session of the New Jersey Annual Conference of the African Methodist Episcopal Church signed a resolution that spoke to the national political crisis. Outlining "integrity and honesty in government are absolutely essential if the Nation is to maintain its moral and spiritual health," they stated allegations of political misdeeds "implicate the President of the United States in serious violations of the Constitution." They persisted that Nixon attempted "diversionary maneuvers" to "thwart" investigations. Because of this "aura of corruption and criminality" that might "poison the very processes of government," they resolved at the 102nd Session of the New Jersey Annual Conference to "go on record" with a demand the president "cease and desist from all obstructionist tactics, and fully cooperate with the lawful investigation" by Congress. Mistrust of Nixon and a feeling he hid something from the American people were proving decisive. And they had company among AME members.[28]

An article in the *A.M.E. Church Recorder* detailed how African American voters helped to elect a white Democrat to Congress during a special election in Cincinnati, Ohio, a traditional Republican stronghold. On March 5, 1974, Thomas Luken won by just over 4,000 votes out of a little over 102,000 votes cast. More than 17,000 votes for Luken came from black voters (92 percent of the African American vote). The article emphasized the importance of black voting, particularly by its AME readers. The anonymous writer explained Congressman Andrew Young traveled to Cincinnati and particularly campaigned for black preachers to use their pulpits to encourage voting, especially because of Nixon's cutting of social programs that assisted minority communities. Black voters, including AME members, elected a Democrat, a "stunning rebuke to Richard Nixon. The Watergate scandals and Nixon's performance in office were the main issues in the election" of Luken to office. The AME not only rebuked the White House publicly but also celebrated political activities it thought would bring about change.[29]

The African Methodist Episcopal Church continued to steer its own course in the 1970s as it related to Watergate. It reported less on the matter than other church bodies and periodicals studied here, for vague reasons not concretely explained in the archival material. Perhaps its members and leaders grew weary of the controversy, or perhaps they felt uneasy about constant condemnations of the president. They mixed a conservative theology of individual conversion that would in turn help save the nation with a public and sharp criticism of the president. They therefore placed themselves in both an evangelical camp theologically and a liberal Protestant stance politically.

The Ground under Conservatives Moves

At this point in the Watergate scandal, it became impossible for conservatives to maintain their previously cautious and somewhat optimistic attitude about President Nixon and his White House. Unlike liberal Protestants, who found confirmation of their perceptions in the White House transcripts, the tapes proved to be a smoking gun for conservative Protestants. Instead of a moral man upholding American values and wrongly besieged by liberals and the media, conservative Christians confronted a profane and vindictive president seeking to save his presidency and nothing else. To be sure, their comments remained milder and their hope for repentance strong, but their support was compromised, and they staked out a permanent place in politics to try to avoid future problems.

Christianity Today, which began to question the president earlier than many of its conservative peers, stated the transcripts "show him to be a person who had failed gravely to live up to the moral demands of our Judeo-Christian heritage. We do not expect perfection, but we rightly expect our leaders, and especially our President, to practice a higher level of morality than the tapes reveal." That the editors questioned his morality based on this new evidence did not mean they were changing their political stripes. Adding a touch of continued right-leaning politics, the next line recommended those who "mercilessly pursued him" should also "examine their own souls." The editorial, which urged Nixon to resist resignation and instead allow the impeachment process to determine his fate, explained, "Repentance might not win Mr. Nixon acceptance by all, but it could get him off to a new start if his exit from the stage is deferred until January, 1977." Still somewhat cautious, the periodical took the conservative lead in denouncing the president, but this time plenty of others joined the fray.[30]

A number of periodicals from the Southern Baptist Convention echoed similar sentiments after reading the White House transcripts. L.

H. Moore, editor of the *Ohio Baptist Messenger*, listed Watergate along with such problems as media cynicism, rumor mills, and the language in the tapes that were taking the nation "down the road to moral and spiritual bankruptcy." Moore found it distressing "we no longer require moral excellence as a requisite of leadership"; he explained that, far from the "gutter language," the "moral climate such dialogue exposes" alarmed him more. Yet this shift in feelings against the president brought a now familiar solution: national sorrow and repentance if accompanied by "a dedication under God to do better." C. J. Daley Jr. at the *Western Recorder* first emphasized, "This is not a political editorial," and his message went beyond partisan politics to instead take up the moral state of the country. He wrote the transcripts "are shocking" because of the "profane language and the spirit of the conversations" they reveal, but the true problem lay in the spirit of the discussions, not in the words themselves. It represented a degeneration of the American government and prompted Daley to wonder if such profanity always existed, then "the exalted image most of us have had for the United States President is destroyed. Even the stars and stripes of old glory seem soiled and the language of men in high places is more appropriate for pool rooms and beer joints than for the White House." Clearly the release of the White House tapes sent conservatives into a reassessment of their views.[31]

And if Southern Baptist editors made harsh statements, it only asserted what the SBC's most prominent leaders felt about the transcripts. The June conference of Southern Baptist pastors in Dallas, Texas, brought an opportunity for SBC leaders to speak to a national audience. H. Edwin Young, pastor of First Baptist Church in Columbia, South Carolina, gave a speech in which he called the Watergate tapes "one of the most pornographic and vulgar and blasphemous documents you have ever heard and the words have come from the lips of the highest elected man on the face of the earth." He therefore labeled Nixon's conduct "an abomination unto the Lord." Like SBC editors, he worried about the president's lack of a moral compass, finding only "all sorts of political chicanery and intrigue and payoff and backbiting and subtleties and vulgarities." At least in the eyes of this pastor, Nixon had fallen completely out of favor. No less than Jaroy Weber, pastor of First Baptist Church in Lubbock, Texas, and the newly elected SBC president, said much the same thing. While the profanity offended him, "even worse" was "the apparent way the President has manipulated people" and conveyed himself in a sinful manner as president. While Weber stopped short of demanding a resignation and wanted "to follow due process," he found the transcripts shocking. What the investigations and evidence failed to accomplish to this point, the White House tapes achieved overnight: conservative Protestants no longer trusted their president.[32]

Profanity was one issue, but there were others. A number of evangelical periodicals, including *Christianity Today* and several Baptist publications, lamented the revelation the Nixons gave little to charities. In 1974, Nixon published his tax returns that revealed his dearth of giving. Tithing was a crucial component of the faith life of many conservatives and a monetary help for the less fortunate, as Jesus instructed. Charles King, a seventy-eight-year-old African American and the first black officer in the Southern Baptist Convention, articulated additional grounds for distrust. King declared he would rather have the racist George Wallace as president because "at least black people knew where Wallace stands." In contrast, Nixon lived in a world of confusion and subterfuge and "has done more damage to this country than any other presidents since 1896." Referencing Nixon's recent trip to the Middle East, he wished "the Egyptians would 'keep Nixon with them. They like him so much.'"[33]

Despite increasing forays into criticizing Nixon, a basic respect for the presidency and Nixon as a fellow human shaped conservative Protestant commentaries. In other words, many refused to go to the extent their liberal colleagues did in condemning him. A letter to the editor of the *Alabama Baptist* warned, "Watergate should be no concern to the church" because of its political nature, countering SBC president Jaroy Weber's remarks with support for Nixon. Such sentiments also persisted with the argument Nixon deserved due process of the law and a full investigation before the public, and especially the churches, convicted him.[34]

In the end, Watergate remained but the symptom of a much deeper malady, a disease of immorality that would crush the United States without repentance. *Christianity Today* decried the idea that "religion is and should be a private affair and that ethics must follow suit," because it led to people seeking personal gain over greater good and the general state of immorality in politics currently crippling the nation. Lutheran Church—Missouri Synod president J. A. O. Preus "puzzled" at the unethical behavior of national leaders but reminded one layperson, "Our Lord Jesus warned us that in the last days many would fall from the faith." His statement aligned him with evangelical thinking about the end times and using dire warnings to bolster faith and create converts. It also indicated a thinking that, perhaps, Watergate and the moral collapse were unavoidable as the nation cascaded toward the apocalypse. To another constituent, Preus wrote a more hopeful note that read, "We are indeed a nation that should give priority to repentance, the sincere recognition of all our sins, both personal and as a nation." He pondered, "Perhaps our Lord is chastising us to do so in these troubled and violent times." While the questioning of the president changed with the release of the transcribed tapes, the basic theology behind conservative thinking and Watergate remained anchored to mass conversion and revival in America.[35]

Fellow conservatives in the Southern Baptist Convention asserted the same theology. In an article about contemporary youth culture that primarily castigated the younger generation, Albert McClellan wondered, "How far do we have yet to fall before we hit the bottom?" He complained about how the streaking fad signaled "we are falling faster and faster into a deeper and blacker pit," but also the "sex revolution, moral relativity, corruption in politics, the increasing irresponsibility of many of our elected leaders, and the breakdown of business integrity" further degraded the United States. He more pointedly indicted politics by stating, "Without a set of Ten Commandments and all that they imply, and without a vital integrated New Testament morality, any political system is destined to be ground up in its own green bile." In other words, sin had taken over the nation, which desperately needed to repent. Jimmy Allen, the pastor of First Baptist Church in San Antonio, Texas, preached during Home Missions Week and returned to the typical conservative response, saying, "The time has come for the people of God to humble ourselves and realize our responsibility" because "nobody wins out of Watergate. Everybody loses. We need to pray and pray and pray" in order to make the country a more righteous one.[36]

In the spring and summer of 1974, the White House tapes revealed Nixon to be far less a Christian and far more a man of sin than previously known, and conservative Protestants reacted in horror. While still somewhat cautious about impeachment, many conservatives crossed a bridge from trust to condemnation. A theological change of heart, how-ever, did not follow. Conservatives still prescribed prayer and repentance to save the country from God's wrath. Indeed, an intensified emphasis on America as a Christian nation and a conservative role in politics be-came the primary way of hoping to maintain this honored status.

The Persistence of Christian America

The Cold War created a patriotic country as Americans remained in a state of war readiness; questioning of the United States often became tantamount to treason, even into the 1970s and 1980s despite too many histories now relegating such extremism to McCarthyism of the 1950s. However, the majority opinion in this regard disintegrated amid 1960s and 1970s controversies surrounding youth culture, the Vietnam War, the continued struggle over civil rights, and, finally, Watergate. Too many issues called into question a blind trust in the government for too many people. Yet conservative Americans clung to their faith in the country. As the left challenged universal patriotism, conservative Americans dug in with their traditional point of view. Republican The-ology buttressed them because it protected their government and their faith at the same time. Conservative America crafted an intensified view of America as uniquely Christian to counter a perceived assault on American values amid the continued Cold War. More and more, this notion blurred the line between faith and patriotism, turning the country into a Christian state as it opposed communist atheism and dubiously insisting the founders intended to govern through Christian-ity. If anything, Watergate intensified the way right-leaning people of faith conceived of the United States as favored by God as a way to save a country on the brink.

In fact, conservatives took their pietism and applied it to America. As Jim Young explained to the Southern Baptist Convention in the pages of *Home Missions*, "The need to reevaluate church commitment to govern-ment and to define the responsibilities for redemptive activities within the political environment has seldom been more pressing." The current crisis demanded that saving the United States required faith in the pub-lic realm. This notion circulated widely among Baptists and was not an isolated declaration. Dr. Warren Hultgren preached the same message on a broadcast of *The Baptist Hour* in July: "As a nation and as individuals, we must assume a greater responsibility for government and in electing the right kind of political leadership." The SBC Christian Life Commission drove this point home in its annual report to the convention that summer. A nation seeking morality in government and honest politicians needed Christian prayers to bring God's intercession in order to deliver America "from the current malignancy of deceit, distrust, and discord." Christians must further expose "evil at every level of government" and "bring to justice" those who violated the law. Quoting Isaiah, the commission declared, "Righteousness exalts a nation, but sin is a reproach to any people." Few Americans would disagree the country faced a dangerous moment in spring and summer 1974 as Watergate threatened the Nixon administration. Christians, however, disagreed on what could bring about the needed change. In their call for Christians to assert themselves, conservatives mirrored leftist calls for religious institutional intervention, but their employment of that principle combined Christianity and the government differently.[37]

For example, conservatives blurred the lines between religion/faith and government; they wanted this merging, which crafted itself more and more into a participation by the church in politics. Editor J. Everett Sneed told the *Arkansas Baptist Newsmagazine*, "No nation can long survive apart from Christian ideals. The best we can give to our nation today and to the generations of the future is to commit ourselves completely to Christ and his purposes." Applying their faith to the government was essential. The Reverend Tim Nichols explained, "I don't see any inconsistency whatever in the Christian faith and politics" except the public realm had fallen too far away from Christian principles. The Kentucky pastor wanted the SBC faithful to unite their religious principles and the government so they commingled to create a stronger Christian nation. Baptist Press reported how a majority of SBC clergy agreed. A pastors confab reminded SBC leaders "they have a responsibility to help lead America out of its lapse of political integrity and into a climate where the spiritual principles of justice, equality, and morality will flourish." In their eyes, America must become, or maintain, itself as a country where people blended their government and their Christian God.[38]

No Southern Baptist leader was better positioned to express this idea for his denomination than James E. Wood Jr. As director of the Baptist

Joint Committee of Public Affairs, he oversaw the entity that brought together seven national Baptist church bodies in order to lobby in Washington, DC, for various causes and shared ideas. A mix of faith and patriotism naturally came to his job, and needing to explain why the Baptist Joint Committee joined the newly formed Religious Committee for Integrity in Government provided him the opportunity as Watergate climaxed. With an "erosion of integrity" in government and the subsequent mistrust of politicians, Wood warned of the "serious threat to the survival of democracy." With "the very foundations of this nation" threatened, Wood demanded responsible Baptists bring their ethical and spiritual outlook to the government in order to save America. The United States had fallen from grace, and Baptists could lift the nation up to an integrity more worthy of its heritage. As he explained to readers of his *Report from the Capital*, "The Christian witness needed is not one of cynicism, but one that affirms the Christian's obligation to exercise his religious liberty through responsible citizenship and concern for integrity in government which is committed to liberty and justice." He assumed a traditional Christian role in American government that had somehow lapsed and thus led to Watergate, therefore demanding, "*The times require the renewal of the Christian's commitment to the legitimate role of the political process.*" He concluded, "The current crisis in American government is clearly a moral as well as constitutional one. Without integrity no democratic government can endure." Integrity in this case was articulated through a Baptist faith point of view written onto the national government.[39]

Journalist and editor Everett Hullum contributed a similar jeremiad in a lengthy article for the SBC's *Home Mission*. He first quoted US Representative Andrew Young of Georgia, who explained that praying "thy kingdom come" in the Lord's Prayer meant his work in Congress was to bring "about the kingdom. We're partnered with God, and through implication, to continue the work of Christ here on earth." In this point of view, Congress served as a church, a house of worship, through which Baptists must bring their faith to the world. Hullum criticized Baptists for being too silent in voicing opinions about government, in part because Baptists represented many points of view and disdained top-down polity. Interestingly, Hullum warned that "civil religion" created a false worship of the presidency, that in turn lapsed into confusion when the now deified president sinned, because it was "like discovering God has made a mistake." He asserted this ideology honored a generic concept of democracy, not nation worship or praise for a single individual. His comment blurred the lines between Christianity and the function of US government.[40]

The Religious Committee for Integrity in Government, a subgroup of the Southern Baptist Convention's Christian Life Commission, organized to address the unethical behavior of the government and to offer its solution to the problems. To that end, the committee sent a communication to US senators and representatives advocating campaign reform to prevent moneyed interests from having a disproportionate influence on elections. The letter asserted such action by Congress "will go a long way to place our system of campaign financing under a fair and just process. It will free candidates from the threat of compromising obligation." Yet, more noticeably, it implied a natural link between Baptist ethical convictions and what the government needed. Southern Baptists sought to influence politicians to save American democracy, and thus preserve not only political freedom but also religious freedom. This argument demonstrated perfectly how the SBC espoused Republican Theology during Watergate. To worship freely meant defending the United States from corrupting influences, thus blending religion and politics.[41]

C. Welton Gaddy of the Christian Life Commission, which sponsored Christian Citizenship Sunday, explained too many individuals, including prominent people in the government, warned young people to stay away from politics in order to maintain their purity and morality. Gaddy decried this advice and insisted, "No Christian can heed these words and remain true to either the concept of democracy or the Christian faith." In one sentence, he solidified the link between the Baptist faith and American democracy, while simultaneously blurring the lines of worship between the two. Adhering to one necessitated reverence for the other. He instructed SBC members, "From every church and political precinct in our nation the call is for active political involvement for persons with integrity so public confidence in government may be restored." After establishing that a Christian must blend faith in God and government, he extrapolated such behavior would heal the nation's woes and direct the United States onto a more righteous path. The SBC campaign to get all of its churches to commemorate this special Sunday commingled patriotism and Christianity in an effort to get Christians involved in politics. No doubt the calamity of a nation on the brink contributed to Baptist angst about the future. Christian Citizenship Sunday's faith in Christianized democracy would save America.[42]

The culmination of conservative Protestant linkages between Watergate and crafting America as a Christian country came with their planning for the nation's 1976 Bicentennial. Organizations and people throughout the country began planning for the Bicentennial well in advance, with the preparations in 1974 prompting reflections about the meaning of the United States and its future amid Watergate. For example, a priest at Our Lady of Arlington Novitiate in Arlington Heights, Illinois, succinctly summarized this case: "I ask that all Christian journals make a concerted appeal to its [sic] readers and the country to make 1975 a year of healing—forgiveness in preparation for the Bicentennial. The first call is to every Christian to seek healing from Christ—and then become another Christ, his instrument." Personal conversion and more careful adherence to faith promised to save the nation in a grand Bicentennial celebration that would bring the nation closer to God, and thus out of the Watergate pit. Baptist Press Release added to this idea and perhaps infused a prophetic note into the conversation in its reporting about Jimmy Carter's address to the Southern Baptist National Convention in June. The current governor of Georgia and future president of the United States called Watergate a "national tragedy and embarrassment" but saw the issue as "a temporary aberration." Carter trusted the "higher ideals" of the American people and noted the two hundredth anniversary of the nation caused "a hunger" for the honesty of its Founding Fathers, which could come about if Christians engaged more forcefully in the political process. If they committed to "shaping the standards and quality of public life" through faith, the country could return to the values of George Washington and Thomas Jefferson. Carter's words blurred the lines between nation and God, between faith and reverence for country. He, too, wanted the upcoming Bicentennial to repudiate the current sin of Watergate with a stronger Christian conviction for the United States.[43]

Hope for renewal of national pride through the Bicentennial merged with evangelical pietism to create a conservative Christian veneration of the United States during the final days of Watergate. The evidence against the Nixon administration had become too great to continue to ignore or hope something would prove the accusations wrong. But rather than dwell in misery, conservative Christians searched for a means of hope and discovered it in God's favor for America. Faith in God and nation blurred to give them both personal hope and divine trust their nation could survive the dangerous moment. It would survive in part with their firm commitment to maintain a more active political role.

Charles Colson

Charles Colson continued to give conservative Christians a unique perspective from which to view Watergate with his previous stint inside the White House combined with his subsequent born-again conversion. The specific example of one individual became the embodiment of what conservatives sought for the entire nation. To Colson, living in sin contributed to the collapse of the country, but his evangelical awakening righted his own moral ship and in that way assisted the country in becoming more godly.

Charles Colson embraced this role. His correspondence with a variety of people in June 1974 revealed his understanding of this narrative. He often reminded people about the magnitude of his personal conversion because it so profoundly changed him. Indeed, his previous addiction to alcohol and especially to the power he gained from manipulating the political process transformed into an addiction for personal piety and his brand of Christianity. Once a saved man, Colson claimed he contributed to healing the nation through his testimonies. In this regard, he became a messianic figure in his own mind and in the view of others, because his faith might very well save the United States. However, far from becoming a completely new person, Colson converted his dogma into a religious zeal that kept him in the public spotlight and maintained his sense of high status.

Colson often referenced his personal conversion in letters, perhaps reminding himself of its importance as much as he communicated it to readers. At first, he found it difficult to handle Watergate because "I could not fully and completely testify about everything I knew because I had to defend myself." He admitted a previous "excess of loyalty to many causes," but "now found the one that a person cannot be too loyal to" and therefore was "relying on the Lord to vindicate me." Whenever he explained his actions, he reminded the reader, "I truly believe the Lord has shown me the way." In other words, God guided his actions, not personal desire or sin.[44]

Once converted, Colson felt led to handle Watergate differently because "it is my conviction that the time is long overdue for all of the truth about the Watergate to come out and I intend to do my part." Doing his part was also "my obligation both as a Christian and as a citizen." Like many of his conservative colleagues in Christianity, he blended this notion into a form of Christian citizenship that might set the nation on a better course. This altered approach to Watergate, from protecting himself exclusively to testifying based on his Christian conviction, turned him into God's appointed minister, at least in his own eyes. As he stated to the Honorable Michael Alison of the House of Commons in England, "I now feel freer than I have in years, not only free in the eyes of God which I was before, but also free now to tell the truth to my countrymen in a way that I think will help bring this ordeal to an end." As a matter of political and theological conviction, he announced, "The country needs to be helped in any way possible out of the Watergate morass; that is a matter of political conviction with me. As a matter of theological conviction, I could not see myself remaining a defendant and not being free to tell exactly the truth." He repeated this idea frequently, altering it slightly here and there and sometimes attempting to add a humble phrase, but always with the same salvation for the country his revelations might bring. To another person he proclaimed, "I really feel I was led by the Lord to do it and I only pray that it will help the country in some small way to find an end to the Watergate agonies." Colson crafted a new sense of his importance by declaring his faith in Christ converted him into the messenger who could end Watergate and heal the nation.[45]

Evangelicals embraced Colson as an agent of national healing as shown by *Christianity Today* in its June 21, 1974, issue. Edward E. Plowman, the news editor, reported on the influence of God in the Watergate proceedings and asserted, "There's been a lot of soul searching on the part of many slogging around in the morass of Watergate. In their search some have found God, and the outcome so far has been profound." He noted James McCord, who oversaw security for CREEP, wrote the letter to a judge that became the impetus for his becoming a lead witness after hearing a sermon. Stating Colson's guilty plea "set off shock waves in Washington," Plowman approved his "decision" and noted that the decision and the "wording of his statements were thrashed out in a small prayer group he joined soon after his conversion last August." Colson conferred with a group of high-powered and highly placed individuals in the government on when and how to issue his plea. They explained God guided their decisions. Thus, Colson's story affirmed the pietist theology preached by the periodical as the basis for how to solve the nation's problems.[46]

Even the left-leaning *Christian Century* agreed, despite its regular condemnation of conservative theology as naive. After Colson was sentenced to prison, a July news item stated Colson "has been converted, and until his behavior proves otherwise, he is entitled to be believed," and that his conversion "transformed his life and has opened the way for him to apply his intellect to the complex issues of secular society." It also explained it would refrain from assessing the authenticity of his new faith because "what matters is that one who was lost now testifies that he has been found. We rejoice with Mr. Colson in his new beginning." The periodical's neutrality left open the possibility their joy could vanish later, but the *Christian Century* supported the idea that Colson had a divinely appointed role in Watergate.[47]

Colson played a central role in almost all of the illegal White House dealings culminating in the Watergate explosion. His key contribution to the downfall of the Nixon administration led to his own ouster from the inner circle and to his prison sentence. His political afterlife was as a born-again servant of national healing, a role cherished in conservative circles. To them, one man's coming to Christ changed the course of history and saved the United States.

Conclusion

By summer 1974, the investigations by Congress, the judicial branch, and the American media brought the Watergate scandal to a head. The evidence that mounted into an unanswerable case hardly surprised liberal Protestantism, which long suspected Nixon's trustworthiness. Moderate Christian entities also became adamant in their denunciations because they too were convinced of Nixon's guilt. Conservatives in the end abandoned all hope they could rely on the president and wanted a full investigation. They had trusted Nixon's administration to champion Republican Theology but instead woke up to the reality of an immoral federal government that had embarrassed them.

For two years, Protestant America followed the Watergate caper, much like American citizens writ large, and with the same diversity of opinions about it. Vast differences separated them along theological and political lines, though throughout they sought to influence American life in general and politics specifically. By summer 1974 they came to agree a major problem existed, that it was rooted in the White House, and President Nixon lay at the heart of it. That basic agreement disintegrated soon thereafter, as their deeply held quarrels continued to separate them. Liberal Protestants called for the church to assert itself more forcefully in the public realm in order to restore moral and ethical behavior in the government, and they were joined by many moderates. In contrast, conservative Protestants persisted with mass conversion being the solution, highlighting the story of Charles Colson as proof positive.

But collectively, Protestant America proclaimed its voice in an attempt to both heal the Watergate nightmare and demonstrate its moral authority over the country, even if it proved a disparate and uneven contribution because of these differences. This very diversity of solutions represented typical US Christian history. Religious pluralism remained a bedrock of American freedom, even if it hindered a uniform response. And yet Protestants *were* now uniform in one thing: they dove into the political fray and were there to stay. As Nixon's Watergate drama ended with his resignation, Protestants characteristically followed through on their desire to influence the aftermath and change minds, if not hearts. They now operated comfortably and regularly in politics, a way of being that did not dissipate after Watergate ended.

Conclusion

Nixon's Resignation and Final Thoughts

The resignation of Richard M. Nixon as president of the United States on August 8, 1974, brought immediate reactions from liberal to moderate to conservative Protestants that paralleled one another more than at any other time during the Watergate crisis. To be sure, differences persisted, and a close look reveals them. But the actual moment of resignation brought a sigh of relief, as well as a desire to move the nation beyond this divisive episode. But August 8 lacked a sense of finality because many unresolved issues continued to trouble Christians, the solutions to which divided conservatives and liberals. Protestants thus decided not to exit the political stage in their commentary despite Nixon's departure, and they remain enmeshed in it to this day.

Editorials in *Christianity Today* and the *Christian Century* indicated liberals and conservatives still felt too much about Watergate remained unknown. Prior to Nixon's resignation, *Christianity Today* had desired an impeachment trial so the facts might reveal the truth of what happened and assess the degree of presidential criminality. Even so, the periodical shifted its stance on Nixon from its longtime support to measured reproach as the weight of evidence in the spring and summer of 1974 tilted against him. Editors explained Nixon's acknowledged attempt to halt the investigation, the White House tapes, and other evidence revealed "political reasons" along with Nixon's claim of national security for his behavior. His preemptory resignation meant "unresolved problems remain," such as whether or not Nixon should be sentenced for a crime. The editors concluded, "Until these questions have been answered satisfactorily the unsavory odor of Watergate will linger." A piece in the *Christian Century* by Franklin H. Littell, professor of religion at Temple University, concurred that the serious "constitutional crisis" of Watergate devolved into "popular outrage" that removed the commander in chief, not careful legal arguments or an effort to dig into the totality of Watergate wrongdoing. Littell argued, "Tribal witches are dealt with by popular emotion, but in a mature republic even the most revolting crime receives due process of law." Many Christians lamented how Watergate ended. An "inevitable trial" would have allowed the needed closure about Watergate and its grander meaning for Americans.[1]

In contrast, leaders of the Southern Baptist Convention almost desperately sought to make the resignation the very closure these leading Protestant periodicals claimed it failed to offer. A Baptist Press Release explained denominational leaders, speaking as individuals and not on behalf of the entire convention, "agreed with Nixon's decision to resign, [but] expressed no bitterness toward the ex chief executive while recognizing a lapse in integrity which led to his demise." Baptists also hoped August 1974 would become a launching point to move America toward a brighter, more morally acceptable future. SBC president Jaroy Weber wanted the political process to return to "some absolutes" and glide away from thinking "everything is relative," an obvious reference to situational ethics; he called for national repentance to lead to a "cleansing restoration" that would "move up" to public officials. He even implied prayer and conversion had already led the nation to this important juncture because "the believer always has hope." Still, others expressed "a note of sadness." Showing signs of the dissension that split the SBC in the 1980s, Foy Valentine, the executive secretary of the SBC Christian Life Commission, stated he "joined Christians across the land in praying for him [Nixon] and his family and all persons and families caught in the awful web of public immorality which has come to be a reproach to all America." Weber and Valentine disagreed on what the closure from the resignation actually was, but both saw it as a defining time. The strain of Watergate and the general violence and unrest of the previous decade left SBC leaders wanting to put the turmoil in the past, a sentiment that mirrored American Lutheran hopes.[2]

No doubt American Lutheranism's tradition of avoiding intense discord about foreign or domestic policy lay at the core of Lutherans' desire to put Watergate to rest. General fatigue over debates concerning race, gender, the Vietnam War, and other social issues also affected these largely white, middle-class Protestants. Dr. Arnold Michelson, president of Lutheran Council U.S.A., published a statement advocating for the president's resignation to "provide the occasion for the nation to reflect upon the opportunities inherent in new beginnings." Reminding constituents that all people sinned, he asked for mercy and healing because "people of goodwill can work together to rebuild our shaken government, restore our political system and make our land the model of freedom, justice, and honor." The Lutheran Church in America's official publication, *Lutheran*, similarly pushed Lutherans to see this moment as one of reconciliation and healing. Editor Albert P. Stauderman observed Nixon's violation of the law made his "ouster" "inevitable." This mandated his readers "assure the new administration of prayerful support and of willingness to fulfill our responsibilities as citizens" to honorably and faithfully move the country in a new direction. A sampling of letters to the editor indicates at least some readers agreed. Frederick J. Miller pointed out God forgave sins, including Nixon's, and "some millions of the rest of us-so-called 'little people' ought to know this also." Another pastor authored a poem that scolded those wanting vengeance against the disgraced commander in chief, instead offering Americans should "take the risk of mercy / And let a man now heal." In an increasingly rare concurrence of opinion among the spectrum of Lutherans in the 1970s, Lutheran Church—Missouri Synod president J. A. O. Preus telegrammed Nixon himself: "may he bless your labor for peace may he continue to use your devotion and talents in the service of our beloved nation." Weary of the decade-long fighting and unrest both in American society and within Lutheranism, Lutherans earnestly sought to reach a peace accord on the occasion of the president's removal from office.[3]

In short, the tragedy of Nixon's resignation brought mixed reactions from Protestants, some of whom saw it as a cheapened form of justice that denied Americans the total truth, and others of whom seized on it as the chance to push the nation past a bizarre tale once and for all. Of course, in all the postmortem reflections, the divisions and disagreements among American Protestantism came screaming out, as they had throughout the scandal. And their now solidified comfort with discussing politics within the church's realm set the stage for continuing such behavior as they moved beyond Watergate. They had become more vigilant moral and ethical watchdogs, and simultaneously more dogmatic partisan politicians.

The Liberal Solution

Little changed for liberals, in large part because they had already suspected the president at least since his election in 1968. Watergate proved their already well-established suspicions about Nixon and those who worked for him in the White House. As part of the theological critique of pietism and American conservatism in general, liberals asserted the remedy for future Watergates was a new value system focusing on the broader good, social justice, and a less militaristic foreign policy. Liberals inverted Nixon's policies almost completely. The president's resignation prompted liberal to moderate Protestants to once again advocate their vision for a changed America, even as the group entered a period of waning influence. In that way, though, liberals attempted to become even more forceful in asserting political points of view, to try to maintain their once dominant moral vision in the public sphere.

Many leftist religious commentators framed Watergate in the biblical image of a broken covenant because the government's obligation to its citizens for honest government was betrayed by Nixon-era illegal activities. The *Christian Century* naturally and emphatically advocated this point of view. A former senior officer at the Central Intelligence Agency and then director of research at the Institute for the Study of Ethics and International Affairs at Georgetown University, Harold P. Ford, wrote the article entitled "The Sleazing of America." Ford admonished all readers for failing to hold politicians, and particularly Nixon's White House, accountable. People focused on a market economy of individualism and failed to muster enough outrage about the United States' immoral foreign policy. Watergate stemmed from "ethical numbness" that revealed Americans too frequently "looking the other way" and backing "authority" as a matter of convenience and perceived safety. Regarding pietism, Ford wrote, "We tend to concern ourselves with the wrong question: how we may be saved, rather than how we may serve God." This diverted attention from the greater good, and vigilance about the government and its actions. More directly, he proclaimed, "Piety will not suffice. The cultic cop-out of deedless worship has always constituted a trap." And, quoting Reinhold Niebuhr, Ford reminded Americans they "cannot build our individual ladders to heaven and leave the total human enterprise unredeemed of its excesses and corruptions." *Christian Century* editor James M. Wall reflected on Watergate during the fall 1974 elections. He observed, "Watergate came upon us—and consigned us to a kind of hell—because public officials conspired to break the covenant of responsibility to the people" and met "public indifference," which left the electoral process subject to the whims of those in power. As Mary Maher warned *Christian Century* readers, "It does not follow that the death of the ship's captain necessarily gives life to those who are still aboard." Ford, Wall, and Maher thus sought to alter circumstances that led to Watergate with more collective attention regarding right and wrong in the government and a shunning of pietistic individualism.[4]

While this line of thinking established a root cause for the problem and an esoteric solution, liberal to moderate Protestants made more explicit recommendations for reforms. United Church of Christ president Robert V. Moss explained to the Tenth General Synod delegates some government leaders implored him to get the church to respond about the importance of ethics in politics and get individual members to vote for change. Lutheran Church in America president Robert J. Marshall instructed fellow pastors, "Part of Christian responsibility in politics is to speak prophetic criticism against distortion of power" and a lesson that "leap[t]" out of Watergate was that Christians should "be more prepared to deal reasonably and justly" with election issues. He wanted Lutherans to assess carefully all politicians and ask "the right questions about qualifications." Next, Christians should "act faithfully in love, and to sacrifice in order to meet the needs of the neighbor" and to create a "civil righteousness sufficient to the demands of public office," a subtle rebuke of pietism. Leaders such as Moss and Marshall pled with their constituencies to inject more deliberately Christian ethics and morality into American politics moving forward.[5]

A gathering of prominent theologians, professors, and Lutherans at a symposium held at the Lutheran Theological Seminary in Gettysburg, Pennsylvania, in spring 1974 brought this left-leaning Christian reaction into sharp focus. A symposium cochair explained it sought to "explore the relationship of their faith to the troubling developments in the body politic" and to determine what a "believer in Jesus Christ" could do to alter the negative climate. As another commentator declared, "The very air we breathe is charged with an abuse of power." While participants appreciated congressional action to halt executive maleficence, they noted,

"Ours is the time in which the relation between conscience and power is in confrontation." They thus explained Christian duty, included holding the state accountable based on human conscience and love for every individual. A Lutheran leader stated, "It is all too clear that the phenomenon called 'America' has been driven more by the pursuit of private things than it has by the pursuit of public things, private goods rather than public good." Participants all agreed Nixon's resignation purged the country of its immediate problem, but an infusion of Christian concern for the greater good and a sharp turn away from piety was needed to revitalize America.[6]

Liberal Protestants steered clear of gloating, despite their prognostications of doom almost since the day Richard Nixon ascended to the White House, primarily because they viewed the present as such a dark time. They sought a societal shift away from a "me first" attitude to one, guided by Christian conviction, paying more attention to community. Nixon's return to private life began the healing process, but liberal Protestants hoped for a more substantive change to prevent the country from future Watergates. And they vowed to arbitrate more closely the ethical and moral climate of the political realm, thus promising to fight to continue an assertive presence in America as time marched on.

The Conservative Solution

Similar to liberal reactions to Watergate at the moment of Nixon's resignation, the conservative response did not surprise anyone or change the basic trajectory of their thinking. Unlike liberal commentators who made frequent reference to the president's resignation, conservatives almost never mentioned it. Perhaps the silence was out of embarrassment for having backed the president, or they hoped his downfall would not doom conservative politics. Whatever the reason, conservative comment at the moment was directed at healing the nation and issuing calls for piety and prayer. Like their liberal counterparts, they wanted a stronger Christian presence in voting and politics, though the meaning of that participation differed even as it paralleled the promise to be more politically active.

Not surprisingly, conservative commentators started with the notion of sin, on a national and personal level, and blamed Watergate from the initial break-in to the current political climate on this human problem. God punished sin, the United States and its people had sinned, and therefore the nation suffered the consequences. Harold Lindsell reminded historian Ronald A. Wells of this very fact, pointing out all events, including the failed Bay of Pigs invasion, the Vietnam War, the confrontation with communism, and Watergate, embodied a "moral flaw," innate sin that affected personal and collective actions. He insisted any conversation about the current climate begin with this premise. C. Welton Gaddy, the director of Christian Citizen Development for the Southern Baptist Christian Life Commission, regretted a "conviction that winning is everything" created a culture in which "persons become dehumanized—rendered unimportant" and "morality becomes utilitarian." Watergate proved this sinful notion incorrect, according to Gaddy, and also "morally, the end still does not justify the means." A Lutheran Church in America pastor echoed this sentiment, going so far as to say liberal Christian teachings about protest against war and social change contributed to an environment where the "end justifies the means, and has indirectly encouraged disrespect for law by carrying to extremes the concept of obeying God rather than men." Lutheran Church—Missouri Synod theologian and writer James G. Manz concluded, "We reap what we sow. It is sheer folly to put ultimate trust in anyone or anything human."[7]

Conservative theologians directly linked sin to Watergate, though without addressing the specifics about Nixon. Wallace Henley, a first-term staff assistant in the Nixon White House and later pastor of Old Spanish Fort Baptist Church near Mobile, Alabama, felt power corrupted a number of people in the Nixon administration. He further explained, whether a common citizen or those "festooned with the entrapments of the White House," the only salvation possible "is the scriptural theme that, under the transcendent God, morality and truth are absolute." Henley extolled that everyone, and most of all "Washington," "must give ultimate allegiance to Authority transcending finite authorities. Our ultimate allegiance must belong to God. That's a lesson from Watergate!" Evangelicals for Social Action, the left-leaning to moderate organization of neo-evangelicals created to combat a rigid conservatism among their colleagues, agreed but added that all Americans "have winked at our national sins and acquiesced in them." Conservative evangelical theology blamed human sin for God's punishment and used Watergate as the specific example. Now two-plus years into the crisis, the theological construction of what went wrong in America remained the same. The church would now need to more deliberately participate in political discourse to end this nightmare cycle.[8]

Having once again established human sinfulness as the cause for God's punishment, conservative Protestants throughout the United States asked fellow believers to pray for God's grace and for a way out of the national mess. In *Christianity Today*, Harold Lindsell implored people to "pray that God will work in saving power in the hearts of all the people involved in the Watergate tragedy, and that all, like Charles Colson, will openly repent, place their faith in Jesus Christ, and receive forgiveness of their sins." Southern Baptist Convention president Jaroy Weber concurred in a discussion about "an integrity crisis" the United States faced. The nation needed to return to demanding honesty from everyone, from family members to politicians, and to pray for God's guidance in this matter. The Lutheran Church—Missouri Synod joined this chorus, as when Alma Kern, a leader within the Lutheran Women's Missionary League (LWML), authored a responsive prayer for readers of *Lutheran Woman's Quarterly*. She wanted congregants to pray for a more active voice in politics and for individuals to speak out when others condemn the church, morality, or the government. The entire assembly was asked to pray, "Give us Your power, almighty Lord, to go and sin no more. Give us wisdom to choose and support leaders who respect You. Give us courage to stand up and speak out for what is right, instead of going with popular opinion." The Louisiana District of the LWML asked both the LWML International and the Lutheran Church—Missouri Synod as a whole to back a day for prayer for the entire nation. Quoting 2 Chronicles 7:14 and the promise that if God's people called and sought divine assistance, God would "heal their land," the assembly explained, "An earnest and humble plea to Almighty God for divine assistance and guidance is needed now to direct our nation's leaders and citizens to the living faith and hope that undergirded and sustained our Forefathers." Employing a notion of civil religion that assumed the nation "was founded on the principle that its destiny was dependent upon the guidance and protection of Almighty God," they rallied LCMS members to pray for God to bring the nation out of its current turmoil.[9]

Prayer, however, could only take the nation so far. Conservative theology therefore, once again, looked toward a broad-based revival in America. SBC adherents articulated this hope, in part because they believed "the nation's integrity crisis" amounted to the top religious news story of 1974, for the first time in four years topping SBC member concerns about the split taking place within the denomination. Brooks Hays, a former congressman and former SBC president, explained Christians were "duty bound to confront economic and political authorities with the demand they obey God's laws of righteousness and justice." More Christians making this demand would heal the nation. *Alabama Baptist* editor Hudson Baggett hoped the country learned from Watergate "that some things are right and that some things are wrong no matter who does them." But he also warned against a cynical view that painted all politicians negatively and prone to lying, instead asking Christians to involve themselves in politics to add a strong Christian message. James E. Wood Jr. more pointedly warned the church's "prophetic role is the highest service religion can render the nation state, since it places all human authority and all nation states under judgment." SBC adherents had to inculcate politics with a moral fervor and thereby enact "the Christian's obligation actively to support justice, truth, and integrity in government," with a loud and consistent voice. Wood, too, called for a pietistic conversion of the United States, or at least an assertion of conservative evangelical principles as the means to blend honest work back into the political system.[10]

Conservative evangelicals likewise took the opportunity to distance themselves from liberals regarding situational ethics. An article in *Christianity Today* drove home this point. Erwin W. Lutzer, senior pastor at Edgewater Baptist Church in Chicago, claimed Watergate stemmed from situational ethics because "their guiding principle was to win at any price," which he claimed situational ethics condoned. He doubled down on the proposition with "situationally, there is nothing wrong with winning at any price if winning is the best for the greatest number." Conservative morality and its sometimes absolutist approach clashed with liberal theology, with both sides asserting the other created the climate for Watergate to flourish.[11]

While many conservatives came to distrust Richard Nixon and/or anguished over the state of politics in the nation, their basic message remained the same. Sin, rooted deeply in humanity, caused such calamities, and the only force powerful enough to vanquish it came from a God believers needed to exhort through prayer to intercede on behalf of a growing number of contrite Christians who recognized the nation's failure. Once prayer prevailed, individual Christians and churches could revive America, its people, and its government. In this way, Watergate marked a change because conservatives determined to be more active in making this revivalism happen within politics.

African Methodist Episcopal Church Solutions

As we have seen, the African Methodist Episcopal Church charted a unique course through Watergate. President Nixon's resignation did not alter the denomination's antipathy to his indifference to racial and social justice policies. The AME's political progressivism was matched with a theology that approached that of other evangelicals: individual Americans must convert and profess their belief in a Christian God before the faith could redeem the public realm and mend myriad problems facing the nation, in part with political action from a religious sphere.

No one in the African Methodist Episcopal Church voiced much sympathy for the disgraced president, or any surprise over his resignation. Presiding elder Jonathan A. Dames addressed the Ninety-Second Session of the AME Chicago Annual Conference to declare "Watergate refused to go away until after" Nixon resigned and doubted "the stain of Watergate, like the blood on the hands of Lady McBeth [*sic*], will ever, by fiat or automatic decree, go completely away." He pronounced the entire government crisis, orchestrated by Nixon, as the "worst of all our woes." Another commentator noted the American people shared some blame because they failed to consider "what the President needed. Namely, a deep sense of morality, plus an abiding Love for Truth and Humanity." Lacking these Christian attributes, she concluded the nation doomed itself with Nixon's selection to the problems it faced at the moment. A sharper rebuke came from the Fortieth Session of the General Conference, when Vernon E. Jordan Jr., then the executive director of the National Urban League, claimed the 1960s social policies such as the War on Poverty and civil rights initiatives "didn't fail" but were instead "murdered by the same forces that tried to kill democracy in the Watergate adventure." This problem and the Nixon administration resulted in an age "marked by ethical retardation, and by the passive tolerance of racism and poverty." Rather than sending Nixon on his way in peace or voicing a sense of forgiveness, the AME continued to identify his character flaws and America's election of him as willingness to accept his sinning.[12]

Yet more like conservative Protestants, the AME emphasized the primacy of human sin, followed by a pietist call for repentance, individual adherence to Christian principles, and more conversions. Numerous pastoral and lay leaders within the church explained all Americans needed to turn to God, because "He has the solution to our twisted lives and the cure for this sin that is killing us." Reverend T. S. Clements offered a guest editorial to the *A.M.E. Church Recorder* that reduced all sin in politics to the lack of honesty. Christians knew the importance of honesty in their lives as a means of living out their faith and remaining true to God.[13]

But in a slightly different turn on the conservative mantra of individual conversion leading to national rehabilitation, the AME centered its message of individuals forming the body of the church, and the AME then fostering the environment to save the country. In other words, their theology went a step further than that of many evangelical conservatives, who stopped at collecting individual salvation as a way to build capital with God in order to save the nation. As with civil rights activism from the last fifty-plus years, AME commentators understood collective action achieved more results than individual angst. The East Tennessee Annual Conference of the Thirteenth District that met in July 1974 explained as much. The Social Action Committee reminded participants the decline in morality at the highest levels of government demanded "the church must forever be the rock, the star, the salt of the earth." Linking a person's conversion to the greater church action, it continued, "The church must put into use its main objective—the spreading of redemptive love of God and man. We must point the way where people can see a stone of hope even in times like these." Similarly, the East Florida Annual Conference in the Eleventh District issued a report from the Committee on the State of the Church, which direly warned "the church is fraught with conditions and responsibilities never before in the history of mankind experienced" because "truly our nation is sorely troubled and we believe this to be a sickness of the spirit." It then charged the church with bringing a voice of hope and Christian commitment to society in order to protect it.[14]

Similar to liberal Protestants, the AME experienced little movement in its position regarding Watergate and Richard Nixon from his reelection in 1972 to his resignation in August 1974, though their rhetoric against him became less and less cautious over the years. AME constituents and leaders never trusted the president, and his resignation drove home this point. As always, Christian faith and the church's leadership needed to lead the country out of the mess. The AME had already participated in politics because of the civil rights movement, but Watergate meant it expanded this interest to a wider political arena.

Final Thoughts

A Baptist pastor hoped "Watergate was the shock, the bucket of cold water that will awake Washington to the need of reforming the White House system, and, better, of seeing men reformed." But Wallace Henley declared this awakening only occurred "through an encounter with Christ." Conservatives such as Henley had traversed Watergate as supporters of Nixon through much of the scandal, scolding the criminals, and then expressing astonishment when they could no longer deny the president's guilt. From beginning to end, little changed in their essential pietism, which had held sway among evangelicals throughout American history. Henley's reiteration that "the most valid answer" to Watergate was "through prayer" echoed thousands of voices from the past. He worried the nation's capital was "a place incredibly blind to the limitations of man caused by sin" and thus, until massive "spiritual reform" swept across Washington, DC, nothing would change for the United States. His reflection mirrored other aspects of conservative theology and Watergate. Conservatives almost never admitted particular guilt in the matter, except to assert everyone sinned, including the president and themselves. This thinking avoided introspection in the face of mounting evidence against the president, a president whom conservatives saw as their best advocate of Republican Theology. Denial kept them from seeking political reform until summer 1974, when the transcripts and other evidence forced them to distance themselves from Nixon. Throughout, they called for prayer and a highly emotional form of personal conversion. But it also instilled in them a more concerted effort to engage politics and believers more intimately. It was a pivotal moment in the rise of the Religious Right, a way of being that helped set the stage for modern evangelical conservative politics. It was also another episode of putting blinders on to the moral failings of a president because he otherwise backed their chosen causes.[15]

Rebuking the conservative approach, James M. Wall of the *Christian Century* observed, "Watergate has forced this capital city to look for the meaning of morality beyond a surface pietism that has served as a rhetorical shield for office-seekers." In giving voice to liberal and many moderate Protestants, Wall explained, "a President makes only 'political' decisions based upon what he feels is in the public interest. Those political decisions, however, are informed by the character of the man who makes them, and that character is shaped by a moral commitment or by its absence." Since news of the initial break-in became public, and really from the beginning of his presidency, liberal Protestants had questioned the morality of Richard Nixon and found it wanting. Watergate confirmed the point they made about Nixon from the outset, that his demeanor and policies were ruinous for the United States. Wall, perhaps hoping to maintain mainline Protestant authority over America even as it slipped away, wanted Christians to analyze the character of politicians, despite it being "a dangerous road," because "it is a road we must travel if we are to emerge from a politics of piety that has used religion to cover up rather than reveal the nature of the men—and, hopefully soon, the women, we consider for the White House." Our recent American political scene indicates Wall's hope went unfulfilled, but not without liberal Christians attempting to bring its theology centered on social justice and doing right for the greater good into the public sphere. Throughout Watergate, they added their voice to the opposition, and with the church's moral authority sought to heal the United States and save democracy. They have continued that activity into the present, despite a waning influence as mainline Protestantism lost adherents, and now stand as a regular constituent within liberal politics.[16]

The United States faced a constitutional crisis during the Nixon administration. Lies, deceit, underhanded tactics, and winning at any cost pervaded the White House, ultimately leading to Watergate and the serious threat to democracy. Most histories, rightfully so, applaud three primary elements that saved the country: the judicial branch, Congress, and the media. But a fourth element proves just as important. The American people needed to back these investigations and to believe in them. Without popular support, these entities may have succumbed to Nixon or failed to pursue their agendas. Christian America contributed to public trust, a fourth institution of national strength. American democracy aided it in carrying on the Protestant heritage of working to add their vision of a godly society to the situation. Whether liberal, moderate, or conservative, the church led a crucial conversation about morality and ethics during these dark days of the 1970s. Protestant leaders, periodicals, and laypeople jointly crafted a theology that addressed the crisis in America politics and, though their impact is impossible to measure precisely, influenced many to back the other three key components that exposed Watergate. They struggled to reconcile their desire for strong Christian ethics to guide the nation when people within the government failed on this point. Indeed, evidence suggested not only did these entities lead, but they gave voice to a section of American society that otherwise was quiet. That these lay sources paralleled the ideas of Christian leaders demonstrates an agreement with their points of view, and that Protestants wanted to address constructively the Watergate crisis. They all had embraced the notion religious institutions had to move into politics to protect society's ethical integrity.

Moreover, Watergate launched a new era of Christian involvement in American politics. The necessity of commenting on a moral and ethical political crisis led Christians to a renewed comfort in partisan political activity, one that had been subdued for much of the twentieth century. Literature on the rise of the Religious Right has already revealed its buildup from the 1960s, through the 1970s, and its blasting onto the political stage during Ronald Reagan's administration. But the slow burn toward that moment included Watergate surging it forward, helping to explain further why evangelical Americans and other conservative Christians became a monumental political force from the 1980s to the present. Liberal Christians countered as best as possible, given their declining numbers and subsequent loss of influence. Having determined they had to insert themselves in political issues such as the civil rights movement and the Vietnam War, Watergate kept them firmly planted in politics as they sought to contribute to solving the national problem. And as the right stayed in politics afterward, mainline and liberal Christians held steady to counter their influence.

In both cases, Nixon as a polarizing politician led Christians to either condemn or support him throughout Watergate, another shift in that their political commentary became more comfortable with specifying favored and disliked candidates, political parties, and movements. This factor, too, continued after Watergate. Studies of American religion since the 1980s are rife with the ways Christians became political constituents, players, and factions, to the point their political activity has become the norm. For example, the Religious Right became a staple of Republican Party politics, a key faction virtually all Republicans placate to this day. Almost every candidate for office now declares their religious affiliation quite publicly, where once it was considered a more private affair. Bill Clinton used religion to assist his political career after revelations of an affair in office by enlisting Billy Graham and others as pastoral mentors to guide him toward a more righteous path. Politicians must sometimes even respond to remarks from their church's leaders, as Barack Obama famously did regarding Jeremiah Wright, as if the pastor spoke on behalf of the candidate and not himself or God. No constituency more faithfully supported Donald J. Trump, no matter what he did or said, than evangelical Christians because of his support for their political aims. In today's political landscape, Christianity and politics blur together in one of the nation's most intensified eras of religion and politics commingling. Once again, Protestants lined up to denounce or applaud a president mired in unethical and immoral activities. Watergate led to this resurgent Christian political action in a significant way.

As we have seen, while American Protestant institutions were not unified in their approach to the Watergate controversy, many were impelled by the event to become more politically active, seeking to save the nation from its moral crisis. Their focus on morality and ethics helped to undergird the nation's democratic institutions. Now as then, religious Americans belong in this struggle. In our current era, religious institutions can again support elements of American democracy and protect the Constitution. While diversity of theologies and politics will always make it impossible for Christians to unite fully, let alone be harmoniously joined by other faiths, religious communities are well positioned to address politics in turbulent times. They must advocate for the moral and ethical leadership that will protect democracy. But this requires, within the Christian comfort of mixing religion and politics, they put morality first and politics a distant second.

ACKNOWLEDGMENTS

Now in my third go-round at it, I still find writing the acknowledgments page the most daunting task of writing a book. Not because I find it tedious or unimportant, but because the opposite holds true. So many people, groups, and institutions contributed to bringing this study to fruition over the last fifteen years, I will inevitably forget someone or underreport the value they added to my work. The mistakes are mine alone, but this book's success owes a debt to a multitude of others.

Archivists in particular humble me at every turn. In every archive I visited, I found friendly faces and people willing to go above and beyond the norm to assist my search for information. They dug into materials, opened new boxes for me, and made my time among them a pleasure. The following archives assisted this book and provided open access to all materials: the African Methodist Episcopal Church Department of Research and Scholarship, the Billy Graham Center Archives, the Concordia Historical Institute, the Evangelical Lutheran Church in America Archives, the Gerald R. Ford Presidential Library, the Richard M. Nixon Presidential Library, the National Archives and Records Administration in Washington, DC, the Southern Baptist Historical Library and Archives, the Southern Illinois University Archives, and the United Church of Christ Archives.

Travel grants from the Southern Baptist Historical Library and Archives and the Gerald R. Ford Presidential Library and Archives assisted tremendously in making this book possible. Even more consequential, Concordia University Chicago awarded a series of summer travel grants and a sabbatical that facilitated my research. Quite literally, without CUC's financial assistance, *Evil Deeds in High Places* would not exist. As the university continues to strive for its talented professors to contribute research to our fields, monetary assistance remains essential.

Several people added in meaningful ways to this book. Concordia University Chicago's Department of History, Philosophy, and Political Science provides a great home for any scholar. David Bates, Robert Hayes, William Pierros, and Kurt Stadtwald are wonderful and supportive colleagues. I rely on our department meetings to get me through the semester. Indeed, my colleagues at the university overall uplift my research in many ways: by attending the research symposia at which I present, chatting in the halls, and making CUC such a kind and caring place to work. The following individuals contributed to my research more than others, for which I thank you: Jill Gill, John Hink, Michelle Morkert, Jule Nyhuis, Jon Pahl, and Elisabeth Unruh. Even more, Kurt Stadtwald and Jenny Smith edited this book with care, precision, and tremendous insight. Kurt Stadtwald, more than a mere department chair and colleague, marked it up from top to bottom and somehow made me laugh while editing all of his suggestions into it. His work went above and beyond the call of duty and made this a much better study. Jenny Smith, too, had me laughing with her comments as she improved what I had originally written.

Coming back to New York University Press was comfortable and wonderful. The entire staff supported me and helped to make this the best book possible. Outside readers assisted greatly, especially with sharpening my thesis and pulling out of me the meaning of what I investigated. My editor, Jennifer Hammer, is the most understanding and forgiving person in the business. I cannot write enough about how much I appreciate working with her, and the way she crafted this into a much better book than I at first submitted.

My students inspire me. Working with history majors, minors, and those interested in my discipline reminds me why I love teaching them so much. Directing the CUC Honors Program brings me into contact with passionate, scholarly, and magnificent people every day. Your passion and enthusiasm push me to do better, to model in some way the compassionate and brilliant professionals I see in all your futures.

My friends, family, and dogs too are a big part of my research. I love every minute I spend with you. I love how you support me, nurture me, and love me. Thank you.

I dedicate this book to the loving memory of my father, Allen D. Settje. He noticed my passion for history clear back in grade school, where together we explored more history than a young mind could hope to see in a lifetime. His patience and guidance inspired me. He further championed my love for history by financially supporting me through my undergraduate career and well into my graduate studies. He always wanted to hear about my latest projects and about what I was reading at the moment. No one was prouder of my successes, without ever seeming to take credit for how much he made them happen for me. I cannot imagine more love and support from a father. I miss him terribly but find some comfort in knowing he lives in these pages. I love you, Dad.

NOTES

INTRODUCTION

1 The historiography regarding Watergate suggests the need for a study of more average American reactions. Historian Andreas Killen's *1973 Nervous Breakdown* characterizes the importance of the 1970s as an overlooked decade that incubated much of the world in which we live today. It nurtured and led to the rise of neoconservatism and culminated in the unraveling of American mythologies of greatness, largely because of the Vietnam War and Watergate. For Killen, Watergate raised suspicions about malevolent government so profound they continue today. Many Americans went from trusting their government during much of the Cold War to cynically suspecting it of undermining their values to protect those in power. Killen frames Watergate as the worst example of institutional failure from that year. Intensified Protestant political behavior because of Watergate provides a window into how Americans assessed Killen's "nightmare" moment.

Killen's call coincides with other scholars who argue for better analysis of religion and American politics, such as historians Mark A. Noll and Luke E. Harlow. In *Religion and American Politics*, they detail the need to recognize "the enduring importance of religion in American political life and the necessity of understanding that significance with sophistication." The constitutional separation of church and state has never divorced individuals or even institutions from engaging in politics based on faith. Watergate forced even the most reluctant of the faithful to confront politics because it was a moral crisis, traditionally the church's realm of public influence. Noll and Harlow, *Religion and American Politics*, 4, 7.

A study from the 1980s that delves into the evangelical reaction to Watergate also indicates the need for this book. Political scientist Robert Booth Fowler's analysis of evangelical political thought from 1966 to 1976 argues that Watergate revealed both hope and a sense of failure among conservative thinkers. While the political system's moral failure dismayed them, the rhetoric about conversion and national healing offered hope. Primarily examining *Christianity Today*, Fowler found that evangelical Christians were reluctant to abandon Nixon until the release of the tapes exposed the vulgarity of the administration and subsequent evidence proved White House guilt. Then the evangelical magazine committed to a theological analysis that blamed situational ethics from which the nation needed to be saved. Fowler, *A New Engagement*.

There has been a dearth of scholarship on general American responses to Watergate, whether religious or secular in orientation. An older study started the conversation but stands relatively alone. Sociologist Michael Schudson's examination focused on how America contextualized Watergate in its aftermath. He notes it affected people's political affiliation and views of the government in the decade following Nixon's resignation, to the point that almost everything was then viewed through a Watergate lens. But its post-Watergate focus does not explain people's reactions at the moment, and its sociological nature freezes it in the 1990s. Schudson, *Watergate in American Memory*.

2 This study buttresses Robert Wuthnow's thesis regarding the shift in Christian America from strong denominational identities to more political affiliations. The United States was not secularizing even as traditional mainline churches lost influence. Rather, the merging of morality and politics altered their ways of being Christian by becoming more political. My thesis about Watergate demonstrates how that moment in American history intensified Wuthnow's argument. Wuthnow, *Restructuring of American Religion*.

3 Historiography has firmly established the 1960s and 1970s as a time of profound political instability and movement. A small sampling of examinations that parallel my argument in this regard includes Kruse, *White Flight*; Kruse and Zelizer, *Fault Lines*; and Lassiter, *Silent Majority*. The studies cited in note 1 also belong in this list.

4 The basic trajectory of religion and politics outlined in this paragraph and the remainder of the introduction comes from numerous sources, in terms of both survey work on American religion and specific studies of people, denominations, movements, and topics. See Allitt, *Religion in America since 1945*; Lambert, *Religion in American Politics*; Noll and Harlow, *Religion and American Politics*; Preston, Schulman, and Zelizer, *Faithful Republic*.

5 My commentary on a lull in religious activity and politics should not be read as the absence of religion in politics. Several studies have shown how Christianity exerted influence on US politics no matter the decade. Darren Dochuk reveals the influence of evangelical thinking on business and politics during the 1930s. Still, if one considers the broader narrative of some decades compared with others, and scrutinizes the public force of Christianity, it becomes clear how the impact was not consistent at all times. The studies of how religion did exert influence include Dochuk, *From Bible Belt to Sun Belt*; Dochuk, *Anointed with Oil*; Williams, *God's Own Party*; and Kruse, *One Nation under God*.

6 Some of the content in this introduction is drawn from the introduction in Settje, *Faith and War*, or Settje, *Lutherans and the Longest War*.

7 Of the numerous studies of Nixon's career and public image, the following stand out as especially useful: Greenberg, *Nixon's Shadow*; Perlstein, *Nixonland*; Reeves, *President Nixon*; and Small, *Presidency of Richard Nixon*.

8 Reliable guides to Watergate include Emery, *Watergate*; Olson, *Watergate*; Reeves, *President Nixon*; and Small, *Presidency of Richard Nixon*.

9 Lynerd, *Republican Theology*. The conservative apocalypse analysis stems from the excellent study by historian Matthew Avery Sutton, *American Apocalypse*.

10 For a good review of *Christianity Today's* history and efforts to influence the public, political, and diplomatic realm, see Hart, *That Old-Time Religion in Modern America*. Quentin J. Schultze's *Christianity and the Mass Media in America* also employed a comparison of *Christianity Today* and the *Christian Century* to gain a sense of religious effects on American society, in his case the interaction between the Christian press and the mass media. By using *Christianity Today*, the *Christian Century*, and a variety of denominational periodicals, this study coincides with such successful surveys of American attitudes by adding how the Christian press addressed Watergate. Marietta Chicorel, ed.. *Ulrich's International Periodicals Directory*, vol. 2, *Arts, Humanities, Business, and Social Sciences*, 12th ed. (New York: R. R. Bowker, 1968), 1045.

11 Hart, *That Old-Time Religion in Modern America*, 151.

12 Chicorel, *Ulrich's International Periodicals Directory*, 779. Historian David A. Hollinger articulated the perception of mainline Protestantism at this moment as liberalizers struggling to relate to a secularizing world but in the process becoming bridge builders for many Americans to new ideas, from an older, isolated individualism toward a more evolved Enlightenment that included the notion of other truths existing and therefore being taken seriously. Hollinger, *After Cloven Tongues of Fire*. Mark Hulsether's *Building a Protestant Left* provides an excellent model for using one periodical to represent liberal Protestantism, as this book does with the *Christian Century*.

13 For the history of the *Christian Century*, see Hutchison, *Between the Times*, and Coffman, *The Christian Century and the Rise of the Protestant Mainline*, 3. Coffman notes that, while the periodical often drove society forward in terms of its global outlook and acceptance of diversities, the "resolutely forward looking mainline leaders too seldom glanced over their shoulders to see if anyone was following them," which led to declining mainline numbers as those who felt isolated from their liberalizing church leaders left to find a more moderate Christian outlook.

14 The best and most recent summary of American Lutheranism is Granquist, *Lutherans in America*. For a complete guide to Lutheran church bodies in the United States, see Wiederaenders, *Historical Guide to Lutheran Church Bodies of North America*; Lagerquist, *The Lutherans*; Cimino, *Lutherans Today*.

15 W. Kent Gilbert's *Commitment to Unity* provides a solid overview of the LCA's activities during its existence from 1962 to 1988. See also Klein, *Politics and Policy*; Benson Y. Landis, ed., *Yearbook of American Churches: Information on All Faiths in the U.S.A.* (New York: National Council of Churches of Christ, 1965), 61; Constant H. Jacquet Jr., ed., *Yearbook of American Churches: Information on All Faiths in the U.S.A.* (New York: National Council of Churches of Christ, 1970), 50; Jacquet, ed., *Yearbook of American and Canadian Churches, 1974* (Nashville, TN: Abingdon Press, 1974), 234.

16 Jaquet, *Yearbook of American and Canadian Churches, 1974*, 234. The best history of the LCMS is Mary Todd's *Authority Vested*. For other overviews of the Lutheran Church—Missouri Synod during this period, see Suelflow, *Heritage in Motion*; Graebner, *Uncertain Saints*; Pankow and Pankow, *75 Years of Blessings*.

17 *Statistical Abstract of the United States 90th Annual Edition* (Washington, DC: US Department of Commerce, 1969), 41; this membership number is from 1967.

18 Fletcher, *Southern Baptist Convention*; Leonard, *Baptists in America*; Morgan, *New Crusades*; Porterfield, *Conceived in Doubt*.

19 *Statistical Abstract*, 1969: 42; for a reason not described in the *Statistical Abstract*, the reporting on denominational membership for the AME was for the year 1951 and was never updated throughout the years of this study, 1964–75.

20 Gregg, *History of the African Methodist Episcopal Church*; Lincoln and Mamiya, *Black Church in the African American Experience*; Pinn and Pinn, *Fortress Introduction to Black Church History*.

21 *Statistical Abstract*, 1969: 42; these figures were for the year 1967.

22 Gunnemann, *Shaping of the United Church of Christ*; Gunnemann, *United and Uniting*.

23 Foley, *Dear Dr. Spock*. I combed through the periodicals page by page, examining every reference to politics in general, to the president individually, and to Watergate or corruption as a topic. I saw all editorials, guest columns, featured articles, book reviews, and letters to the editor for each issue. All of the periodicals included in this study commented frequently on these matters; I chose a representative sampling from these editorials and articles to quote and cite because they encapsulated the vast amount of commentary for each journal. This approach offered a solid overview of the publication and its general approach to Watergate. I also researched in archives for unpublished letters to the editor when available, as well as editorial correspondence and private memos to gain a broader perspective about the journals. Again, the letters I cite herein are a representative sampling unless I indicate otherwise. Similarly, I spent weeks in the denominational archives for the AME, LCA, LCMS, SBC, and UCC. I uncovered as much material as they had preserved to include in this study. From private letters from laypeople to denomination leaders, to churchwide resolutions, I gathered as much information as possible to gain a holistic view of that particular denomination's views on the moral climate in Washington, DC, and the nation in general. When I quote someone, whether denominationally or from a periodical, either that person/entity was a good representative of something that I saw in multiple locations or I note in the text that it was from a unique voice. For example, I used lay letters to the editor that voiced an opinion heard from several lay sources, while I allowed a denominational leader to speak on her or his own, knowing that readers would recognize the particular nature of that opinion. Researching American Protestantism can be a haphazard enterprise, but I strove to overcome this challenge with a breadth of material to give as complete a sense as possible of each of the entities I examined.

1. A PRESIDENTIAL ELECTION AND THIRD-RATE BURGLARY

1 Thomas Bentz, "The Election of a President: An Interview with Two Friends Fighting in Good Christian Fellowship," *A.D.* 1 (November 1972): 70–72; Robert W. Hirsch and Cecil D. Andrus, "Your Choice in '72: Two Lutherans Speak," *Lutheran Witness* (hereafter *LW*) 91 (October 15, 1972): 18–19.

2 Lynerd, *Republican Theology*; Jack Hamm, "To Which We Owe Our Position," *California Southern Baptist* (hereafter *CSB*) 31 (June 29, 1972): 4; Cyril E. Bryant, Press Release, 1971 (?), Southern Baptist Historical Library and Archives (hereafter SBHLA), Fred B. Rhodes Papers, Box 2, "Folder 49"; Richard M. Nixon, typed book inscription copy, 1970s, SBHLA, Fred B. Rhodes Papers, Box 2, "File 49."

3 Hudson Baggett, "No Endorsement Intended," *Alabama Baptist* (hereafter *AB*) 137 (August 3, 1972): 2; Hudson Baggett, "On Choosing a President," *AB* 137 (July 13, 1972): 2; Hudson Baggett, "Politics and Principles," *AB* 137 (October 26, 1972): 2.

4 Donald T. McGregor, "Freedom to Vote," *CSB* 31 (November 2, 1972): 3; Donald T. McGregor, "We Are Free," *CSB* 31 (July 6, 1972): 4; J. Everett Sneed, "How Can Christians Influence Government?," *Arkansas Baptist Newsmagazine* (hereafter *ABN*) 71 (October 5, 1972): 3; L. H. Moore, "Voting Is a Must," *Ohio Baptist Messenger* (hereafter *OBM*) 20 (September 28, 1972): 4.

5 Foy Valentine, "Patriotism and Piety," *Home Missions* (hereafter *HM*) 43 (July 1972): 3–7; Don Murdock, "July Fireworks," *HM* 43 (September 1972): 47; James E. Wood Jr., "The Commitment and Witness of Baptists in Public Affairs," *Report from the Capital* (hereafter *RC*) 27 (October 1972): 2, 7; Phil Strickland, "Political Involvement: Try It, You'll Like It," Baptist Press Release (hereafter BPR), September 27, 1972, SBHLA.

6 Southern Baptist Convention (hereafter SBC), "Resolution on the Bill of Rights," SBC Resolutions, June 1972, www.SBC.net; SBC, "Resolution on Religious Liberty and No Establishment of Religion," SBC Resolutions, June 1972; SBC, "Resolution on Christian Citizenship," SBC Resolutions, June 1972, www.SBC.net.

7 Reverend R. Gary Heikkila to Harold Lindsell, 1972, Billy Graham Center Archives (hereafter BGCA), Collection 8, Records of *Christianity Today* (hereafter *CT*) International, Box 19, Folder 19; Harold Lindsell to Mark O. Hatfield, February 12, 1969, BGCA, Collection 8, Records of *CT* International, Box 17, Folder 65.

8 B. J. Nolen, "Spiritual Vitality, Religion, and Politics Highlight the First Six Months of 1972," *Christian Recorder* (hereafter *CR*) 123 (August 1, 1972): 5, 8. Barbara Dianne Savage has delineated the conflicted path within African American Christianity about its role in political discourse, with some denominations moving faster and more readily than others. Savage, *Your Spirit Walks beside Us*; "A.M.E.'s Announce National Voter Registration Drive," *CR* 123 (September 26, 1972): 1, 7.

9 Robert E. Van Deusen, ed., "The New Politics," *Focus on Public Affairs* (hereafter *FPA*) 6 (August 1, 1972): 1–2.

10 Albert P. Stauderman to Charles T. Carson, October 13, 1972, Evangelical Lutheran Church in America Archives (hereafter ELCA), Albert P. Stauderman Papers (hereafter ASP), Box B88, "C-D 1972"; Albert P. Stauderman, "Editor's Opinion," *Lutheran* 10 (August 16, 1972): 50; "Calendar of Intercessory Prayer," *Lutheran Women* (hereafter *LWomen*) 10 (October 1972): 31.

11 Frank D. Starr, "Faith and Public Life," *LW* 91 (July 2, 1972): 5–7 (emphasis in original; deletions in original); J. A. O. Preus, "Brother to Brother: From the Desk of the President," October 26, 1972, Concordia Historical Institute (hereafter CHI), Preus Administration, "*Brother to Brother: LCMS. Office of the President. Preus*"; "A Summary of Speaking to the Issues: Reports of 1971 Regional Conferences," Minute and Reports, Board of Parish Education, 1972, CHI, Bound Volumes.

12 Huber F. Klemme, "The Next Four Years," *Social Action* (hereafter *SA*) 39 (September 1972): 3–5.

13 Among the best studies about the movement of conservative religion into the Republican Party after World War II are Burkee, *Power, Politics, and the Missouri Synod*; Dochuk, *From Bible Belt to Sun Belt*; Miller, *Billy Graham and the Rise of the Republican South*; Schulman and Zelizer, *Rightward Bound*; and Smith, *Rise of Baptist Republicanism*.

14 "Louisiana Baptist Pastors Overwhelmingly Support Nixon," BPR, October 30, 1972, SBHLA; "National Baptist President Supports Nixon," BPR, *Western Recorder* (hereafter *WR*) 146 (September 23, 1972): 19; Harold Lindsell, "Editor's Note," *CT* 17 (October 27, 1972): 3.

15 Settje, *Faith and War*; David E. Kucharsky, "The Unlikely Summit," *CT* 16 (June 9, 1972): 29; Paul F. Swartz, "Moderate Stand on Peace Taken at Ohio Convention," *Lutheran* 10 (August 2, 1972): 40; Albert P. Stauderman to Howard L. Logan, April 10, 1972, ELCA, ASP, Box B89, "L 1972."

16 Harold Lindsell to Richard M. Nixon, March 30, 1972, BGCA, Collection 8, Records of *CT* International, Box 20, Folder 16; Harold Lindsell to Dr. Henry Kissinger, March 30, 1972, BGCA, Collection 8, Records of *CT* International, Box 19, Folder 25.

17 Thomas J. Houser, "The Case for Nixon," *Christian Century* (hereafter *CC*) 89 (November 1, 1972): 1092–96 (emphasis in original).

18 Robert E. Van Deusen, "Busing: A Hot Issue Gets Hotter," *Lutheran* 10 (June 7, 1972): 20; Martin L. Nissly to the *Lutheran*, September 5, 1972, ELCA, ASP, Box B90, "N-O 1972." For thorough treatments of Nixon's record on civil rights, see Kotlowski, *Nixon's Civil Rights*; and Reeves, *President Nixon*.

19 Settje, *Faith and War*; Gill, *Embattled Ecumenism*; and Hall, *Because of Their Faith*.

20 Alan Geyer, "Nixon Confounds the Gloomy Prophets," *CC* 89 (June 14, 1972): 680–81; Roger L. Shinn, "Our Cause Is Not Just," *CC* 89 (November 1, 1972): 1099–103 (emphasis in original); United Church of Christ Press Release, June 2, 1972, United Church of Christ Archives (hereafter UCC), Office of Communication, Box 4, "July 1969–1975"; "Minutes of the Council of Instrumentality Executives,"

UCC Center for Social Action, May 10, 1972, UCC, Center for Social Action, Box 2002.20.10, No File Label.

21 Virginia Toth to Albert P. Stauderman, June 10, 1972, ELCA, ASP, Box B90, "T-U-V 1972"; James Armstrong, "The Case for McGovern," *CC* 89 (November 1, 1972): 1096–98.

22 Martin E. Marty, "The Ennui in Miami," *CC* 89 (September 6, 1972): 883; Martin E. Marty, "M.E.M.O: Amicable Bombing," *CC* 89 (October 11, 1972): 1027 (emphasis in original).

23 "Black Baptist Organization Condemns Nixon," BPR, *WR* 146 (September 23, 1972): 19; W. F. McIntosh Jr., "Black Methodists Endorse McGovern," *CR* 123 (August 29, 1972): 1, 3; "A.M.E. Bishop Comments on Protest Barring Edward Nixon Speaking," *CR* 123 (August 22, 1972): 3. The documents do not indicate which brother attempted to attend.

24 James Armstrong, "The Case for McGovern," *CC* 89 (November 1, 1972): 1096–98; artist unknown, editorial cartoon, *CC* 90 (September 26, 1972): 940.

25 Mike Gravel, "The Secrecy System," *SA* 38 (May 1972): 13–20; Huber F. Klemme, "The People's Right to Know," *SA* 38 (May 1972): 3–4 (emphasis in original).

26 Claude W. Ash to the Editor, June 29, 1972, ELCA, ASP, Box B88, "A—1972"; "Objective: 1600 Pennsylvania Avenue," *CT* (July 28, 1972): 24.

2. A FADING ISSUE OR SINISTER PLOT?

1 Peter J. Ediger, "Illusion," *CC* 89 (November 22, 1972): 1176; "The Watergate Wrangle," *CT* 17 (13 April 1973): 31.

2 Miller, *Billy Graham and the Rise of the Republican South*; Gibbs and Duffy, *The Preacher and the Presidents*.

3 "Make Bible 'Touchstones' of Life, Nixon Asks," *WR* 146 (November 18, 1972): 14; Richard M. Nixon to Mrs. F. O. Smith, January 9, 1973, National Archives and Records Administration (hereafter NARA), Richard M. Nixon Papers (hereafter RMNP), White House Central Files (hereafter WHCF)—Subject Files, Religious Matters, Box 3, "Religious Matters 1-1-73/7-31-74."

4 J. A. O. Preus to Mrs. Murray (Nancy) Chotiner, January 10, 1973, CHI, Executive Offices Records, 1904–1981, Box 52, "President: correspondence" (JAOP), 1973; Calvin W. Franz, "Eye-to-Eye Platform," *A.D.* 2 (January 1973): 68; William B. Bradshaw to James M. Wall, November 20, 1972, Southern Illinois University Archives (hereafter SIU), *Christian Century* Files (hereafter CCF), Box 171, Folder 3.

5 "Peace Must Begin in Men's Hearts, President Nixon Says," *Lutheran* 11 (March 7, 1973): 30; "LCMS President Preus Comments on Peace Agreement," January 24, 1973, News Release, LCMS Department of Public Relations, CHI; "Synod Leader Hails Peace," *LW* 92 (February 18, 1973): 20; SBC, "Resolution on Southeast Asia," SBC Resolutions, June 1973, www.SBC.net.

6 Charles W. Colson to Patrick J. Buchanan, July 10, 1973, BGCA, Collection 275, Papers of Charles Wendell Colson, Box 86, Folder 1; J. Frederick Rossell to Eugene

A. Brodeen (President of the New England Synod), June 23, 1973, ELCA, ASP, Box B92, "Q-R 1973."

7 SBC, "Annual of the Southern Baptist Convention," June 12–14, 1973, SBHLA: 85; Robert Sternloff, "Freeing the Press," *Lutheran* 11 (April 18, 1973): 49.

8 "A Morality That Did Not Communicate," *CC* 89 (November 15, 1972): 1143–44; J. Martin Bailey, "Comment," *A.D.* 2 (January 1973): 70–71.

9 Kotlowski, *Nixon's Civil Rights*; Settje, *Faith and War*.

10 United Church of Christ Press Release, January 16, 1973, UCC, Office of Communication, Box 4, "January 1973–February 1973"; "A.M.E. Bishops Protest Pres. Nixon's Actions," *CR* 122 (March 5, 1973): 1–2; "Bishop Hickman Honored; Hits Nixon Administration," *CR* (March 19, 1973): 1–2.

11 Swartz, *Moral Minority*; Ronald J. Sider to _____, November 14, 1972, BGCA, Collection 37, Evangelicals for Social Action (hereafter EvangSA), Box 1, Folder 4; Stephen Charles Mott to Dr. W. T. Miller, January 5, 1973, BGCA, Collection 37, EvangSA, Box 1, Folder 4.

12 G. S. Gordon to editors, February 5, 1973, SIU, CCF, Box 175, Folder 3; James M. Wall, "Politics and Morality: A Postelection Interview with George McGovern," *CC* 90 (January 31, 1973): 119–24; Erwin D. Canham, "What Are These Freedoms?," *A.D.* 2 (April 1973): 27–35; "Most Americans Oppose Amnesty," *Lutheran* 11 (4 April 1973): 26.

13 Huber Klemme, "Church Pronouncements Need Interpretation," *Engage/Social Action* (hereafter *ESA*) 1 (January 1973): 50–52; "NAACP 'Crisis' Comments on Watergate," *CR* 122 (July 2, 1973): 5.

14 UCC Office of Communication, "BHM Supports Universalists in Pentagon Papers Affair," *A.D.* 1 (December 1972): 80; Karl H. Hertz to Editor, April 26, 1973, ELCA, ASP, Box B91, "H 1973."

15 James M. Wall, "Watergate and Secrecy," *CC* 90 (April 18, 1973): 444; Franklin H. Littell, "Reflections on a Constitutional Crisis," *CC* 90 (May 30, 1973): 621–22; Reese Cleghorn, "Watergate: 'Just Politics'?," *CC* 90 (May 30, 1973): 620–21.

16 Hart, *That Old-Time Religion in Modern America*, 206; Finstuen, *Original Sin and Everyday Protestants*; Settje, *Faith and War*.

17 Letters to the editor, *LW* 91 (November 26, 1972): 27; Robert E. Karstendiek to the editor, June 4, 1973, ELCA, ASP, Box B92, "K—1973."

18 "Presidency Called Victim of 'Idolatrous Expectations,'" *Lutheran* 11 (June 20, 1973): 24; "Redeeming the System," *Capital Baptist* (hereafter *CB*) n.v. (May 24, 1973): 4; Gaines S. Dobbins, "The Christian in a Time of Crisis," *AB* n.v. (May 31, 1973): 9.

19 "Politics on the Ethical Periphery," *CT* 17 (November 24, 1972): 29.

20 Albert P. Stauderman, "Editor's Opinion," *Lutheran* 11 (June 6, 1973): 50.

21 James E. Wood Jr., "Lessons from Watergate," *RC* 28 (June 1973): 2, 8.

22 Catherine Allen and Orville Scott, "Democracy Is on Trial in USA Moyers Tells WMU Convention," BPR, June 12, 1973, SBHLA; "Former Press Secretary Bill Moyers Blasts 'Civil Religion,' Watergate," BPR, *WR* 147 (June 23, 1973): 17.

23 Harold Lindsell, Untitled Speech, n.d., BGCA, Collection 192, Papers of Harold Lindsell, Box 8, Folder 2; Owen Cooper, "Annual President's Address," June 12, 1973, SBHLA, Southern Baptist Press Kit Collection, "1973—Addresses."

24 "Calendar of Intercessory Prayer," *LWomen* 10 (November 1972): 31; Albert P. Stauderman to Norman Martinson, December 7, 1972, ELCA, ASP, Box B89, "M 1972"; Hudson Baggett, "Morality in Government," *AB* 138 (May 3, 1973): 2.

25 J. R. White, "Nathan: The Crisis of Moral Decay," *AB* 138 (June 28, 1973): 14; Theo Sommerkamp, "SBC Religious Educators Assess Watergate Affair," BPR, June 12, 1973, SBHLA; "'Watergate' Reflects What Churches Teach, Educators Told," *WR* 147 (June 23, 1973): 18.

26 Donald T. McGregor, "Principles of Politics," *CSB* 32 (May 10, 1973): 4; "Avoid Corruption in High Places, Heed Bible, Baptist Educators Told," BPR, June 11, 1973, SBHLA; Ralph H. Langley, "Do You Let Your Christianity and Politics Mix?," *Baptist Program* (hereafter *BP*) (June 1973): 10–11 (emphasis in original).

27 "The President Asks for Our Prayers," *CT* 17 (February 16, 1973): 35; L. H. Moore, "Independence Day, July 4, 1973," *OBM* 21 (June 28, 1973): 4.

28 Daniel R. Grant, "Can Any Good Come from Watergate?," *ABN* 72 (June 7, 1973): 2; J. A. O. Preus, "President's Address," Lutheran Church—Missouri Synod, Convention Minutes, July 6–13, 1973, CHI, 55–57.

29 James M. Dunn, "Watergate!," *WR* 147 (June 2, 1973): 3.

30 "Political Espionage," *CT* 17 (May 25, 1973): 33.

31 Foy Valentine, "The Moral Word in the Gospel," June 14, 1973, SBHLA, Southern Baptist Press Kit Collection, "1973—Addresses."

32 For good histories of liberal Christian theology in the twentieth century, see Coffman, *The Christian Century and the Rise of the Protestant Mainline*; Finstuen, *Original Sin and Everyday Protestants*; Gunnemann, *United and Uniting*; Hollinger, *After Cloven Tongues of Fire*; Hulsether, *Building a Protestant Left*; and Settje, *Faith and War*.

33 Dr. H. Eberhard von Waldow to Robert J. Marshall, January 9, 1973, ELCA, Robert J. Marshall Papers (hereafter RJMP), Box C-134, "LCA, Office of the President/Bishop, Dr. Robert J. Marshall, 1973–1976"; Edgar R. Trexler, "Editor's Opinion," *Lutheran* 11 (July 11, 1973): 50.

34 J. Martin Bailey to L. D. Layman, March 16, 1973, Presbyterian Historical Society (hereafter PHS), A.D. Records, J. Martin Bailey Papers, Box 2, Folder "La"; "Only in America," *A.D.* 2 (June 1973): 54; "Minutes of the Executive Council of the United Church of Christ," March 8–11, 1973, UCC, Executive Minutes, Box 1970–1973, "3/8–11/73, Set 1, Folder 1."

35 Reverend Doctor Gabriel Fackre, United Church of Christ Press Release, May 6, 1973, UCC, Office of Communication, Box 4, "May–July 1973."

36 Therion E. Cobbs, "Methodists Protest Watergate," *CR* 122 (June 25, 1973): 4; Herblock, political cartoon, *ESA* (January 1973): 23.

37 Robert Jewett, "Whispered in Private Rooms . . . Shouted from the Housetops: Reflections on Watergate in Light of Luke 12:2–3," *CC* 90 (June 6, 1973): 648–50.

38 Martin E. Marty, "Watergate and the Godfather-Ethic," *CC* 90 (May 16, 1973): 583; E. Paul Weaver to Editors, May 14, 1973, SIU, CCF, Box 181, Folder 2.

39 "Nixon Heads Watergate Prosecution," *Washington Report* (hereafter *WashRep*) 3 (May 3, 1973): 2; Allan R. Brockway, "The Necessary Corollary of Naming the Evil," *ESA* 1 (July 1973): 2–4.

40 "Moss Speaks Out on Watergate Issue," *A.D.* 2 (July 1973): 45; Robert V. Moss, Statement at the Christian Theological Seminary in Indianapolis, IN, May 23, 1973, UCC, Robert V. Moss Papers, UCC 90-3, Box 1, "Moss Speeches, Folder 4" (emphasis in original).

41 James M. Wall, "Early Warning on Watergate's Aftermath," *CC* 90 (May 23, 1973): 587–88.

42 Robert J. Marshall to All LCA Pastors, July 1, 1973, ELCA, LCA Office of the President, Box C-200, "Dear Partners, 1972–1974"; "Build on Truth, Editor Urges," *Interchange* 7 (July 1973): 1; Martha A. Kopra to Albert P. Stauderman, June 4, 1973, ELCA, ASP, B92, "K—1973."

43 "Issues Coming Up—Independent Elections Commission," *WashRep* 3 (June 14, 1973): 3; Raymond A. Heine, "Michigan Takes Action on Amnesty, Watergate," *Lutheran* 11 (June 20, 1973): 33.

44 Robert H. Heinze (*A.D.* publisher), "An Award Given," *A.D.* 2 (June 1973): 35. In July 1973, they gave the first award to Peter Bridge for an article he wrote for the *Newark Evening News* that led to a jail sentence, which he served, for refusing to divulge a source. Appeals of his case went all the way to the US Supreme Court, which declined to hear it. The article was about a possible bribe received by a Newark Housing Authority Commissioner.

45 Robert V. Moss, "A Message for the Pilgrims," Address to the Ninth General Synod, June 22, 1973, "Minutes of the Ninth General Synod," UCC, General Synod Collection: 98–101.

46 Mary Elizabeth Anderson, "Christians Must Bear Witness," *CR* 123 (July 16, 1973): 2–3, 5.

47 "Ninth General Synod, Advanced Materials, Section III," June 22–26, 1973, UCC, General Synod Collection: 51; "Ninth General Synod, Advanced Materials, Section III," June 22–26, 1973, UCC, General Synod Collection: 52; "Minutes of the Ninth General Synod," June 22–26, 1973, UCC, General Synod Collection: 48.

48 "Minutes of the Executive Council of the United Church of Christ," June 21, 1973, UCC, Executive Minutes, Box 1970–1973, "6/21/73."

49 "Minutes of the Executive Council of the United Church of Christ," June 21, 1973, Executive Minutes, Box 1970–1973, "6/21/73"; UCC, "Minutes of the Ninth General Synod," June 22–26, 1973, UCC, General Synod Collection: 47.

50 "Minutes of the Executive Council of the United Church of Christ," June 21, 1973, UCC Executive Minutes, Box 1970–1973, "6/21/73."

51 "Minutes of the Executive Council of the United Church of Christ," June 27–28, 1973, UCC, Executive Minutes, Box 1970–1973, "6/27–28/73, Set 1 and 2."

52 J. Martin Bailey, "Delegates Reject Watergate Statement," *A.D.* 2 (August 1973): 45.

53 Miriam Wallach to the Editor, June 1, 1973, ELCA, ASP, Box B93, "W-X-Y-Z 1973."

54 James M. Wall, "Pietism and the Climate for Corporate Sin," *CC* 90 (May 30, 1973): 619.

55 "An Ethics Student Rationalizes Watergate," *CC* 90 (July 4, 1973): 723–24.

56 Hudson Baggett, "Keeping Patriotism Alive," *AB* 138 (June 28, 1973): 2.

57 SBC, "Resolution on Integrity and Morality in the American Political System," SBC Resolutions, June 1973, www.SBC.net (emphasis in original).

58 Winn T. Barr, "Salt Needed!," *WR* 147 (June 2, 1973): 6; C. Welton Gaddy, "Celebrate Christian Citizenship!," May 11, 1973, SBHLA, Christian Life Commission (hereafter CLC), "Christian Citizenship, 1970–1973"; "Christian Citizenship Sunday 1973," Poster, June 1973, SBHLA, CLC.

59 Albert W. Galen, "Appeal to Peal," *LW* 92 (June 24, 1973): 4.

60 Robert E. Van Deusen, "Patriotism Today," *LW* 92 (June 24, 1973): 6–7; Robert E. Van Deusen, "Reflections on Watergate," *FPA* 7 (July 1, 1973): 1–2.

61 "Editorials," *A.D.* 2 (July 1973): 42.

62 James M. Wall, "On Seeing the Presidency as Sacred," *CC* 90 (May 16, 1973): 555–56.

63 William Henry Young to James M. Wall, May 15, 1973, SIU, CCF, Box 181, Folder 2; Immanuel Nielsen to James M. Wall, May 26, 1973, SIU, CCF, Box 181, Folder 2.

3. A FAVORABLE PRESIDENT OR MOST DANGEROUS MAN?

1 "The Sowing of Watergate," *CC* 90 (August 1, 1973): 774–75; Brooks Hays, "The Moral Implications of the Watergate Affair," BPR, August 12, 1973, SBHLA.

2 Aitken, *Charles W. Colson*; Colson, *Born Again*; Dean, *Nixon Defense*; Emery, *Watergate*; and Small, *Presidency of Richard Nixon*.

3 Charles W. Colson to Neil Kvasnak, August 22, 1973, BGCA, Collection 275, Papers of Charles Wendell Colson (hereafter PCWC), Box 2, Folder 11; Charles W. Colson to Edward J. Gurney, September 20, 1973, BGCA, Collection 275, PCWC, Box 2, Folder 12; Charles W. Colson to Honorable Edward J. Gurney, September 20, 1973, BGCA, Collection 275, PCWC, Box 8, Folder 2; Charles W. Colson to John E. Elliott, August 2, 1973, BGCA, Collection 275, PCWC, Box 2, Folder 11; Charles W. Colson to Richard Nixon, October 26, 1973, BGCA, Collection 275, PCWC, Box 2, Folder 13. See also Friedman and Levantrosser, *Watergate and Afterward*, 87.

4 Floyd M. Stephens, "Letters and Opinions," *AB* 138 (August 2, 1973): 3.

5 "The Case of Spiro T. Agnew," *CT* 18 (October 26, 1973): 47.

6 Hilda Schoenig to the Editor, July 26, 1973, ELCA, ASP, Box B92, "Sa-Si 1973"; Nels V. Bonn to Edgar Trexler, July 16, 1973, ELCA, ASP, Box B91, "B 1973" (emphasis in original); Berte Jens, "Keep Away from Watergate," *Lutheran* 11 (August 8, 1973): 49.

7 James C. Dickert to the Editor, July 13, 1973, ELCA, ASP, Box B91, "C-D 1973"; Louis L. Mast to Gentlemen, July 14, 1973, ELCA, ASP, Box B92, "M—1973"; J. Hebert to Editor, July 20, 1973, ELCA, ASP, Box B91, "H 1973"; William Kopf to

Albert P. Stauderman, September 22, 1973, ELCA, ASP, Box B92, "K—1973" (emphasis in original).

8 William Kopf to the Editor, August 7, 1973, ELCA, ASP, Box B92, "K—1973" (emphasis in original); James C. Dickert, "Keep Away from Watergate," *Lutheran* 11 (August 8, 1973): 49; John P. Banta, "Keep Away from Watergate," *Lutheran* 11 (August 8, 1973): 49.

9 Lee D. Rustin, "Readers React to 'The Necessary Corollary of Naming the Evil,'" *ESA* 1 (September 1973): 60–61; Kelly Janes, "Readers React to 'The Necessary Corollary of Naming the Evil,'" *ESA* 1 (September 1973): 61; Ernest D. Smith to J. Martin Bailey, September 12, 1973, PHS, A.D. Records, J. Martin Bailey Papers, Box 4, Folder "Sm" (emphasis in original).

10 Ralph P. Ley to J. Martin Bailey, July 25, 1973, PHS, A.D. Records, J. Martin Bailey Papers, Box 2, Folder "Le"; J. W. Steinman to J. Martin Bailey, August 6, 1973, PHS, A.D. Records, J. Martin Bailey Papers, Box 4, Folder "St" (emphasis in original); J. W. Steinman, "Hierarchical Naiveté," *A.D.* 2 (October 1973): 64 (emphasis in original).

11 Victor P. Croftchik to J. Martin Bailey, September 1973, PHS, A.D. Records, J. Martin Bailey Papers, Box 1, Folder "C"; J. Martin Bailey to Victor P. Croftchik, October 2, 1973, PHS, A.D. Records, J. Martin Bailey Papers, Box 1, Folder "C."

12 Floyd A. Craig, "Telling All the Story Is the Best Practice," *WR* 147 (July 21, 1973): 4; William L. Bennett, "It Happened at the Watergate," *ABN* 72 (August 9, 1973): 8–9; Max E. Shirk, "Watergate," *CSB* 32 (September 6, 1973): 2.

13 Charles W. Colson to Gerald R. Ford, October 11, 1973, BGCA, Collection 275, PCWC, Box 2, Folder 13; Walden Howard to Ronald J. Sider, August 24, 1973, BGCA, Collection 37, EvangSA, Box 1, Folder 12; "Watergate and Religion," *CT* 17 (August 31, 1973): 27–28.

14 "Watergate and Religion," *CT* 17 (August 31, 1973): 27–28; Harold Kuhn, "Personal Pietism and Watergate," *CT* 17 (September 28, 1973): 61–62.

15 Baptist Joint Committee on Public Affairs, "A Statement of Concern," *RC* 28 (October and November 1973): 1.

16 "Baptists Call for Return to Morality in Public Life," BPR, October 5, 1973, SB-HLA; "Baptists Assert All Government Officials Bound to Obey Law," BPR, *WR* 147 (October 27, 1973): 2.

17 Engleman, editorial cartoon, *CC* 90 (August 15–22, 1973): 80.

18 William F. Moore, "Salvation for Richard Nixon," *A.D.* 2 (September 1973): 47; "Nixon Integrity Now Doubted," *WashRep* 3 (September 6, 1973): 1.

19 Marlette, cover art, *CC* 90 (September 26, 1973): Cover; James M. Wall, "Needed: Leadership, Not Deception," *CC* 90 (September 12, 1973): 875–76; Lowell A. Anderson to James M. Wall, September 5, 1973, SIU, CCF, Box 186, Folder 3.

20 Tran Van Dinh, "'A People That No Longer Trusts Its Rulers,'" *CC* 90 (October 17, 1973): 1021; Mary Turnbull, "Weeds and Watergate," *A.D.* 2 (September 1973): 24. For histories that delineate White House arrogance and a feeling of being above

the law, see Dean, *Nixon Defense*; Emery, *Watergate*; Reeves, *President Nixon*; Small, *Presidency of Richard Nixon*.

21 Albert Vorspan, "Toward a Coalition of Concern," *CC* 90 (29 August 1973): 827–28; Frederick L. Hofrichter to All Members of the House of Representatives, 10 September 1973, UCC, 2002.20.51, "Washington Report and Other Mailings, 1973."

22 Allan R. Brockway, "How Many Facts Are Needed?" *ESA* 1 (September 1973): 2–3.

23 Dennis E. Shoemaker, "From Watergate to Witherspoon: A Special Report Prepared Especially for *A.D.*," *A.D.* 2 (September 1973): 11–16.

24 Carolyn Keefe, "Watergate Funhouse," *CC* 90 (July 18, 1973): 755; "Litany for Unity," *A.D.* 2 (August 1973): 3; "Editor Labels 1973 'Year of Retrenchment,'" *Interchange* 7 (October 1973): 2.

25 UCC Press Release, August 17, 1973 (?), UCC, Office of Communication, Box 4, "August 1972–October 1972." For background on LaRue, see Emery, *Watergate*; Dean, *Nixon Defense*.

26 For a solid overview of Nixon's religious faith, including his background and affiliation as a Quaker, see Holmes, *Faiths of the Postwar Presidents*, 99–123. Milton Mayer, "Disownment: The Quakers and Their President," *CC* 90 (October 10, 1973): 1000–1003; Forrest Fitzhugh to Editors, October 19, 1973, SIU, CCF, Box 189, Folder 1; David P. Gaines to Editors, October 9, 1973, SIU, CCF, Box 187, Folder 5; Arnold P. Von der Porten to Editors, October 21, 1973, SIU, CCF, Box 150, Folder 7; T. Eugene Coffin, "Richard Nixon and the Quaker Fellowship," *CC* 91 (January 2–9, 1974): 5–6.

27 Albert P. Stauderman to Nels V. Vonn, July 23, 1973, ELCA, ASP, Box B91, "B 1973"; William E. Diehl to the Editor, August 18, 1973, ELCA, ASP, Box B91, "C-D 1973"; William E. Diehl, "Watergate Must Be Aired," *Lutheran* 11 (September 19, 1973): 33.

28 J. Martin Bailey to Ralph P. Ley, August 3, 1973, PHS, A.D. Records, J. Martin Bailey Papers, Box 2, Folder "Le"; J. Martin Bailey to J. W. Steinman, August 20, 1973, PHS, A.D. Records, J. Martin Bailey Papers, Box 4, Folder "St"; Ralph Douglas Hyslop, "Judgment on Watergate," *A.D.* 2 (October 1973): 64; Anna B. Robertson, "The Prophet's Voice," *A.D.* 2 (September 1973): 47.

29 Duane R. Miller, "Watergate and the Thought of Jacques Ellul," *CC* 90 (September 26, 1973): 943–46.

30 "Mourn Moral Breakdown," *A.D.* 2 (August 1973): 32–33.

31 "Minutes of the Administrative Committee Meeting," September 6–8, 1973, UCC, Administrative Committee Minutes, Box 1956–September 1973, "9/6–8/73, Folder 1."

32 Executive Council of the United Church of Christ, "Statement of Concern about Corruption in Government," UCC, 2002.20.51, "Washington Report and Other Mailings, 1973"; "Minutes of the Executive Council of the United Church of Christ," October 28–31, 1973, UCC, Executive Minutes, Box 1970–1973, "10/28–31/73, Set 1" (emphasis in original).

33 James M. Wall to Theologians, August 8, 1973, Special Collections Research Center—Morris Library—SIU, CCF, Box 185, Folder 3; Earl Brewer to James M. Wall, August 16, 1973, SIU, CCF, Box 185, Folder 3; Joseph Fletcher to James M. Wall, August 17, 1973, SIU, CCF, Box 185, Folder 3; James M. Wall to Theologians, September 6, 1973, SIU, CCF, Box 185, Folder 3.

34 "Watergate: Religious Issues and Answers: A National Symposium," *CC* 90 (September 26, 1973): 937–42. Quoted passages from this special issue of Christian Century are from the source cited in this note.

35 Settje, *Faith and War*, 153.

36 Chicago Annual Conference, African Methodist Episcopal Church (hereafter AME), 91st Session of the Annual Conference Minutes, September 18–21, 1973, AME Department of Research and Scholarship (hereafter AMEDRS), Nashville, TN; A. Lewis Williams, "The President Has Lost the Country," *CR* 123 (November 5, 1973): 4; Marvyn M. Dymally, "Telegram," *CR* 123 (July 16, 1973): 6.

37 Michigan Annual Conference, AME, 87th Session of the Annual Conference Minutes, August 28–31, 1973, AMEDRS, Nashville, TN; Illinois Annual Conference, AME, Annual Conference Minutes, September 23–28, 1973, AMEDRS, Nashville, TN.

38 E. P. Wallace, "America's Image 'Blighted,' Judge Jones," *CR* 123 (August 20, 1973): 2; B. J. Nolen, "Think on It," *CR* 123 (July 30, 1973): 4.

39 Indiana Annual Conference, AME, 135th Session of the Annual Conference Minutes, September 4–7, 1973, AMEDRS, Nashville, TN; Indiana Annual Conference, AME, 135th Session of the Annual Conference Minutes, September 4–7, 1973, AMEDRS, Nashville, TN.

40 William R. Wilkes, "The Scandal of 'Watergate,'" *CR* 123 (September 10, 1973): 5.

41 Gregg, *History of the African Methodist Episcopal Church*; Lincoln and Mamiya, *Black Church in the African American Experience*; Pinn, *Fortress Introduction to Black Church History*; Savage, *Your Spirit Walks beside Us*; Settje, *Faith and War*.

42 J. Elliott Corbett, "Closing the Watergate," *ESA* 1 (July 1973): 53–55; Karl K. Quimby to James M. Wall, September 29, 1973, SIU, CCF, Box 187, Folder 1; Michigan Annual Conference, AME, 87th Session of the Annual Conference Minutes, August 28–31, 1973, AMEDRS, Nashville, TN.

43 "What Good from Watergate?," *CT* 17 (August 10, 1973): 27; Arthur B. Rutledge, "Christian Citizenship," *HM* 44 (July–August 1973): 60.

44 "Christian Life Commission Confronts Social Issues," BPR, September 14, 1973, SBHLA; Cecil E. Sherman and Foy Valentine to Senators and Congressional Representatives, September 12, 1973, SBHLA, CLC, "Christian Citizenship, 1970–1973."

45 "Prayers of the Social Awakening: For Public Officers," *A.D.* 2 (September 1973): 9; "Pray for . . . Skepticism," *Interchange* 7 (October 1973): 4.

46 Philip C. Becker, "Watergate Must Be Aired," *Lutheran* 11 (September 19, 1973): 33; "Watergate Hearings Continue," *WashRep* 3 (September 27, 1973): 3.

47 "Minutes of the Administrative Committee Meeting," September 6–8, 1973, UCC, Administrative Committee Minutes, Box September 1973–1983, "9/6–8/73, Folder 2."

48 James M. Wall, "The Agnew Case and Christian Realism," *CC* 90 (October 24, 1973): 1043–44. A very good summary of Agnew's rightward swing and overall history is Justin P. Coffey, "Spiro T. Agnew: The Decline of Moderates and the Rise of the Republican Right," in Gifford and Williams, *Right Side of the Sixties*, 243–59.

49 Ralph L. Moellering, "Civil Religion, the Nixon Theology and the Watergate Scandal," *CC* 90 (September 26, 1973): 947–51.

4. THE CHURCH AS PROPHET VERSUS PRAYING FOR THOSE IN AUTHORITY

1 Robert Jewett, "The Law Is No Respecter of Persons," *CC* 90 (November 14, 1973): 1116.

2 J. Everett Sneed, "The Hour of Prayer," *ABN* 73 (January 17, 1974): 3.

3 John Collins, "Dealing with Nixon," *CC* 91 (January 16, 1974): 54 (emphasis in original); Larry E. Dixon, "Dealing with Nixon," *CC* 91 (January 16, 1974): 54; James M. Wall, "An Inflexible Leader Cannot Lead," *CC* 91 (February 13, 1974): 171–72.

4 Susan B. King, "No Substitute for Campaign Reform," *ESA* 2 (March 1974): 36–42; Huber F. Klemme, "The Price of Pettiness," *ESA* 2 (March 1974): 55–56.

5 David E. Kyvig offers by far the best summary of the impeachment history as it relates to Nixon and Watergate. Kyvig, *Age of Impeachment*, 141–77; quotation on 143.

6 "The Alternative to Impeachment," *CC* 90 (November 14, 1973): 1115–16; "Impeachment in the Global Village," *CC* 91 (17 April 1974): 411–12; John A. Cappon, "Impeachment Delay Opposed," *CC* 91 (17 April 1974): 436–37; W. F. Roberts, "Impeachment Delay Opposed," *CC* 91 (17 April 1974): 436.

7 James M. Wall, "The Assassination of the Presidency," *CC* 90 (November 21, 1973): 1139–40; "Political Euphemisms Debase and Deceive," *CC* 91 (January 23, 1974): 60–61.

8 Allan R. Brockway, "On Not Leaving It to the Courts," *ESA* 1 (December 1973): 2–3; "One Year Is Enough," *ESA* 2 (March 1974): 2–3.

9 "The President and the Law," *ESA* 1 (December 1973): 11; "UCC Agency Approves Impeachment Study," *A.D.* 3 (January 1974): 70.

10 Howard Schomer to Peter W. Rodino Jr., January 4, 1974, PHS, A.D. Records, J. Martin Bailey Papers, Box 4, Folder "Sch."

11 Kenneth A. Coates, "Reader Reaction Continues to July Editorial on 'The Necessary Corollary,'" *ESA* 1 (December 1973): 58 (emphasis in original); Dov Peretz Elkins, "A Neglected Consideration about Impeachment," *CC* 91 (March 13, 1974): 277–78.

12 Swartz, *Moral Minority*.

13 "The Office of the Presidency," Action Proposal, November 23, 1973, BGCA, Collection 37, EvangSA, Box 2, Folder 9; "Action Proposal," November 23, 1973, BGCA, Collection 37, ES, Box 1. Folder 8.

14 "Presidential Appointee Believes in Rule of Law," BPR, *WR* 147 (November 10, 1973): 3; "Moral Leadership Question Skirted by Vice President," BPR, *WR* 148 (January 19, 1974): 6; Anonymous, "On Prayer for Nixon," *ABN* 73 (February 14, 1974): 5. Regarding Foy Valentine's moderate stances, see Settje, *Faith and War*.

15 Fred L. Hofrichter and Tilford E. Dudley to A Few UCCers, 8 April 1974, UCC, 2002.20.51, "Washington Report and Other Mailings, 1973–1974"; Charles F. Gregg to J. Martin Bailey, May 17, 1974, PHS, A.D. Records, J. Martin Bailey Papers, Box 1, Folder "Gr." For information on the illegal use of funds by CREEP, see Emery, *Watergate*.

16 William Nelson, "Serving in 1974 between Despair and Hope," *A.D.* 3 (January 1974): 12–13; "Time for Action, Time for Hope," *A.D.* 3 (January 1974): 22–23.

17 J. Elliott Corbett, "A Question of Integrity," *ESA* 1 (December 1973): 46–48; "Washington Presence," *Keeping You Posted* 10 (April 1, 1974): 17.

18 J. Martin Bailey to Mrs. C. Robert Frye, January 11, 1974, PHS, A.D. Records, J. Martin Bailey Papers, Box 1, Folder "Fr."

19 Jim Scurlock, "Reader Reaction Continues to July Editorial on 'The Necessary Corollary,'" *ESA* 1 (December 1973): 57; Sydney J. Neal, "We Are Watergate," *A.D.* 3 (February 1974): 59.

20 Larold K. Schulz, "The Judgment upon Us," *ESA* 1 (December 1973): 6–10, 14; Schulz specifically cited 1 Kings 22; 2 Chronicles 18. For information on Archibald Cox, see Emery, *Watergate*; Small, *Presidency of Richard Nixon*.

21 James M. Wall, "Christian Hope in a Watergate World," *CC* 90 (December 12, 1973): 1219; Robert B. Padley, "Servant or Lord?," *CC* 90 (November 28, 1973): 1181.

22 "Govt. Integrity Packet Available," *WashRep* 4 (4 April 1974): 3; Larold K. Schulz, "The Judgment upon Us," *ESA* 1 (December 1973): 6–10, 14; Barbara W. McCall, "The Pilgrim Synod: Cause or Effect," *A.D.* 2 (December 1973): 65 (emphasis in original).

23 Carroll R. Chambliss, "An Acceptable State of Affairs," *A.M.E. Church Review* (hereafter *AMECR*) 106 (1974): 38–43.

24 ". . . Meets in Capital Torn by Watergate," *CR* 123 (January 21, 1974): 7; Thelma A. Wills, "Mrs. Wilkes Addresses Women of Ebenezer, Nashville," *CR* 123 (September 24, 1973): 1–2, 5.

25 "Special Resolution Committee Report, 87th Session of the Michigan Annual Conference," *CR* 123 (November 12, 1973): 3.

26 "Even the Bible Tells of Water Gate Confessions," *AMECR* 106 (January–March 1974): 24–25.

27 Opal Dargan, "Musings," *AMECR* 106 (October–December 1973): 55–56; E. William Judge, "'Watergate and the A.M.E. Church,'" *CR* 123 (January 7, 1974): 4–5.

28 "1973 Convention Concern," *First District Clarion* (hereafter *FDC*) 1 (December 15, 1973): 7. Even most histories of Watergate mention Wills only in passing, sometimes simply as a security guard without recording his name. Emery at least gives a more thorough account of his actions that night (*Watergate*, 132–34).

29 Lonnie C. Wormley, "'Social Action Report,'" *CR* 123 (January 14, 1974): 8.

30 Michael Thompson to Patrick Buchanan, November 21, 1973, NARA, RMNP, WHCF—Subject Files, Religious Matters, Box 3, "Religious Matters 1-1-73/7-31-74."

31 [Howard Dean?] to Terrence O'Donnell, December 10, 1973, NARA, RMNP, WHCF—Subject Files, Religious Matters, Box 3, "Religious Matters 1-1-73/7-31-74" (the research was initialed by "HCD," which the archivists guessed was Howard Dean); Terrence O'Donnell to Michael Thompson, December 12, 1973, NARA, RMNP, WHCF—Subject Files, Religious Matters, Box 3, "Religious Matters 1-1-73/7-31-74."

32 E. M. Cullen, "Prayer for Nixon," WR 148 (January 26, 1974): 15; Franklin Owen, "Leadership Fellowship," WR 148 (March 16, 1974): 6.

33 Dr. Herschel H. Hobbs, "The Problem of National Crisis," March 31, 1974, SBHLA.

34 John A. Huffman Jr., "Biblical Lessons from Watergate," CT 18 (March 15, 1974): 8–12. For Nixon's Key Biscayne purchases, see Small, Presidency of Richard Nixon, 225.

35 "The Appeal to Resign," CT 18 (November 23, 1973): 41.

36 R. W. Wicker, "Reader Reaction Continues to July Editorial on 'The Necessary Corollary,'" ESA 1 (December 1973): 57–58; Raymond T. Moreland Jr., "Reader Reaction Continues to July Editorial on 'The Necessary Corollary,'" ESA 1 (December 1973): 57; C. L. Leighton, "Reader Reaction Continues to July Editorial on 'The Necessary Corollary,'" ESA 1 (December 1973): 60–61.

37 Richard M. Nixon to Dr. and Mrs. Lavender, January 14, 1974, NARA, RMNP, WHCF—Subject Files, Religious Matters, Box 17, "Religious Service in the White House 1/1/73–5/74"; Richard M. Nixon to Mrs. Lee Souers, February 11, 1974, NARA, RMNP, WHCF—Subject Files, Religious Matters, Box 6, "Prayers-Prayer Periods 1-1-73."

38 Charles W. Colson to Hirsh Freed, March 18, 1974, BGCA, Collection 275, PCWC, Box 9, Folder 1; Charles W. Colson, Discussant comments in Friedman and Levantrosser, Watergate and Afterward, 87; Charles W. Colson to W. Clement Stone, 9 April 1974, BGCA, Collection 275, PCWC, Box 9, Folder 1. For secondary accounts of Colson, see Aitken, Charles W. Colson; Colson, Born Again; Dean, Nixon Defense; Emery, Watergate; Small, Presidency of Richard Nixon.

39 "The Message to the President," CT 18 (November 9, 1973): 40–41.

40 "Bicentennial Blues," LW 92 (November 18, 1973): 5. An excellent study of the Bicentennial that makes these points is Gordon, Spirit of 1976; see also Christopher Capozzola, "'It Makes You Want to Believe in the Country': Celebrating the Bicentennial in an Age of Limits," in Bailey and Farber, America in the Seventies, 29–49.

41 L. H. Moore, "Still Cause for Thanks!," OBM 21 (November 22, 1973): 4; Gould Wickey to Editors, November 7, 1973, SIU, CCF, Box 150, Folder 7; Elmer L. Gray, "After Watergate," CSB 33 (25 April 1974): 4.

42 "The Appeal to Resign," CT 18 (November 23, 1973): 41 (emphasis in original); Hudson Baggett, "The Challenge of a Crisis," AB 138 (November 1, 1973): 2.

43 Hudson Baggett, "Pray for Country," *AB* 139 (February 7, 1974): 2; "Ohio Baptists Urge Prayer, Not Criticism, for Leaders," BPR, November 12, 1973, SBHLA; L. H. Moore, "Day of Prayer," *OBM* 22 (January 17, 1974): 4.

44 "A Declaration of Evangelical Social Concern," November 25, 1973, Chicago, Illinois, BGCA, Collection 37, EvangSA, Box 1, Folder 9. For the history of this group, see the section titled "The President Reviled" in chapter 4.

45 Lillian Dresser to J. A. O. Preus, November 3, 1973, CHI, Executive Offices Records, 1904–1981, Box 71, "General Correspondence: DO."

46 "The Morality of Presidents," *CT* 18 (November 23, 1973): 41–42; L. H. Moore, "Prayer to Do Right," *OBM* 21 (December 13, 1973): 4.

47 "Baptists Urge Governmental Integrity," BPR, *WR* 147 (November 10, 1973): 16.

48 James E. Wood Jr. to Honorable Sam J. Ervin, October 15, 1973, *Congressional Record—Senate*, November 7, 1973, 36122; Baptist Joint Committee on Public Affairs, "A Statement of Concern," *RC* 28 (October and November 1973): 1.

49 "Colorado Baptists Speak on Morality, Elect President," BPR, November 16, 1973, SBHLA; Bob Terry, "Power of the People," *WR* 147 (November 3, 1973): 4–5; C. R. Daley Jr., "More Integrity Instead of More Rules," *WR* 148 (January 19, 1974): 4–5.

50 Dr. Herschel H. Hobbs, "A Meddlesome Prophet," Broadcast 6 January 1974, SBHLA, Baptist Hour Sermons, Box 3, "January–June 1974"; Dr. Herschel H. Hobbs, "A Word That Weighs a Ton," Broadcast 13 January 1974, SBHLA, Baptist Hour Sermons, Box 3, "January–June 1974"; Dr. Herschel H. Hobbs, "The Bell Tolls for You," Broadcast 27 January 1974, SBHLA, Baptist Hour Sermons, Box 3, "January–June 1974"; Dr. Herschel H. Hobbs, "The Problem of National Crisis," Broadcast 31 March 1974, SBHLA, Baptist Hour Sermons, Box 3, "January–June 1974." The quotations about Hobbs's sermons in this paragraph and the next two come from these same sources.

51 Charles W. Colson to Gail W. Ledwig, January 23, 1974, BGCA, Collection 275, PCWC, Box 3, Folder 1; Charles W. Colson to Wesley Powell, January 24, 1974, BGCA, Collection 275, PCWC, Box 3, Folder 3; Friedman and Levantrosser, *Watergate and Afterward*, 87.

52 Charles W. Colson to Reverend Wallace Henley, January 23, 1974, BGCA, Collection 275, PCWC, Box 3, Folder 1; Charles W. Colson to Major John Grinalds, January 24, 1974, BGCA, Collection 275, PCWC, Box 2, Folder 16; Charles W. Colson to Ms. Becky Reading, January 23, 1974, BGCA, Collection 275, PCWC, Box 3, Folder 3.

53 Charles W. Colson to Winston O. Weaver, March 7, 1974, BGCA, Collection 275, PCWC, Box 2, Folder 18; Charles W. Colson to Thomas L. Phillips, March 7, 1974, BGCA, Collection 275, PCWC, Box 9, Folder 1; Charles W. Colson to Emily Billings, March 22, 1974, BGCA, Collection 275, PCWC, Box 9, Folder 1; Charles W. Colson to John K. Andrews Jr., April 5, 1974, BGCA, Collection 275, PCWC, Box 2, Folder 19.

54 Edward E. Plowman, "Religion in Washington: An Act of God," *CT* 18 (January 4, 1974): 48–49; Edward E. Plowman to Charles W. Colson, December 26, 1973, BGCA, Collection 275, PCWC, Box 3, Folder 3.

55 Robert J. Marshall to Mr. Clarence A. Glotfelty, November 27, 1973, ELCA, RJMP, Box C-130, "Miscellaneous, 1973–78."

56 Albert P. Stauderman, "War, Politics and the Will of God," *Lutheran* 11 (November 7, 1973): 34; Albert P. Stauderman, "Anno Domini 1974," *Lutheran* 12 (January 2, 1974): 34.

57 "Minutes of the Division for Mission in North America: Report from the Department for Church and Society," Lutheran Church in America (hereafter LCA), January 24–25, 1974, ELCA, ACC 87-344, Box 2, "LCA/Management Committee—Minutes." I could not find evidence that this report ever went beyond this preliminary stage. Later minutes indicate that Gerhard Elston, director of Church and Society's Center for Ethics and Society, primarily authored it.

58 This article by Empie appeared in a variety of places, including LCUSA publications, the national inter-Lutheran agency that coordinated endeavors between Lutheran denominations on which they agreed, and the *Lutheran*: Paul C. Empie, "National Issues/Christian Responsibility," *FPA* 7 (November 1, 1973): 1–2; Paul C. Empie, "Needed: A New World Now," *Lutheran* 12 (January 23, 1974): 8–10.

59 Robert Marshall responded to them that he agreed entirely with their thoughts, but also that he and others had made statements, within the confines of their offices and the workings of the church. See below for Marshall's feelings about Watergate during this period. Church Council of Holy Communion Lutheran Church, Racine, WI, to Robert. J. Marshall, December 12, 1973, ELCA, RJMP, Box C-126, "File 1."

60 Paul Simon, "Church and Society—1973," *Lutheran Social Concern* (hereafter *LSC*) 13 (Winter 1973): 16–21 (emphasis in original). Simon, a Lutheran, formerly served in Illinois as a state legislator and lieutenant governor and at the time was running for a seat in the House of Representatives.

61 Robert E. Van Deusen, "Power and Watergate," *FPA* 7 (November 15, 1973): 1–2.

62 Robert J. Marshall to Gerald R. Ford, December 21, 1973, ELCA, RJMP, Box C-125, "File 1"; Robert J. Marshall, "How You Can Help Your Church," *Lutheran* 12 (January 2, 1974): 4–6.

5. THE BLEEP HEARD ROUND THE WORLD

1 James M. Wall, "After the Fall," *CC* 91 (August 21–28, 1974): 787–88; L. H. Moore, "A Time to Repent and Pray," *OBM* 22 (August 15, 1974): 4.

2 Martin E. Marty, "Bleep!," *CC* 91 (May 8, 1974): 519 (emphasis in original).

3 "Waiting for Godot in the Oval Office," *CC* 91 (May 15, 1974): 523–24; Douglas G. Ebert, "Public Financing Not the Answer," *ESA* 2 (June 1974): 60.

4 James M. Wall, "Reporters in a Lonely Search for Truth," *CC* 91 (June 12–19, 1974): 627–28. Though historians believe they exaggerated their role in bringing down

the Nixon White House, because Congress and the judicial branch also played key roles, Bernstein and Woodward told their story well in *All the President's Men*.

5 Tilford E. Dudley to Members of the House Judiciary Committee, May 1, 1974, UCC, 2002.20.51, "Washington Report and Other Mailings, 1973–1974"; J. Elliott Corbett, "Scenario to Impeach," *ESA* 2 (August 1974): 50–52; Marge Roberts, "Morality or Security," *CC* 91 (May 1, 1974): 484–85.

6 J. Martin Bailey, "Too Little and Too Much," *A.D.* 3 (September 1974): 48; J. Martin Bailey, "Comment," *A.D.* 3 (May 1974): 57. As outlined later in this chapter, of course, conservatives had a much different outlook. It should be noted here, however, that some of those conservatives came from within the United Church of Christ. In response to calling Nixon "repulsive," a letter to the editor blasted Bailey as "un-Christian" and chastised him for publishing such a harsh statement in a "Christian magazine." R. A. Bradberg continued that "it is a terrible thing to refer to anyone as repulsive, and you dwell only on his weaknesses, ignoring the great things that he did." R. A. Bradberg, "You Should Be Ashamed," *A.D.* 3 (November 1974): 11.

7 "Spragg Says Church Should Lead U.S. from 'Morass,'" *A.D.* 3 (July 1974): 55.

8 James M. Wall, "The Value System of a Faithless People," *CC* 91 (May 29, 1974): 579–80.

9 Robert E. Van Deusen, "1974: Year of National Crisis," *LW* 93 (July 7, 1974): 5.

10 J. Martin Bailey, "Demons and Scapegoats," *A.D.* 3 (August 1974): 64; Allan R. Brockway, "The Dying of a Myth," *ESA* 2 (August 1974): 2–4, 45.

11 Huber F. Klemme, "Unfamiliar Sounds," *ESA* 2 (August 1974): 53–54; Martin E. Marty, "M.E.M.O.," *CC* 91 (September 18, 1974): 863 (emphasis in original).

12 Robert E. Van Deusen, "Moral Crisis in Washington: What Can a Christian Do about It?," *Lutheran* 12 (June 19, 1974): 12–14; Walter M. Wick to Robert J. Marshall, June 12, 1974, ELCA, RJMP, Box C-129, "General Correspondence, 1972–78"; Carl T. Uehling, "How American Is American?," *Lutheran* 12 (May 1, 1974): 34.

13 Robert E. Van Deusen, "Moral Crisis in Washington: What Can a Christian Do about It?," *Lutheran* 12 (June 19, 1974): 12–14; Byron L. Schmid, "Editorially Speaking," *LSC* 14 (Spring 1974): 4–5 (emphasis in original).

14 Albert P. Stauderman, "The Qualities of Leadership," *Lutheran* 12 (June 19, 1974): 34; Edgar R. Trexler, "The Voice of the Church," *Lutheran* 12 (July 10, 1974): 34; Michael Novak, "The Way We Really Are," *Lutheran* 12 (5 June 5, 1974): 10–13.

15 Robert J. Marshall, "Report of the President," Minutes of the Seventh Biennial Convention of the LCA, July 3–10, 1974, ELCA: 26–37 (boldface in original); "Dr. Marshall Urges Moral Stamina to Endure Crisis Facing Nation," Religious News Service, August 8, 1974, ELCA, LCUSA 16/6/2, Box 12, "Government—White House, 1962–1979"; Robert J. Marshall to All LCA Pastors, June 5, 1974, ELCA, LCA Office of the President, Box C-200, "Dear Partners, 1972–1974."

16 "Report of the Committee on the Report of the President," LCA, "Minutes of the Seventh Biennial Convention of the LCA," July 3–10, 1974, ELCA: 746–48; LCA, "Minutes of the Seventh Biennial Convention of the LCA," July 3–10, 1974, ELCA:

297; LCA, "Minutes of the Seventh Biennial Convention of the LCA," July 3–10, 1974, ELCA: 724.

17 For the complete discussion about academic and minority Bicentennial commemorations, see Gordon, *Spirit of 1976*.

18 Sydney E. Ahlstrom, "Bicentennial Reflections" (address given at the LCA Convention, Baltimore, MD, July 3–10, 1974), copy at ELCA, LCA—DMNA, Department of Church and Society, Subject Files, Box 1, no file title.

19 Sydney E. Ahlstrom, "Some Thoughts on the Bicentennial," Consulting Committee on the Bicentenary, Division for Mission in North America, LCA, 1974, ELCA, LCA/DPS Aids in Mission, Box 2, "November 1974."

20 Edna S. Nielsen to the Editor, August 5, 1974, ELCA, ASP, Box B95, "N-O 1974"; Erling P. Redal, "Write Your Congressman?," *Lutheran* 12 (July 10, 1974): 33; Kenneth L. Nerenz, "Write Your Congressman?," *Lutheran* 12 (July 10, 1974): 33.

21 Wallace E. Fisher to Robert J. Marshall, April 18, 1974, ELCA, RJMP, Box C-124, "File 3."

22 Walter E. Fisher to All Pastors on the LCA Clerical Roll and the Lay Delegates to the Seventh Biennial Convention of the LCA, May 1, 1974, ELCA, RJMP, Box C-124, "File 3."

23 Kenneth L. Nerenz to Clergy and Lay Delegates to 1974 LCA Convention, May 15, 1974, ELCA, RJMP, Box C-124, "File 3."

24 J. W. "Jack" Berry to Robert J. Marshall, May 8, 1974, ELCA, RJMP, Box C-124, "File 3"; LCA, "Minutes of the Seventh Biennial Convention of the LCA," July 3–10, 1974, ELCA: 38, 391, 394–95, 419–20.

25 Robert J. Marshall to Wallace E. Fisher, April 26, 1974, ELCA, RJMP, Box C-124, "File 3"; Robert J. Marshall to Rev. C. Marcus Engdahl, June 13, 1974, ELCA, RJMP, Box C-124, "File 3."

26 "Mission to the World," *Lutheran* 12 (August 14, 1974): 4–6, 15–19; Wallace E. Fisher to Robert J. Marshall, July 4, 1974, ELCA, RJMP, Box C-124, "File 3."

27 Hope Barham, "The Eternal Optimist," *AMECR* 107 (1974): 44–46; A. Lewis Williams, "Let Us Preach Christ," *CR* 123 (May 13, 1974): 4–5; Dr. Charles E. Wells, "Phase II," *FDC* 1 (May 15, 1974): 6–7.

28 "Nixon Urged to Come Clean," *FDC* 1 (May 15, 1974): 1.

29 "Black Voters Decisive in Congressional Election of National Significance," *AMECR* 123 (May 27, 1974): 7.

30 "Should Nixon Resign?," *CT* 18 (June 7, 1974): 28–29.

31 L. H. Moore, "If My People . . . ," *OBM* 22 (May 23, 1974): 4; C. J. Daley Jr., "The Hidden Will Be Uncovered," *WR* 148 (May 18, 1974): 4.

32 "Pastors Confab Elects Officers; Urged to Set Ethical Example," BPR, *WR* 148 (June 22, 1974): 22–23; Jack Brymer, "Watergate Spills Over into Pastor's Conf.," *AB* 139 (June 20, 1974): 5; "New President Fends Reporters Questions about Watergate, Ordinations, Theological 'Storms.'" BPR, *WR* 148 (June 22, 1974): 6–7; "Nixon Manipulates People New SBC President Declares," BPR, June 12, 1974, SBHLA.

33 "Kentuckian Becomes First Black Elected to SBC National Office," BPR, *WR* 148 (June 22, 1974): 7.

34 M. G. Toliver, "Letters and Opinions," *AB* 139 (July 18, 1974): 3.

35 "Watergate: How Widespread?," *CT* 18 (May 10, 1974): 43; J. A. O. Preus to Mrs. Mary Maynar, July 1, 1974, CHI, Executive Offices Records, 1904–1981, Box 73, "General Correspondence: Matthias-May"; J. A. O. Preus to Walter F. Hupfer, February 12, 1974, CHI, Executive Offices Records, 1904–1981, Box 72, "General Correspondence: HUM-HUX."

36 Albert McClellan, "Where Did Streaking Go?," *BP* (May 1974): 31; Toby Druin, "Baptist Conferees Listen, React to Nixon's Farewell," BPR, August 9, 1974, SB-HLA.

37 Jim Young, "The Line," *HM* 45 (July–August 1974): 32–38, 40; Dr. Warren Hultgren, "The Ramparts We Watch," Broadcast 2 July 1974, SBHLA, Baptist Hour Sermons, Box 3, "July–December 1974"; SBC, "Annual of the Southern Baptist Convention," "Christian Life Commission Report—A Statement with Accompanying Recommendations," June 11–13, 1974, SBHLA: 207–11.

38 J. Everett Sneed, "Taking the Long Look for Our Nation," *ABN* 73 (June 27, 1974): 3; Tim Nichols, "Masters of the Myth," *HM* 45 (July–August 1974): 48–51; "Pastors Confab Elects Officers; Urged to Set Ethical Example," BPR, *WR* 148 (June 22, 1974): 22–23.

39 James E. Wood Jr., "Integrity in Government," *RC* 29 (May 1974): 2 (emphasis in original).

40 Everett Hullum, "Beyond the Ballot Box," *HM* 45 (July–August 1974): 13–15, 18–22.

41 Religious Committee for Integrity in Government to Senators and Congressional Representatives, Draft of 1974 Letter, SBHLA, CLC, "Integrity in Government 1974"; Lynerd, *Republican Theology*.

42 C. Welton Gaddy, "Christian Citizen: America Needs You!," June 1974, SBHLA, CLC, "Christian Citizenship, 1970–1973."

43 Rev. Thomas Sullivan to Harold Lindsell, June 25, 1974, BGCA, Collection 8, Records of *Christianity Today* International, Box 25, Folder 8; "Watergate Called 'National Tragedy and Embarrassment,'" BPR, June 14, 1974, SBHLA.

44 Charles W. Colson to Honorable Michael Alison, June 4, 1974, BGCA, Collection 275, PCWC, Box 1, Folder 1; Charles W. Colson to Leighton S. Bishop, June 10, 1974, BGCA, Collection 275, PCWC, Box 4, Folder 3; Charles W. Colson to Mrs. Mary Vredewoogd, June 10, 1974, BGCA, Collection 275, PCWC, Box 3, Folder 2; Charles W. Colson to Hurd Baruch, June 14, 1974, BGCA, Collection 275, PCWC, Box 67, Folder 4; Charles W. Colson to Hurd Baruch, June 14, 1974, BGCA, Collection 275, PCWC, Box 2, Folder 19.

45 Charles W. Colson to Honorable Michael Alison, June 4, 1974, BGCA, Collection 275, PCWC, Box 1, Folder 1; Charles W. Colson to Leighton S. Bishop, June 10, 1974, BGCA, Collection 275, PCWC, Box 4, Folder 3; Charles W. Colson to Mrs. Mary Vredewoogd, June 10, 1974, BGCA, Collection 275, PCWC, Box 3, Folder 2; Charles W. Colson to Hurd Baruch, June 14, 1974, BGCA, Collection

275, PCWC, Box 67, Folder 4; Charles W. Colson to Hurd Baruch, June 14, 1974, BGCA, Collection 275, PCWC, Box 2, Folder 19.

46 Edward E. Plowman, "God and Watergate," *CT* 18 (June 21, 1974): 40.

47 "A New Beginning for Charles Colson," *CC* 91 (July 3–10, 1974): 691.

CONCLUSION

1 "Fifteen Turbulent Years," *CT* 18 (August 30, 1974): 24–25; Franklin H. Littell, "Who Is Above the Law?," *CC* 91 (September 18, 1974): 839.

2 "SBC Leaders Agree with Resignation; Register Sadness," BPR, August 9, 1974, SBHLA; "SBC Leaders React with Sadness to Resignation," BPR, *WR* 148 (August 24, 1974): 9, 15.

3 "A Time for 'New Beginnings' Says Lutheran Council President," Religious News Service, August 12, 1974, ELCA, LCUSA 16/6/2, Box 12, "Government—White House, 1962–1979"; Albert P. Stauderman, "End of a Chapter," *Lutheran* 12 (September 4, 1974): 34; Frederick J. Miller to the Editors, August 16, 1974, ELCA, ASP, Box B94, "M 1974"; Reverend Richard Bansemer to Albert P. Stauderman, August 10, 1974, ELCA, ASP, Box B93, "B—1974"; J. A. O. Preus to Richard M. Nixon, August 9, 1974, CHI, Executive Offices Records, Box 66, "United States Government Offices—Correspondence," 1973–1975.

4 Harold P. Ford, "The Sleazing of America," *CC* 91 (August 21–28, 1974): 796–98; James M. Wall, "The Voter and Four Levels of Hell," *CC* 91 (November 6, 1974): 1027; Mary Maher, "Can He Carry Our Sins?," *CC* 91 (September 18, 1974): 839–40.

5 Robert V. Moss, "Jesus Christ Frees and Unites: The Context of Our Meeting," Address to the Tenth General Synod, June 27, 1975, "Minutes of the Tenth General Synod," UCC, General Synod Collection: 124–27; Robert J. Marshall to All LCA Pastors, November 1, 1974, ELCA, LCA Office of the President, Box C-200, "Dear Partners, 1972–1974."

6 *Bulletin*, Lutheran House of Studies, Washington, DC, 1974 Spring Symposium, Vol. 54 (November 1974). This was published by Lutheran Theological Seminary, Gettysburg, PA. This version of the symposium was called "The Use and Abuse of Political Power: Ethical Reflections."

7 Harold Lindsell to Ronald A. Wells, December 27, 1974, BGCA, Collection 8, Records of *Christianity Today* International, Box 25, Folder 21; "Truthfulness Cited as Chief Watergate Lesson," BPR, September 24, 1974, SBHLA; Reverend Kenneth L. Nerenz to Albert P. Stauderman, August 30, 1974, ELCA, ASP, Box B95, "N-O 1974"; James G. Manz, "The Power That Holds," *LW* 93 (October 6, 1974): 4–5.

8 Wallace Henley, "White House 'Superaides' Hold 'Amoral' Philosophy," BPR, September 30, 1974, SBHLA; "A Resolution," Proposal, November 1974, BGCA, Collection 37, EvangSA, Box 2, Folder 16.

9 Harold Lindsell, "Editor's Note," *CT* 18 (August 30, 1974): 3; Jaroy Weber, "Let the Bells Ring," June 10, 1975, SBHLA, Southern Baptist Press Kit Collection, "1975—Addresses"; Alma Kern, "Bridge over Troubled Waters," *Lutheran Woman's*

Quarterly 33 (Winter 1974–75): 20c–20d; Vida L. Laporte to J. A. O. Preus, December 15, 1974, CHI, American Bicentennial Committee, Box 1, Second Binder.

10 "Integrity Crisis Ranks as Top 1974 BP Story," BPR, December 30, 1974, SBHLA; Erwin L. McDonald, "Hays Calls for Moral Leadership by the Religious," BPR, October 8, 1974, SBHLA; Hudson Baggett, "Beyond Watergate," *AB* 139 (August 29, 1974): 2; James E. Wood Jr., "A Nation in Crisis," *RC* 29 (August–September 1974): 1–2.

11 Erwin W. Lutzer, "Watergate Ethics," *CT* 18 (September 13, 1974): 27.

12 Jonathan A. Dames, "The Presiding Elder's Message at the 92nd Session of the Chicago Annual Conference," *CR* 124 (November 18, 1974): 6; Mrs. Anna Scott (King) Ransaw, "'What the World Needs'—The Hope of a Universal Love," *CR* 124 (June 16, 1975): 2–3, 5 (emphasis in original); AME, "Minutes of the Fortieth Session of the General Conference," June 1976, AMEDRS, Nashville, TN, 308–13, Vernon E. Jordan Jr., address on June 17, 1976.

13 "America, Land of the 'Spree,' Home of the 'Knave,'" Committee on the State of the Country, Eleventh Episcopal District South Florida Annual Conference, 1974, AME; T. S. Clements, "Objective Reflections," *AMECR* 124 (October 7, 1974): 4.

14 "Social Action," *AMECR* 124 (September 9, 1974): 7; "State of the Church," *AMECR* 124 (September 30, 1974): 4–5; "The State of the Church," *CR* 124 (October 28, 1974): 1–2.

15 Wallace Henley, "White House Reality Distorted by 'Warp,'" BPR, September 20, 1974, SBHLA.

16 James M. Wall, "Morality Talk along the Potomac," *CC* 91 (October 9, 1974): 923–24.

BIBLIOGRAPHY

PRIMARY MATERIALS

Periodicals and Newspapers
A.D. (UCC)
Alabama Baptist
A.M.E. Church Review
Arkansas Baptist Newsmagazine
Baptist Program
California Southern Baptist
Capital Baptist
Christian Century
Christianity Today
Christian Recorder (AME)
Congressional Record
Engage (UCC)
Engage/Social Action (UCC)
First District Clarion (AME)
Focus on Public Affairs (LCUSA)
Home Missions (SBC)
Interchange (LCUSA)
Keeping You Posted (UCC)
Lutheran (LCA)
Lutheran Social Concern (LCA)
Lutheran Witness (LCMS)
Lutheran Woman's Quarterly (LCMS)
Lutheran Women (LCA)
Ohio Baptist Messenger
Report from the Capital (Baptist)
Social Action (UCC)
United Church Herald (UCC)
Washington Report (UCC)
Western Recorder (Kentucky Baptist)

Archives

African Methodist Episcopal Church, Nashville, TN. Department of Scholarship and
  Research.
Billy Graham Center, Wheaton, IL. Evangelical Archives and Repository.
Concordia Historical Institute, St. Louis, MO. Archives.
Concordia University Chicago, River Forest, IL. Library.
Evangelical Lutheran Church in America Headquarters, Chicago, IL. Department of
  Denominational Archives.
Gerald R. Ford Library, Ann Arbor, MI.
Lutheran Theological Seminary, Gettysburg, PA. A. R. Wentz Library.
National Archives and Research Administration, College Park, MD. Nixon Presidential
  Materials.
Presbyterian Historical Society, Philadelphia, PA. Presbyterian Church (USA).
Richard Nixon Library, Yorba Linda, CA.
Southern Baptist Convention Headquarters, Nashville, TN. Historical Library and
  Archives.
Southern Illinois University, Carbondale, IL. *Christian Century* Archives.
United Church of Christ Headquarters, Cleveland, OH. Archives.

ARTICLES, BOOKS, AND DISSERTATIONS

Adams, David L., and Ken Schurb, eds. *The Anonymous God: The Church Confronts
  Civil Religion and American Society*. Saint Louis, MO: Concordia Publishing House,
  2004.
Ahlstrom, Sydney E. *A Religious History of the American People*. New Haven, CT: Yale
  University Press, 1972.
Aitken, Jonathan. *Charles W. Colson: A Life Redeemed*. Colorado Springs, CO: Water-
  Brook Press, 2005.
———. *Nixon: A Life*. Washington, DC: Regnery, 1993.
Allitt, Patrick. *Religion in America since 1945: A History*. New York: Columbia Univer-
  sity Press, 2003.
Ambrose, Stephen E. *Nixon*. Vol. 1, *The Education of a Politician, 1913–1962*. New York:
  Touchstone Books, 1987.
———. *Nixon*. Vol. 2, *The Triumph of a Politician, 1962–1972*. New York: Simon and
  Schuster, 1989.
———. *Nixon*. Vol. 3, *Ruin and Recovery, 1973–1990*. New York: Touchstone Books,
  1991.
Anderson, Terry H. *The Movement and the Sixties: Protest in America from Greensboro
  to Wounded Knee*. New York: Oxford University Press, 1995.
Andrew, John A., III. *The Other Side of the Sixties: Young Americans for Freedom and
  the Rise of Conservative Politics*. New Brunswick, NJ: Rutgers University Press, 1997.
Avery, William O. *Empowered Laity: The Story of the Lutheran Laity Movement*. Minneapolis, MN: Augsburg Fortress Press, 1997.

Bachmann, E. Theodore. *The United Lutheran Church in America, 1918–1962*. Minneapolis, MN: Fortress Press, 1997.

Bailey, Beth, and David Farber, eds. *America in the Seventies*. Lawrence: University Press of Kansas, 2004.

Bailey, Julius H. *Race Patriotism: Protest and Print Culture in the AME Church*. Knoxville: University of Tennessee Press, 2012.

Balmer, Randall. *God in the White House: A History: How Faith Shaped the Presidency from John F. Kennedy to George W. Bush*. New York: HarperOne, 2008.

Bellah, Robert N. *The Broken Covenant: American Civil Religion in Time of Trial*. 2nd ed. Chicago: University of Chicago Press, 1992.

Bendroth, Margaret. *The Last Puritans: Mainline Protestants and the Power of the Past*. Chapel Hill: University of North Carolina Press, 2015.

Bennett, David H. *The Party of Fear: The American Far Right from Nativism to the Militia Movement*. New York: Vintage Books, 1988.

Berkowitz, Edward D. *Something Happened: A Political and Cultural Overview of the Seventies*. New York: Columbia University Press, 2006.

Bernstein, Carl, and Bob Woodward. *All the President's Men*. New York: Warner Books, 1974.

Blackburn, Simon. *Being Good: A Short Introduction to Ethics*. New York: Oxford University Press, 2001.

Bloodworth, Jeffrey. *Losing the Center: The Decline of American Liberalism, 1968–1992*. Lexington: University Press of Kentucky, 2013.

Blumhofer, Edith L., ed. *Religion, Politics, and the American Experience: Reflections on Religion and American Public Life*. Tuscaloosa: University of Alabama Press, 2002.

Booraem, Hendrik, V. *The Education of Gerald Ford*. Grand Rapids, MI: William B. Eerdmans, 2016.

Bothwell, Cecil. *The Prince of War: Billy Graham's Crusade for a Wholly Christian Empire*. 2nd ed. Asheville, NC: Brave Ulysses Books, 2010.

Bowler, Kate. *Blessed: A History of the American Prosperity Gospel*. New York: Oxford University Press, 2013.

Boyer, Paul. *When Time Shall Be No More: Prophecy Belief in Modern American Culture*. Cambridge, MA: Harvard University Press, 1992.

Braun, Mark E. *A Tale of Two Synods: Events That Led to the Split between Wisconsin and Missouri*. Milwaukee, WI: Northwestern Publishing House, 2003.

Brekus, Catherine A., and W. Clark Gilpin, eds. *American Christianities: A History of Dominance and Diversity*. Chapel Hill: University of North Carolina Press, 2011.

Brennan, Mary C. *Turning Right in the Sixties: The Conservative Capture of the GOP*. Chapel Hill: University of North Carolina Press, 1995.

Brett, Edward T. *The U.S. Catholic Press on Central America: From Cold War Anticommunism to Social Justice*. Notre Dame, IN: University of Notre Dame Press, 2003.

Buggeln, Gretchen. *The Suburban Church: Modernism and Community in Postwar America*. Minneapolis: University of Minnesota Press, 2015.

Burkee, James C. *Power, Politics, and the Missouri Synod: A Conflict That Changed American Christianity*. Minneapolis, MN: Fortress Press, 2011.

Busch, Andrew E. *Reagan's Victory: The Presidential Election of 1980 and the Rise of the Right*. Lawrence: University Press of Kansas, 2005.

Campbell, James T. *Songs of Zion: The African Methodist Episcopal Church in the United States and South Africa*. Chapel Hill: University of North Carolina Press, 1998.

Campbell, Karl E. *Senator Sam Ervin, Last of the Founding Fathers*. Chapel Hill: University of North Carolina Press, 2007.

Cannon, James. *Time and Chance: Gerald Ford's Appointment with History*. Ann Arbor: University of Michigan Press, 1994.

Caplow, Theodore, Howard M. Bahr, John Modell, and Bruce A. Chadwick. *Recent Social Trends in the United States, 1960–1990*. Montreal: McGill-Queen's University Press, 1991.

Carpenter, Joel A. *Revive Us Again: The Reawakening of American Fundamentalism*. New York: Oxford University Press, 1997.

Carroll, Peter N. *It Seemed Like Nothing Happened: America in the 1970s*. New Brunswick, NJ: Rutgers University Press, 1982.

Carter, Dan T. *The Politics of Rage: George Wallace, the Origins of the New Conservatism, and the Transformation of American Politics*. Baton Rouge: Louisiana State University Press, 1995.

Cimino, Richard, ed. *Lutherans Today: American Lutheran Identity in the 21st Century*. Grand Rapids, MI: William B. Eerdmans, 2003.

Cline, David P. *From Reconciliation to Revolution: The Student Interracial Ministry, Liberal Christianity, and the Civil Rights Movement*. Chapel Hill: University of North Carolina Press, 2016.

Coffman, Elesha J. The Christian Century *and the Rise of the Protestant Mainline*. New York: Oxford University Press, 2013.

Colodny, Len, and Robert Gettlin. *Silent Coup: The Removal of a President*. New York: St. Martin's Press, 1991.

Colson, Charles W. *Born Again*. Grand Rapids, MI: Chosen Books, 1995.

Consulting Committee on the Bicentenary of the United States, Division for Mission in North America, Lutheran Church in America. *Equality and Justice for All: Christian Calling in an Age of Independence*. New York: Lutheran Church in America, 1976.

Corrigan, John, and Winthrop S. Hudson. *Religion in America*. 8th ed. Upper Saddle River, NJ: Prentice Hall, 2010.

Critchlow, Donald T. *Phyllis Schlafly and Grassroots Conservatism: A Woman's Crusade*. Princeton, NJ: Princeton University Press, 2005.

Crockett, H. Dale. *Focus on Watergate: An Examination of the Moral Dilemma of Watergate in the Light of Civil Religion*. Macon, GA: Mercer University Press, 1982.

Crouter, Richard. *Reinhold Niebuhr: On Politics, Religion, and Christian Faith*. New York: Oxford University Press, 2010.

Crowley, Monica. *Nixon in Winter: His Final Revelations about Diplomacy, Watergate, and Life Out of the Arena*. New York: Random House, 1998.

Dallek, Robert. *Nixon and Kissinger: Partners in Power*. New York: HarperCollins, 2007.

Davis, Flora. *Moving the Mountain: The Women's Movement in America since 1960*. Urbana: University of Illinois Press, 1999.

Dean, John W., III. *Blind Ambition: The White House Years*. New York: Simon and Schuster, 1976.

———. *The Nixon Defense: What He Knew and When He Knew It*. New York: Viking, 2014.

DeBenedetti, Charles, and Charles Chatfield. *An American Ordeal: The Antiwar Movement of the Vietnam Era*. Syracuse, NY: Syracuse University Press, 1990.

Dochuk, Darren. *Anointed with Oil: How Christianity and Crude Made Modern America*. New York: Basic Books, 2019.

———. *From Bible Belt to Sun Belt: Plain-Folk Religion, Grassroots Politics, and the Rise of Evangelical Conservatism*. New York: W. W. Norton, 2011.

Dudley, William, ed. *Watergate: Examining Issues through Political Cartoons*. San Diego: Greenhaven Press, 2002.

Ebel, Jonathan H. *G.I. Messiahs: Soldiering, War, and American Civil Religion*. New Haven, CT: Yale University Press, 2015.

Ehrlichman, John. *Witness to Power: The Nixon Years*. New York: Simon and Schuster, 1982.

Emery, Fred. *Watergate: The Corruption of American Politics and the Fall of Richard Nixon*. New York: Times Books, 1994.

Erling, Maria, and Mark Granquist. *The Augustana Story: Shaping Lutheran Identity in North America*. Minneapolis, MN: Augsburg Fortress Press, 2008.

Espinosa, Gaston, ed. *Religion and the American Presidency: George Washington to George W. Bush with Commentary and Primary Sources*. New York: Columbia University Press, 2009.

Fackre, Gabriel. *Believing, Caring, and Doing in the United Church of Christ: An Interpretation*. Cleveland, OH: United Church Press, 2005.

Farber, David. *The Rise and Fall of Modern American Conservatism: A Short History*. Princeton, NJ: Princeton University Press, 2010.

Finke, Roger, and Rodney Starks. *The Churching of America, 1776–1990: Winners and Losers in Our Religious Economy*. New Brunswick, NJ: Rutgers University Press, 1992.

Finstuen, Andrew S. *Original Sin and Everyday Protestants: The Theology of Reinhold Niebuhr, Billy Graham, and Paul Tillich in the Age of Anxiety*. Chapel Hill: University of North Carolina Press, 2009.

Finstuen, Andrew, Anne Blue Wills, and Grant Wacker, eds. *Billy Graham: American Pilgrim*. New York: Oxford University Press, 2017.

Firestone, Bernard J., and Alexej Ugrinsky, eds. *Gerald R. Ford and the Politics of Post-Watergate America*. 2 vols. Westport, CT: Greenwood Press, 1993.

Fitts, Leroy. *A History of Black Baptists*. Nashville, TN: Broadman Press, 1985.

Flamm, Michael W. *Law and Order: Street Crime, Civil Unrest, and the Crisis of Liberalism in the 1960s*. New York: Columbia University Press, 2005.

Fletcher, Jesse C. *The Southern Baptist Convention: A Sesquicentennial History*. Nashville, TN: Broadman and Holman, 1994.

Flowers, Elizabeth H. *Into the Pulpit: Southern Baptist Women and Power since World War II*. Chapel Hill: University of North Carolina Press, 2012.

Flynt, Wayne. *Alabama Baptists: Southern Baptists in the Heart of Dixie*. Tuscaloosa: University of Alabama Press, 1998.

Foley, Michael Stewart. *Dear Dr. Spock: Letters about the Vietnam War to America's Favorite Baby Doctor*. New York: New York University Press, 2005.

———. *Front Porch Politics: The Forgotten Heyday of American Activism in the 1970s and 1980s*. New York: Hill and Wang, 2013.

Ford, Betty, with Chris Chase. *The Times of My Life*. New York: Harper and Row, 1978.

Ford, Gerald R. *A Time to Heal: The Autobiography of Gerald R. Ford*. New York: Berkley Books, 1979.

Fowler, Robert Booth. *A New Engagement: Evangelical Political Thought, 1966–1976*. Grand Rapids, MI: William B. Eerdmans, 1982.

Fox, Richard W. *Jesus in America: Personal Savior, Cultural Hero, National Obsession*. San Francisco: HarperCollins, 2005.

Franklin, H. Bruce. *M.I.A. or Mythmaking in America: How and Why Belief in Live POWs Has Possessed a Nation*. Brooklyn: Lawrence Hill Books, 1992.

Frick, Daniel. *Reinventing Richard Nixon: A Cultural History of an American Obsession*. Lawrence: University Press of Kansas, 2008.

Friedman, Leon, and William F. Levantrosser, eds. *Watergate and Afterward: The Legacy of Richard M. Nixon*. Westport, CT: Greenwood Press, 1992.

Frost, David. *Frost/Nixon: Behind the Scenes of the Nixon Interviews*. New York: Harper Perennial, 2007.

Frost, Jennifer. *Producer of Controversy: Stanley Kramer, Hollywood Liberalism, and the Cold War*. Lawrence: University Press of Kansas, 2017.

Galchutt, Katherine M. *The Career of Andrew Schulze, 1924–1968: Lutherans and Race in the Civil Rights Era*. Macon, GA: Mercer University Press, 2005.

Gardella, Peter. *American Civil Religion: What Americans Hold Sacred*. New York: Oxford University Press, 2014.

Gardner, Eric. *Black Print Unbound: The Christian Recorder, African American Literature, and Periodical Culture*. New York: Oxford University Press, 2015.

Gibbs, Nancy, and Michael Duffy. *The Preacher and the Presidents: Billy Graham in the White House*. New York: Center Street, 2007.

Gifford, Laura Jane. *The Center Cannot Hold: The 1960 Presidential Election and the Rise of Modern Conservatism*. DeKalb: Northern Illinois University Press, 2009.

Gifford, Laura Jane, and Daniel K. Williams, eds. *The Right Side of the Sixties: Reexamining Conservatism's Decade of Transformation*. New York: Palgrave Macmillan, 2012.

Gilbert, James. *Another Chance: Postwar America, 1945–1985*. Belmont, CA: Wadsworth, 1981.

———. *Redeeming Culture: American Religion in an Age of Science*. Chicago: University of Chicago Press, 1997.

Gilbert, W. Kent. *Commitment to Unity: A History of the Lutheran Church in America*. Minneapolis, MN: Fortress Press, 1988.

Gill, Jill K. *Embattled Ecumenism: The National Council of Churches, the Vietnam War, and the Trials of the Protestant Left*. DeKalb: Northern Illinois University Press, 2011.

Goldstein, Warren. *William Sloane Coffin Jr.: A Holy Impatience*. New Haven, CT: Yale University Press, 2004.

Gordon, Tammy S. *The Spirit of 1976: Commerce, Community, and the Politics of Commemoration*. Amherst: University of Massachusetts Press, 2013.

Gordon, William A. *The Fourth of May: Killings and Coverups at Kent State*. Buffalo, NY: Prometheus Book, 1990.

Gorski, Philip. *American Covenant: A History of Civil Religion from the Puritans to the Present*. Princeton, NJ: Princeton University Press, 2017.

Graebner, Alan. *Uncertain Saints: The Laity in the Lutheran Church—Missouri Synod, 1900–1970*. Westport, CT: Greenwood Press, 1975.

Graham, Billy. *Just as I Am: The Autobiography of Billy Graham*. San Francisco: HarperSanFrancisco, 1997.

Granquist, Mark. *Lutherans in America: A New History*. Minneapolis, MN: Fortress Press, 2015.

Greenberg, David. *Nixon's Shadow: The History of an Image*. New York: W. W. Norton, 2003.

Greene, John Robert. *Betty Ford: Candor and Courage in the White House*. Lawrence: University Press of Kansas, 2004.

———. *The Limits of Power: The Nixon and Ford Administrations*. Bloomington: Indiana University Press, 1992.

———. *The Presidency of Gerald R. Ford*. Lawrence: University Press of Kansas, 1995.

Gregg, Howard D. *History of the African Methodist Episcopal Church: The Black Church in Action*. Nashville, TN: AMEC Sunday School Union, 1980.

Grem, Darren E. *The Blessings of Business: How Corporations Shaped Conservative Christianity*. New York: Oxford University Press, 2016.

Gritsch, Eric W. *Fortress Introduction to Lutheranism*. Minneapolis, MN: Fortress Press, 1994.

Gritsch, Eric W., and Robert W. Jenson. *Lutheranism: The Theological Movement and Its Confessional Writings*. Minneapolis, MN: Fortress Press, 1976.

Grzymala-Busse, Anna. *Nations under God: How Churches Use Moral Authority to Influence Policy*. Princeton, NJ: Princeton University Press, 2015.

Gunnemann, Louis H. *The Shaping of the United Church of Christ: An Essay in the History of American Christianity*. Cleveland, OH: United Church Press, 1999.

———. *United and Uniting: The Meaning of an Ecclesial Journey*. New York: United Church Press, 1987.

Guth, James L., John C. Green, Corwin E. Smidt, Lyman A. Kellstedt, and Margaret M. Poloma. *The Bully Pulpit: The Politics of Protestant Clergy*. Lawrence: University Press of Kansas, 1997.

Haberski, Raymond, Jr. *God and War: American Civil Religion since 1945*. New Brunswick, NJ: Rutgers University Press, 2012.

Hagan, John. *Northern Passage: American Vietnam War Resisters in Canada*. Cambridge, MA: Harvard University Press, 2001.

Haldeman, H. R. *The Haldeman Diaries: Inside the Nixon White House*. New York: G. P. Putnam's Sons, 1994.

Hall, Mitchell K. *Because of Their Faith: CALCAV and Religious Opposition to the Vietnam War*. New York: Columbia University Press, 1990.

Hankins, Barry. *Uneasy in Babylon: Southern Baptist Conservatives and American Culture*. Tuscaloosa: University of Alabama Press, 2002.

Hanson, Paul D. *A Political History of the Bible in America*. Louisville, KY: Westminster John Knox Press, 2015.

Harper, Keith, ed. *American Denominational History: Perspectives on the Past, Prospects for the Future*. Tuscaloosa: University of Alabama Press, 2008.

Hart, D. G. *From Billy Graham to Sarah Palin: Evangelicals and the Betrayal of American Conservatism*. Grand Rapids, MI: William B. Eerdmans, 2011.

———. *That Old-Time Religion in Modern America: Evangelical Protestantism in the Twentieth Century*. Chicago: Ivan R. Dee, 2002.

Hartmann, Robert T. *Palace Politics: An Inside Account of the Ford Years*. New York: McGraw-Hill, 1980.

Hartmann, Susan M. *From Margin to Mainstream: American Women and Politics since 1960*. New York: McGraw-Hill, 1996.

Harvey, Paul, and Philip Goff, eds. *The Columbia Documentary History of Religion in America since 1945*. New York: Columbia University Press, 2005.

Heineman, Kenneth J. *God Is a Conservative: Religion, Politics, and Morality in Contemporary America*. New York: New York University Press, 1998.

Henderson, Charles, Jr. *The Nixon Theology*. New York: Harper and Row, 1972.

Herring, George. *America's Longest War: The United States and Vietnam, 1950–1975*. 2nd ed. New York: McGraw-Hill, 1986.

Hibbs, Ben, ed. *White House Sermons*. New York: Harper and Row, 1972.

Hoffmann, Oswald C. J. *What More Is There to Say but Amen: The Autobiography of Dr. Oswald C. J. Hoffmann*. St. Louis, MO: Concordia Publishing House, 1996.

Hollinger, David A. *After Cloven Tongues of Fire: Protestant Liberalism in Modern American History*. Princeton, NJ: Princeton University Press, 2013.

Holmes, David L. *The Faiths of the Postwar Presidents: From Truman to Obama*. Athens: University of Georgia Press, 2012.

Hudnut-Beumler, James. *Looking for God in the Suburbs: The Religion of the American Dream and Its Critics, 1945–1965*. New Brunswick, NJ: Rutgers University Press, 1994.

Hulsether, Mark David. *Building a Protestant Left: Christianity and Crisis Magazine, 1941–1993.* Knoxville: University of Tennessee Press, 1999.

———. *Religion, Culture and Politics in the Twentieth-Century United States.* New York: Columbia University Press, 2007.

Hunter, James Davison. *American Evangelicalism: Conservative Religion and the Quandary of Modernity.* New Brunswick, NJ: Rutgers University Press, 1983.

Hutchison, William R., ed. *Between the Times: The Travail of the Protestant Establishment in America, 1900–1960.* Cambridge: Cambridge University Press, 1989.

Ingle, H. Larry. *Nixon's First Cover-Up: The Religious Life of a Quaker President.* Columbia: University of Missouri Press, 2015.

Jacobs, Meg. *Panic at the Pump: The Energy Crisis and the Transformation of American Politics in the 1970s.* New York: Hill and Wang, 2016.

Jeffreys-Jones, Rhodri. *Peace Now! American Society and the Ending of the Vietnam War.* New Haven, CT: Yale University Press, 1999.

Jenkins, Philip. *Decade of Nightmares: The End of the Sixties and the Making of Eighties America.* New York: Oxford University Press, 2006.

Johnson, Jeff G. *Black Christians: The Untold Lutheran Story.* St. Louis, MO: Concordia Publishing House, 1991.

Johnson, Richard O. *Changing World, Changeless Christ: The American Lutheran Publicity Bureau, 1914–2014.* Delhi, NY: ALPB Books, 2018.

Joireman, Sandra F., ed. *Church, State, and Citizen: Christian Approaches to Political Engagement.* New York: Oxford University Press, 2009.

Kabaservice, Geoffrey. *Rule and Ruin: The Downfall of Moderation and the Destruction of the Republican Party, from Eisenhower to the Tea Party.* New York: Oxford University Press, 2012.

Kadura, Johannes. *The War after the War: The Struggle for Credibility during America's Exit from Vietnam.* Ithaca, NY: Cornell University Press, 2016.

Kalman, Laura. *The Long Reach of the Sixties: LBJ, Nixon, and the Making of the Contemporary Supreme Court.* New York: Oxford University Press, 2017.

Kaufman, Burton I., and Scott Kaufman. *The Presidency of James Earl Carter Jr.* 2nd ed. Lawrence: University Press of Kansas, 2006.

Kent, Stephen A. *From Slogans to Mantras: Social Protest and Religious Conversion in the Late Vietnam War Era.* Syracuse, NY: Syracuse University Press, 2001.

Kersten, Lawrence L. *The Lutheran Ethic: The Impact of Religion on Laymen and Clergy.* Detroit, MI: Wayne State University Press, 1970.

Kidd, Thomas S., and Barry Hankins. *Baptists in America: A History.* New York: Oxford University Press, 2015.

Killen, Andreas. *1973 Nervous Breakdown: Watergate, Warhol, and the Birth of Post-Sixties America.* New York: Bloomsbury USA, 2006.

Kimball, Jeffrey. *Nixon's Vietnam War.* Lawrence: University Press of Kansas, 1998.

Klein, Christa R. *Politics and Policy: The Genesis and Theology of Social Statements in the Lutheran Church in America.* Minneapolis, MN: Fortress Press, 1989.

Kotlowski, Dean J. *Nixon's Civil Rights: Politics, Principle, and Policy*. Cambridge, MA: Harvard University Press, 2001.

Kruse, Kevin M. *One Nation under God: How Corporate America Invented Christian America*. New York: Basic Books, 2015.

———. *White Flight: Atlanta and the Making of Modern Conservatism*. Princeton, NJ: Princeton University Press, 2005.

Kruse, Kevin M., and Julian E. Zelizer. *Fault Lines: A History of the United States since 1974*. New York: W. W. Norton, 2019.

Kutler, Stanley I., ed. *Abuse of Power: The New Nixon Tapes*. New York: Touchstone Books, 1997.

———. *The Wars of Watergate: The Last Crisis of Richard Nixon*. New York: Alfred A. Knopf, 1990.

Kyvig, David. *The Age of Impeachment: American Constitutional Culture since 1960*. Lawrence: University Press of Kansas, 2008.

Lagerquist, L. DeAne. *From Our Mothers' Arms: A History of Women in the American Lutheran Church*. Minneapolis, MN: Augsburg Publishing House, 1987.

———. *The Lutherans*. Westport, CT: Praeger, 1999.

Lahr, Angela M. *Millennial Dreams and Apocalyptic Nightmares: The Cold War Origins of Political Evangelicalism*. New York: Oxford University Press, 2007.

Lambert, Frank. *Religion in American Politics: A Short History*. Princeton, NJ: Princeton University Press, 2008.

Langston, Thomas S. *With Reverence and Contempt: How Americans Think about Their President*. Baltimore: Johns Hopkins University Press, 1995.

Lassiter, Matthew D. *The Silent Majority: Suburban Politics in the Sunbelt South*. Princeton, NJ: Princeton University Press, 2006.

Leonard, Bill J. *Baptists in America*. New York: Columbia University Press, 2005.

———. *God's Last and Only Hope: The Fragmentation of the Southern Baptist Convention*. Grand Rapids, MI: William B. Eerdmans, 1990.

Levang, Joseph H. *The Church of the Lutheran Brethren, 1900–1975: A Believers' Fellowship—A Lutheran Alternative*. Fergus Falls, MN: Lutheran Brethren Publishing, 1980.

Lienesch, Michael. *Redeeming America: Piety and Politics in the New Christian Right*. Chapel Hill: University of North Carolina Press, 1993.

Lincoln, C. Eric, and Lawrence H. Mamiya. *The Black Church in the African American Experience*. Durham, NC: Duke University Press, 1990.

Lindsell, Harold. *The World, the Flesh, and the Devil*. Minneapolis, MN: World Wide Publications, 1973.

Lints, Richard. *Progressive and Conservative Religious Ideologies: The Tumultuous Decade of the 1960s*. Burlington, VT: Ashgate, 2010.

Logevall, Fredrik, and Andrew Preston, eds. *Nixon in the World: American Foreign Relations, 1969–1977*. New York: Oxford University Press, 2008.

Long, Michael G., ed. *The Legacy of Billy Graham: Critical Reflections on America's Greatest Evangelist*. Louisville, KY: Westminster John Knox Press, 2008.

Lutz, Charles P. *Church Roots: Stories of Nine Immigrant Groups That Became the American Lutheran Church*. Minneapolis, MN: Augsburg Publishing House, 1985.

Lynerd, Benjamin T. *Republican Theology: The Civil Religion of American Evangelicals*. New York: Oxford University Press, 2014.

MacIntyre, Alasdair. *A Short History of Ethics: A History of Moral Philosophy from the Homeric Age to the Twentieth Century*. 2nd ed. Notre Dame, IN: University of Notre Dame Press, 1998.

Marsden, George M. *Fundamentalism and American Culture: The Shaping of Twentieth-Century Evangelism, 1870–1925*. New York: Oxford University Press, 1980.

———. *Religion and American Culture*. New York: Harcourt Brace College Publishers, 1990.

Marshall, Jon. *Watergate's Legacy and the Press: The Investigative Impulse*. Evanston, IL: Northwestern University Press, 2011.

Martin, William. *A Prophet with Honor: The Billy Graham Story*. New York: William Morrow, 1991.

Marty, Martin E. *Modern American Religion*. Vol. 3, *Under God, Indivisible, 1941–1960*. Chicago: University of Chicago Press, 1996.

———. *Pilgrims in Their Own Land: 500 Years of Religion in America*. New York: Penguin Books, 1984.

Mason, Robert. *Richard Nixon and the Quest for a New Majority*. Chapel Hill: University of North Carolina Press, 2004.

Matusow, Allen J. *Nixon's Economy: Booms, Busts, Dollars, and Votes*. Lawrence: University Press of Kansas, 1998.

———. *The Unraveling of America: A History of Liberalism in the 1960s*. New York: Harper and Row, 1984.

McBeth, H. Leon. *The Baptist Heritage: Four Centuries of Baptist Witness*. Nashville, TN: Broadman Press, 1987.

McDougall, Walter A. *The Tragedy of U.S. Foreign Policy: How America's Civil Religion Betrayed the National Interest*. New Haven, CT: Yale University Press, 2016.

McGirr, Lisa. *Suburban Warriors: The Origins of the New American Right*. Princeton, NJ: Princeton University Press, 2001.

McManners, John, ed. *The Oxford History of Christianity*. New York: Oxford University Press, 1993.

Melton, J. Gordon. *A Will to Choose: The Origins of African American Methodism*. Lanham, MD: Rowman and Littlefield, 2007.

Mieczkowski, Yanek. *Gerald Ford and the Challenges of the 1970s*. Lexington: University Press of Kentucky, 2005.

Miller, Steven P. *Billy Graham and the Rise of the Republican South*. Philadelphia: University of Pennsylvania Press, 2009.

Mislin, David. *Saving Faith: Making Religious Pluralism an American Value at the Dawn of the Secular Age*. Ithaca, NY: Cornell University Press, 2015.

Mitchell, Greg. *Tricky Dick and the Pink Lady: Richard Nixon vs. Helen Gahagan Douglas—Sexual Politics and the Red Scare, 1950*. New York: Random House, 1998.

Moore, Barrington, Jr. *Moral Purity and Persecution in History*. Princeton, NJ: Princeton University Press, 2000.

Moore, R. Laurence. *Selling God: American Religion in the Marketplace of Culture*. New York: Oxford University Press, 1994.

Morgan, David T. *The New Crusades, The New Holy Land: Conflict in the Southern Baptist Convention, 1969–1991*. Tuscaloosa: University of Alabama Press, 1996.

Mueller, Max. "Prophets, Protests and Politicians: Exploring the Political Theologies of Reinhold Niebuhr and Billy Graham through an Analysis of *Christianity and Crisis* and *Christianity Today*." *Cult/ure: The Graduate Journal of Harvard Divinity School* 3 (2008): 41–66.

Naumann, Cheryl D. *In the Footsteps of Phoebe: A Complete History of the Deaconess Movement in the Lutheran Church—Missouri Synod*. St. Louis, MO: Concordia Publishing House, 2008.

Neiman, Susan. *Evil in Modern Thought: An Alternative History of Philosophy*. Princeton, NJ: Princeton University Press, 2002.

Nelsen, Hart M., and Sandra Baxter. "Ministers Speak on Watergate: Effects of Clergy Role during Political Crisis." *Review of Religious Research* 23 (December 1981): 150–66.

Nelson, E. Clifford, ed. *The Lutherans in North America*. Minneapolis, MN: Fortress Press, 1980.

Newman, Mark. *Getting Right with God: Southern Baptists and Desegregation, 1945–1995*. Tuscaloosa: University of Alabama Press, 2001.

Nixon, Richard M. *The Memoirs of Richard Nixon*. New York: Grosset and Dunlap, 1978.

———. *Richard Nixon: Speeches, Writings, Documents*. Edited by Rick Perlstein. Princeton, NJ: Princeton University Press, 2008.

———. *Six Crises*. New York: Touchstone Books, 1962.

Noll, Mark A. *A History of Christianity in the United States and Canada*. 2nd ed. Grand Rapids, MI: William B. Eerdmans, 2019.

Noll, Mark A., and Luke E. Harlow. eds. *Religion and American Politics: From the Colonial Period to the Present*. 2nd ed. New York: Oxford University Press, 2007.

Olmsted, Kathryn S. *Challenging the Secret Government: The Post-Watergate Investigations of the CIA and FBI*. Chapel Hill: University of North Carolina Press, 1996.

Olson, Keith W. *Watergate: The Presidential Scandal That Shook America*. Lawrence: University Press of Kansas, 2003.

Oppenheimer, Mark. *Knocking on Heaven's Door: American Religion in the Age of the Counterculture*. New Haven, CT: Yale University Press, 2003.

Oudes, Bruce, ed. *From: The President: Richard Nixon's Secret Files*. New York: Harper and Row, 1989.

Pahl, Jon. *Empire of Sacrifice: The Religious Origins of American Violence*. New York: New York University Press, 2010.

———. *Hopes and Dreams of All: The International Walther League and Lutheran Youth in American Culture, 1893–1993*. Chicago: Wheat Ridge Ministries, 1993.

———. *Youth Ministry in Modern America: 1930 to the Present.* Peabody, MA: Hendrickson Publishers, 2000.

Pankow, Fred, and Edith Pankow. *75 Years of Blessings and the Best Is Yet to Come!* St. Louis, MO: International Lutheran Laymen's League, 1992.

Parmet, Herbert S. *Richard Nixon and His America.* New York: Konecky and Konecky, 1990.

Pells, Richard H. *The Liberal Mind in a Conservative Age: American Intellectuals in the 1940s and 1950s.* New York: Harper and Row, 1985.

Peperzak, Adriaan T. *Elements of Ethics.* Stanford, CA: Stanford University Press, 2004.

Perlstein, Rick. *Before the Storm: Barry Goldwater and the Unmaking of the American Consensus.* New York: Hill and Wang, 2001.

———. *Nixonland: The Rise of a President and the Fracturing of America.* New York: Scribner, 2008.

Pierard, Richard. "Billy Graham and Vietnam: From Cold Warrior to Peacemaker." *Christian Scholars Review* 10 (1980): 37–51.

Pinn, Anne H., and Anthony B. Pinn. *Fortress Introduction to Black Church History.* Minneapolis, MN: Fortress Press, 2002.

Pollock, John. *Billy Graham: Evangelist to the World: An Authorized Biography of the Decisive Years.* New York: Harper and Row, 1979.

———. *The Billy Graham Story: The Authorized Biography.* Grand Rapids, MI: Zondervan, 2003.

Porterfield, Amanda. *Conceived in Doubt: Religion and Politics in the New American Nation.* Chicago: University of Chicago Press, 2012.

———. *The Transformation of American Christianity: The Story of a Late-Twentieth-Century Awakening.* New York: Oxford University Press, 2001.

Preston, Andrew, Bruce J. Schulman, and Julian E. Zelizer, eds. *Faithful Republic: Religion and Politics in Modern America.* Philadelphia: University of Pennsylvania Press, 2015.

Raboteau, Albert J. *Canaan Land: A Religious History of African Americans.* New York: Oxford University Press, 1999.

Reeves, Richard. *President Nixon: Alone in the White House.* New York: Simon and Schuster, 2001.

Reinitz, Richard. *Irony and Consciousness: American Historiography and Reinhold Niebuhr's Vision.* Lewisburg, PA: Bucknell University Press, 1980.

Reston, James, Jr. *The Conviction of Richard Nixon: The Untold Story of the Frost/Nixon Interviews.* New York: Three Rivers Press, 2007.

Roof, Wade Clark, and William McKinney. *American Mainline Religion: Its Changing Shape and Future.* New Brunswick, NJ: Rutgers University Press, 1987.

Sandbrook, Dominic. *Mad as Hell: The Crisis of the 1970s and the Rise of the Populist Right.* New York: Alfred A. Knopf, 2011.

Sands, Kathleen M., ed. *God Forbid: Religion and Sex in American Public Life.* New York: Oxford University Press, 2000.

Savage, Barbara Dianne. *Your Spirit Walks beside Us: The Politics of Black Religion.* Cambridge, MA: Harvard University Press, 2008.

Scanlon, Sandra. *The Pro-war Movement: Domestic Support for the Vietnam War and the Making of Modern American Conservatism.* Amherst: University of Massachusetts Press, 2013.

Schmidt, Jean Miller. *Souls or the Social Order: The Two-Party System in American Protestantism.* Brooklyn: Carlson Publishing, 1991.

Schoenwald, Jonathan M. *A Time for Choosing: The Rise of Modern American Conservatism.* New York: Oxford University Press, 2001.

Schudson, Michael. *Watergate in American Memory: How We Remember, Forget, and Reconstruct the Past.* New York: Basic Books, 1992.

Schulman, Bruce. *The Seventies: The Great Shift in American Culture, Society, and Politics.* New York: Da Capo Press, 2001.

Schulman, Bruce J., and Julian E. Zelizer, eds. *Rightward Bound: Making America Conservative in the 1970s.* Cambridge, MA: Harvard University Press, 2008.

Schultze, Quentin J. *Christianity and the Mass Media in America: Toward a Democratic Accommodation.* East Lansing: Michigan State University Press, 2003.

Scott, Joan Wallach. *Gender and the Politics of History.* New York: Columbia University Press, 1988.

Settje, David E. *Faith and War: How Christians Debated the Cold and Vietnam Wars.* New York: New York University Press, 2011.

———. "Lutheran Responses to Watergate." *Lutheran Forum* 46 (Spring 2012): 20–23.

———. *Lutherans and the Longest War: Adrift on a Sea of Doubt about the Cold and Vietnam Wars, 1964–1975.* Lanham, MD: Lexington Books, 2007.

Shafer-Landau, Russ. *Whatever Happened to Good and Evil?* New York: Oxford University Press, 2004.

Sherry, Michael S. *In the Shadow of War: The United States since the 1930s.* New Haven, CT: Yale University Press, 1995.

Small, Melvin. *Johnson, Nixon, and the Doves.* New Brunswick, NJ: Rutgers University Press, 1988.

———. *The Presidency of Richard Nixon.* Lawrence: University Press of Kansas, 1999.

Smith, Andrew Christopher. *Fundamentalism, Fundraising, and the Transformation of the Southern Baptist Convention, 1919–1925.* Knoxville: University of Tennessee Press, 2016.

Smith, Gary Scott. *Religion in the Oval Office: The Religious Lives of American Presidents.* New York: Oxford University Press, 2015.

Smith, Oran P. *The Rise of Baptist Republicanism.* New York: New York University Press, 1997.

Stein, Judith. *Pivotal Decade: How the United States Traded Factories for Finance in the Seventies.* New Haven, CT: Yale University Press, 2010.

Stout, Harry S. *Upon the Altar of the Nation: A Moral History of the Civil War.* New York: Penguin Books, 2006.

Suelflow, August R. *Heritage in Motion: Readings in the History of the Lutheran Church—Missouri Synod*. St. Louis, MO: Concordia Publishing House, 1998.

Sugrue, Thomas J. *The Origins of the Urban Crisis: Race and Inequality in Postwar Detroit*. Princeton, NJ: Princeton University Press, 1996.

Sullivan, Timothy J. *New York State and the Rise of Modern Conservatism*. Albany: State University of New York Press, 2009.

Summers, Anthony. *The Arrogance of Power: The Secret World of Richard Nixon*. New York: Penguin Books, 2000.

Sutton, Matthew Avery. *American Apocalypse: A History of Modern Evangelicalism*. Cambridge, MA: Belknap Press of Harvard University Press, 2014.

Swartz, David R. *Moral Minority: The Evangelical Left in an Age of Conservatism*. Philadelphia: University of Pennsylvania Press, 2014.

Taege, Marlys. *WINGS, Women in God's Service: The 50th Anniversary History of the Lutheran Women's Missionary League of the Lutheran Church—Missouri Synod*. St. Louis, MO: Lutheran Women's Missionary League, 1991.

Todd, Mary. *Authority Vested: A Story of Identity and Change in the Lutheran Church—Missouri Synod*. Grand Rapids, MI: William B. Eerdmans, 2000.

Toulouse, Mark G. *God in Public: Four Ways American Christianity and Public Life Relate*. Louisville, KY: Westminster John Knox Press, 2006.

Tygiel, Jules. *Ronald Reagan and the Triumph of American Conservatism*. New York: Pearson Longman, 2005.

Vinz, Warren L. *Pulpit Politics: Faces of American Protestant Nationalism in the Twentieth Century*. Albany: State University of New York Press, 1997.

Volkan, Vamik D., Norman Itzkowitz, and Andrew W. Dod. *Richard Nixon: A Psychobiography*. New York: Columbia University Press, 1997.

Von Rohr, John. *The Shaping of American Congregationalism, 1620–1957*. Cleveland, OH: Pilgrim Press, 1992.

Wacker, Grant. *America's Pastor: Billy Graham and the Shaping of a Nation*. Cambridge, MA: Belknap Press of Harvard University Press, 2014.

———. "Billy Graham's America," *Church History* 78 (September 2009): 489–511.

Washington, James Melvin. *Frustrated Fellowship: The Black Baptist Quest for Social Power*. Macon, GA: Mercer University Press, 2004.

Weiner, Tim. *One Man against the World: The Tragedy of Richard Nixon*. New York: Henry Holt, 2015.

Werth, Barry. *31 Days: The Crisis That Gave Us the Government We Have Today*. New York: Doubleday, 2006.

White, Theodore H. *Breach of Faith: The Fall of Richard Nixon*. New York: Atheneum, 1975.

Wiederaenders, Robert C., ed. *Historical Guide to Lutheran Church Bodies of North America*. St Louis, MO: Lutheran Historical Conference, 1998.

Williams, Daniel K. *God's Own Party: The Making of the Christian Right*. New York: Oxford University Press, 2010.

Williams, Peter W. *America's Religions: Traditions and Cultures*. New York: Macmillan, 1990.

Wilmore, Gayraud S. *Black Religion and Black Radicalism: An Interpretation of the Religious History of African Americans*. 3rd ed. Maryknoll, NY: Orbis Books, 1998.

Wilsey, John D. *American Exceptionalism and Civil Religion: Reassessing the History of an Idea*. Downers Grove, IL: IVP Academic, 2015.

Woodward, Bob, and Carl Bernstein. *The Final Days*. New York: Simon and Schuster, 1976.

Wuthnow, Robert. *The Restructuring of American Religion: Society and Faith since World War II*. Princeton, NJ: Princeton University Press, 1988.

INDEX

abolitionism, 4

A.D.
activist theology of, 65
anti-Nixon cartoon in, 94
Freedom of the Press Award by, 71–72, 230n44
liberalism of, 49
on morality in politics, 136
prayer in, 123
on the presidential election, 27
prophetic voices in, 108–109
publication of, 102
on the US as a Christian nation, 82–83
on Watergate, 82, 172

African Methodist Episcopal Church. *See* AME

Agnew, Spiro T., 87, 90–91, 124, 133, 162

Ahab and Micaiah (biblical story), 137–138

Ahlstrom, Sydney E., 180–181

Alabama Baptist, 30, 57, 60, 90, 152–153, 190, 209

Allen, Jimmy, 191

All the President's Men, 239–240n4

AME (African Methodist Episcopal Church)
activism of, 120–121, 142
on the civil rights movement, 21, 33
conservatism of, 21–22, 186–187
on conversion, 210–211
on democracy/freedom and Christian convictions, 45–46
history of, 21–22
Nixon opposed by, 42–43, 46, 52, 116–118, 126, 140–145, 168, 186–188, 210–212
pietism of, 211

politics and church blended by, 33
on the prophetic role of Christian bodies, 141
on race, 143–144
on sin, 211
size of, 21
on the Vietnam War, 116
voter registration drive by, 33
voting encouraged by, 187
on Watergate, 116–121, 140–143, 210–212
Wills honored by, 143
See also *Christian Recorder*

A.M.E. Church Recorder, 187

A.M.E. Church Review, 186

American exceptionalism, 29, 150

American Revolution, 4–5

Amos (biblical figure), 157, 159

Anderson, Lowell A., 100

Anderson, Mary Elizabeth, 72

Armstrong, James, 41, 43–44, 114

arrogance of power, 66, 75, 78, 84, 100, 132, 137–138, 160

Baggett, Hudson, 30, 60, 79, 152–153, 209

Bailey, J. Martin
activist theology of, 65
on Christians' role in politics, 136–137
criticism of, 93–94
on the General Assembly, 93
on the General Synod, 75–76
on integrity in government, 174
Nixon criticized by, 52, 93, 172, 240n6
on political commentary in religious periodicals, 108

Banta, John P., 92

ABOUT THE AUTHOR

David E. Settje is Professor of History and Director of the Honors Program at Concordia University Chicago. He is author of *Lutherans and the Longest War: Adrift on a Sea of Doubt about the Cold and Vietnam Wars, 1964–1975* and *Faith and War: How Christians Debated the Cold and Vietnam Wars.*